Contemporary Controversies

Contemporary Controversies

An American Government Reader

Edited by

Robert J. Bresler
Pennsylvania State University–Harrisburg

HarperCollins*College*Publishers

Acquisitions Editor: Maria Hartwell
Project Editor: Diane Rowell
Design Supervisor: Lucy Krikorian
Cover Design: Kay Petronio
Cover Photo: R. Llewellyn/Superstock
Production Manager/Assistant: Willie Lane/Sunaina Sehwani
Compositor: BookMasters, Inc.
Printer and Binder: R. R. Donnelley & Sons Company
Cover Printer: The Lehigh Press, Inc.

For permission to use copyrighted material, grateful acknowledgment is made to the copyright holders on pp. 281–284, which are hereby made part of this copyright page.

Contemporary Controversies: An American Government Reader

Copyright © 1993 by HarperCollins College Publishers

Library of Congress Cataloging-in-Publication Data
Contemporary controversies : an American government reader / edited by
  Robert J. Bresler.
      p. cm.
    Includes bibliographical references.
    ISBN 0-06-501020-5
    1. United States—Politics and government. I. Bresler, Robert
J., 1937–   .
JK21.C73 1992
320.951—dc20   92–29833
                                                              CIP

92 93 94 95 9 8 7 6 5 4 3 2 1

To my mother and father, Dora G. and Joseph D. Bresler, who taught me to treat the serious opinions of others with respect and an open mind.

Contents

Preface

An important measure of one's political education is one's ability to feel comfortable with political controversy. A genuine intellectual life is not a journey to a fixed point but an odyssey, a search for meaning and comprehension. An education should do more than allow one to defend one's prejudices with greater dexterity and persuasiveness. It should open the mind. This requires a receptivity to opposing ideas and an ability to adjust one's thinking to new thoughts, facts, and concepts.

This reader will introduce a wide range of contemporary political controversies. Most of these selections are from the journals of opinion—right, left, and center—where these battles rage. The student may well put this reader down with a greater sense of uncertainty about the ease of finding quick and simple solutions to our problems. These readings are not complete enough to allow one to become an instant expert, but they may inspire one to explore the issues further.

The selections cover a broad variety of issues—some of recent vintage, such as term limitations for members of Congress, and others of a more enduring nature, such as the issue of judicial review. All of them raise important questions about the nature of government and the future direction of our society. You will confront moral and legal questions; for example, does the Constitution protect private consensual sexual behavior between adults, when does the assistance of a member of Congress to a constituent/contributor become undue influence, do affirmative action policies actually benefit minorities? You will also delve into perplexing immediate questions such as why young people appear to be so indifferent to politics and whether political action committees corrupt our political system.

This text is designed to supplement instruction for courses in American government and politics and covers areas included in an introductory American Government course. The selections are not rigidly pro or con on each of the topics covered, but they do represent sharply contrasting points of view. Controversy need not be approached as a highly structured debate, but rather as a free-wheeling and stimulating conversation.

ACKNOWLEDGMENTS

The author wishes to acknowledge the invaluable contribution of my research assistant, Timothy E. Wedig. Tim's numerous suggestions and insights were essential to the successful completion of this book. I would also like to thank the following reviewers: David Louis Cingranelli, SUNY at Binghamton; Terri S. Fine, University of Central Florida; Willoughby Jarrel, Kennesaw State College; and Robert Miewald, University of Nebraska–Lincoln. Also to my editors at HarperCollins, Lauren Silverman, Maria Hartwell, and Diane Rowell for their patience and encouragement.

ROBERT J. BRESLER

Contemporary
Controversies

Chapter
1

Is Judicial Review Democratic?

INTRODUCTION

Democracy involves more than simple majoritarianism—the rule of the majority. It also includes the rule of law, and in the American system the Constitution is the supreme law of the land. Since the historic decision in *Marbury* v. *Madison* (1803) the Supreme Court has had the power to declare laws that violate the Constitution as null and void. This is the power of judicial review, and it gives the Supreme Court the last word in deciding whether a law supported, perhaps by the vast majority, will finally stand.

Interpreting the Constitution is not a simple matter. The document is replete with grandiose phrases that defy a simple meaning. What, for example, constitutes "due process of law" and "equal protection of the law"—rights guaranteed by the Fourteenth Amendment? How can one define "an unreasonable search and seizure"—prohibited by the Fourth Amendment? Critics of judicial review feel that these majestic generalities make it possible for the Court to abuse this power and impose its own preferences and values upon the population.

Supporters of judicial review see no other safeguard from a runaway majority in the legislature that could trample upon provisions and rights guaranteed by the Constitution. Defenders of judicial review argue that if the Constitution is the basic charter of government the courts must guard its integrity against capricious and willful legislatures. In *The Federalist* (No. 78), Alexander Hamilton stated that, "a limited constitution . . . can be preserved in practice no other way than through the medium of the courts of justice, whose duty it must be to declare all acts contrary to the manifest tenor of the constitution void. Without this, all the reservations of particular rights or privileges would amount to nothing."

Robert H. Bork argues in the following that judges can avoid insinuating their own values into the Constitution by carefully following the intent of the Framers. Bork is critical of judges who discover rights, such as the right to privacy, not specifically mentioned in the Constitution, and then give them their own definition. When judges read their own values into the Constitution to overturn laws, Bork feels that they undercut democracy: "As courts intervene more frequently to set aside majoritarian outcomes, they teach the lesson that democratic processes are suspect, essentially unprincipled and untrustworthy."

Eugene V. Rostow sees judicial review as crucial to a functioning democracy. Only through the vigilance of the courts, Rostow argues, can individual rights, the separation of powers, and a system of checks and balances be maintained. Constitutional government demands judicial review. "A written constitution would promote discord," Rostow writes, "rather than order in society if there were no accepted authority to construe it. . . ." Judicial review, according to this argument is a practical condition for the working of constitutional government.

Judicial Review and Democracy

Robert H. Bork

The American ideal of democracy lives in constant tension with the American ideal of judicial review in the service of individual liberties. It is a tension that sometimes erupts in crisis. Thomas Jefferson planned a campaign of impeachments to rid the bench, and particularly the Supreme Court, of Federalist judges. The campaign collapsed when the impeachment of Associate Justice Samuel Chase failed in the Senate. Franklin D. Roosevelt, frustrated by a Court majority that repeatedly struck down New Deal economic measures, tried to pack the Court with additional justices. That effort was defeated in Congress, though the attempt may have persuaded some justices to alter their behavior. In recent years there have been movements in Congress to deprive federal courts of jurisdiction over cases involving such matters as abortion, school busing, and school prayer—topics on which the Court's decisions have angered strong and articulate constituencies.

The problem is the resolution of what Robert Dahl called the Madisonian dilemma. The United States was founded as a Madisonian system, one that allows majorities to govern wide and important areas of life simply because they are majorities, but that also holds that individuals have some freedoms that must be exempt from majority control. The dilemma is that neither the majority nor the minority can be trusted to define the proper spheres of democratic authority and individual liberty.

It is not at all clear that the Founders envisaged a leading role for the judiciary in the resolution of this dilemma, for they thought of the third branch as relatively insignificant. Over time, however, Americans have come to assume that the definition of majority power and minority freedom is primarily the function of the judiciary, most particularly the function of the Supreme Court. This assumption places a great responsibility upon constitutional theory. America's basic methods of policy-making is majoritarian. Thus, to justify exercise of a power to set at naught the considered decisions of elected representatives, judges must achieve, in Alexander Bickel's phrase, "a rigorous general accord between judicial supremacy and democratic theory, so that the boundaries of the one could be described with some precision in terms of the other." At one time, an accord was based on the understanding that judges followed the intentions of the Framers and ratifiers of the Constitution, a legal document enacted by majorities, though subject to alteration only by supermajorities. A conflict between democracy and judicial review did not arise because the respective areas of each were specified and intended to be inviolate. Although this obedience to original intent was occasionally more pretense than reality, the accord was achieved in theory, and that theory stated an ideal to which courts were expected to conform. That is no longer so. Many judges and scholars now believe that the courts' obligations to intent are so highly generalized and remote that judges are in fact free to create the Constitution they think appropriate to today's society. The result is that the accord no longer stands even theoretically. The increasing perception that this is so raises the question of what elected officials can do to reclaim authority they regard as wrongfully taken by the judiciary.

There appear to be two possible responses to a judiciary that has overstepped the limits of its legitimate authority. One is political, the other intellectual. It seems tolerably clear that political responses are of limited usefulness, at least in the short run. Impeachment and Court-packing, having failed in the past, are unlikely to be resorted to again. Amending the Constitution to correct judicial overreaching is such a difficult and laborious process (requiring either two-thirds of both houses of Congress or an application for a convention by the legislatures of two-thirds of the states, followed, in either case, by ratification by three-fourths of the states) that it is of little practical assistance. It is sometimes proposed that Congress deal with the problem by removing federal court jurisdiction, using the exceptions clause of Article III of the Constitution in the case of the Supreme Court. The constitutionality of this approach has been much debated, but, in any case, it will often prove not feasible. Removal of all federal court jurisdiction would not return final power either to Congress or to state legislatures but to 50 state court systems. Thus, as a practical matter, this device could not be used as to any subject where national uniformity of constitutional law is necessary or highly desirable. Moreover, jurisdiction removal does not vindicate democratic governance, for it merely shifts ultimate power to different groups of judges. Democratic responses to judicial excesses probably must come through the replacement of judges who die or retire with new judges of different views. But this is a slow and uncertain process, the accidents of mortality being what they are and prediction of what new judges will do being so perilous.

There exist few, if any, usable and effective techniques by which federal courts can be kept within constitutional bounds. A Constitution that provides numerous checks and balances between president and Congress provides little to curb a judiciary that expands its powers beyond the allowable meaning of the Constitution. Perhaps one reason is that the Framers, though many of them foresaw that the Supreme Court would review laws for constitutionality, had little experience with such a function. They did not remotely foresee what the power of judicial review was capable of becoming. Nor is it clear that an institutional check—such as Senator Robert La Follette's proposal to amend the Constitution so that Congress could override a Supreme Court decision by a two-thirds majority—would be desirable. Congress is less likely than the Court to be versed in the Constitution. La Follette's proposal could conceivably wreak as much or more damage to the Court's legitimate powers as it might accomplish in restraining its excesses. That must be reckoned at least a possibility with any of the institutional checks just discussed and is probably one of the reasons they have rarely been used. In this sense, the Court's vulnerability is one of its most important protections.

If a political check on federal courts is unlikely to succeed, the only rein left is intellectual, the widespread acceptance of a theory of judicial review. After almost two centuries of constitutional adjudication, we appear to be further than ever from the possession of an adequate theory.

In the beginning, there was no controversy over theory. Joseph Story, who was both an associate justice of the Supreme Court and Dane Professor of Law at Harvard, could write in his *Commentaries on the Constitution of the United States*, published in 1833, that "I have not the ambition to be the author of any new plan of interpreting the theory of the Constitution, or of enlarging or narrowing its powers by ingenious subtleties and learned doubts." He thought that the job of constitutional judges was to interpret: "The first and fundamental rule in the interpretation of all instruments is, to construe them according to the sense of the terms and the intention of the parties."

The performance of the courts has not always conformed to this interpretivist ideal. In the last decade or so of the nineteenth century and the first third of the twentieth the Supreme Court assiduously protected economic liberties from federal and state regulation, often in ways that could not be reconciled with the Constitution. The case that stands as the symbol of that era of judicial adventurism is *Lochner* v. *New York* in 1905, which struck down the state's law regulating maximum hours for bakers. That era ended when Franklin D. Roosevelt's appointments remade the Court, and *Lochner* is now generally regarded as discredited.

Nevertheless, if the Court stopped defending economic liberties without constitutional justification in the mid-1930s, it began in the mid-1950s to make other decisions for which it offered little or no constitutional argument. It had been generally assumed that constitutional questions were to be answered on grounds of historical intent, but the Court began to make decisions that could hardly be, and were not, justified on that basis. Existing constitutional protections were expanded and new ones created. Sizable minorities on the Court indicated a willingness to go still further. The widespread perception that the judiciary was recreating the Constitution brought the tension between democracy and judicial review once more to a state of intellectual and political crisis.

Much of the new judicial power claimed cannot be derived from the text, structure, or history of the Constitution. Perhaps because of the increasing obviousness of this fact, legal scholars began to erect new theories of the judicial role. These constructs, which appear to be accepted by a majority of those who write about constitutional theory, go by the general name of the noninterpretivism. They hold that mere interpretation of the Constitution may be impossible and is certainly inadequate. Judges are assigned not the task of defining the meanings and contours of values found in the historical Constitution but rather the function of creating new values and hence new rights for individuals against majorities. These new values are variously described as arising from "the evolving morality of our tradition," our "conventional morality" as discerned by "the method of philosophy," a "fusion of constitutional law and moral theory," or "higher law" of "unwritten natural rights." One author has argued that, since "no defensible criteria" exist "to assess theories of judicial review," the judge should enforce his conception of the good. In all cases, these theories purport to empower judges to override majority will for extraconstitutional reasons.

Judges have articulated theories of their role no less removed from interpretation than those of the noninterpretivist academics. Writing for the Court in *Griswold* v. *Connecticut* in 1965, Justice William O. Douglas created a constitutional right of privacy that invalidated the state's law against the use of contraceptives. He observed that many provisions of the Bill of Rights could be viewed as protections of aspects of personal privacy. These provisions were said to add up to a zone of constitutionally secured privacy that did not fall within any particular provision. The scope of this new right was not defined, but the Court has used the concept in a series of cases since, the most controversial being *Roe* v. *Wade* in 1973.

A similar strategy for the creation of new rights was outlined by Justice William J. Brennan in a 1985 address. He characterized the Constitution as being pervasively concerned with human dignity. From this, Brennan drew a more general judicial function of enhancing human dignity, one not confined by the clauses in question and, indeed, capable of nullifying what those clauses reveal of the Framers' intentions. Thus, Brennan stated that continued judicial tolerance of capital punishment causes us to "fall short of the constitutional vision of human dignity." For that reason, Brennan continues to vote that capital punishment violates the Constitution. The potency of this method of generalizing from particular clauses, and then applying the generalization instead of the clauses, may be seen in the fact that it leads to a declaration of the unconstitutionality of a punishment explicitly assumed to be available three times in the Fifth Amendment to the Constitution and once again, some 77 years later in the Fourteenth Amendment. By conventional methods of interpretation, it would be impossible to use the Constitution to prohibit that which the Constitution explicitly assumed to be lawful.

Because noninterpretive philosophies have little hard intellectual structure, it is impossible to control them or to predict from any inner logic or principle what they may require. Though it is regularly denied that a return to the judicial function as exemplified in *Lochner* v. *New York* is underway or, which comes to the same thing, that decisions are rooted only in the judges' moral predilections, it is difficult to see what else can be involved once the function of searching for the Framers' intent is abandoned. When constitutional adjudication proceeds in a noninterpretive manner, the Court necessarily imposes new values upon the society. They are new in the sense that they cannot be derived by interpretation of the historical Constitution. Moreover, they must rest upon the moral predilections of the judge because the values come out of the moral view that most of us, by definition (since we voted democratically for a different result), do not accept.

This mode of adjudication makes impossible any general accord between judicial supremacy and democratic theory. Instead, it brings the two into head-on conflict. The Constitution specifies certain liberties and allocates all else to democratic processes. Noninterpretivism gives the judge power to invade the province of democracy whenever majority morality conflicts with his own. That is impossible to square either with democratic theory or the concept of law. Attempts have, nonetheless, been made to reconcile, or at least to mitigate, the contradiction. One line of argument is that any society requires a mixture of principle and expediency, that courts are better than legislatures at discerning and formulating principle, and hence may intervene when principle has been inadequately served by the legislative process. Even if one assumes that courts have superior institutional capacities in this respect, which is by no means clear, the conclusion does not follow. By placing certain subjects in the legislative arena, the Constitution holds that the trade-off between principle and expediency we are entitled to is what the legislature provides. Courts have no mandate to impose a different result merely because they would arrive at a trade-off that weighted principle more heavily or that took an altogether different value into account.

A different reconciliation of democracy and noninterpretist judicial review begins with the proposition that the Supreme Court is not really final because popular sentiment can in the long run cause it to be overturned. As we know from history, it may take decades to overturn a decision, so that it will be final for many people. Even then an overruling probably cannot be forced if a substantial minority ardently supports the result.

To the degree that the Constitution is not treated as law to be interpreted in conventional fashion, the clash between democracy and judicial review is real. It is also serious. When the judiciary imposes upon democracy limits not to be found in the Constitution, it deprives Americans of a right that is found there, the right to make the laws to govern themselves. As courts intervene more frequently to set aside majoritarian outcomes, they teach the lesson that democratic processes are suspect, essentially unprincipled and untrustworthy.

The main charge against a strictly interpretive approach to the Constitution is that the Framers' intentions cannot be known because they could not foresee the changed circumstances of our time. The argument proves too much. If it were true, the judge would be left without any law to apply, and there would be no basis for judicial review.

That is not what is involved. From the text, the structure, and the history of the Constitution we can usually learn at least the core values that the Framers intended to protect. Interpreting the Constitution means discerning the principle that the Framers wanted to enact and applying it to today's circumstances. As John Hart Ely put it, interpretivism holds that "the work of the political branches is to be invalidated only in accord with an inference whose starting point, whose underlying premise, is fairly discoverable in the Constitution. That the complete inference will not be found there—because the situation is not likely to have been foreseen—is generally common ground."

This requires that constitutional doctrine evolve over time. Most doctrine is merely the judge-made superstructure that implements basic constitutional principles, and, because circumstances change, the evolution of doctrine is inevitable. The Fourth Amendment was framed by men who did not foresee electronic surveillance, but judges may properly apply the central value of that amendment to electronic invasions of personal privacy. The difference between this method and that endorsed by Justices Douglas and Brennan lies in the level of generality employed. Adapting the Fourth Amendment requires the judge merely to recognize a new method of governmental search of one's property. The justices, on the other hand, create a right so general that it effectively becomes a new clause of the Constitution, one that gives courts no guidance in its application. Modifying doctrine to preserve a value already embedded in the Constitution is an enterprise wholly different in nature from creating new values.

The debate over the legitimate role of the judiciary is likely to continue for some years. Noninterpretivists have not as yet presented an adequate theoretical justification for a judiciary that creates rather than interprets the Constitution. The task of interpretation is often complex and difficult, but it remains the only model of the judicial role that achieves an accord between democracy and judicial review.

The Democratic Character of Judicial Review

Eugene V. Rostow

A theme of uneasiness, and even guilt, colors the literature about judicial review. Many of those who have talked, lectured, and written about the Constitution have been troubled by a sense that judicial review is undemocratic. Why should a majority of nine Justices appointed for life be permitted to outlaw as unconstitutional the acts of elected officials or of officers controlled by elected officials? Judicial review, they have urged, is an undemocratic shoot on an otherwise respectable tree. It should be cut off, or at least kept pruned and inconspicuous. The attack has gone further. Reliance on bad political doctrine, they say, has produced bad political results. The strength of the courts has weakened other parts of the government. The judicial censors are accused of causing laxness and irresponsibility in the state and national legislatures, and political apathy in the electorate. At the same time, we are warned, the participation of the courts in this essentially political function will inevitably lead to the destruction of their independence and thus compromise all other aspects of their work.

I

The idea that judicial review is undemocratic is not an academic issue of political philosophy. Like most abstractions, it has far-reaching practical consequences. I suspect that for some judges it is the mainspring of decision, inducing them in many cases to uphold legislative and executive action which would otherwise have been condemned. Particularly in the multiple opinions of recent years, the Supreme Court's self-searching often boils down to a debate within the bosoms of the Justices over the appropriateness of judicial review itself.

The attack on judicial review as undemocratic rests on the premise that the Constitution should be allowed to grow without a judicial check. The proponents of this view would have the Constitution mean what the president, the Congress, and the state legislatures say it means.[1] In this way, they contend, the electoral process would determine the course of constitutional development, as it does in countries with plenipotentiary parliaments.

But the Constitution of the United States does not establish a parliamentary government, and attempts to interpret American government in a parliamentary perspective break down in confusion or absurdity. One may recall, in another setting, the anxious voice of the *Washington Post* urging President Truman to resign because the Republican Party had won control of the Congress in the 1946 elections.

It is a grave oversimplification to contend that no society can be democratic unless its legislature has sovereign powers. The social quality of democracy cannot be defined by so rigid a formula. Government and politics are after all the arms, not the end, of social life. The purpose of the Constitution is to assure the people a free and democratic society. The final aim of that society is as much freedom as possible for the individual human being. The Constitution provides society with a mechanism of government fully competent to its task, but by no means universal in its powers. The power to govern is parceled out between the states and the nation and is further divided among the three main branches of all governmental units. By custom as well as constitutional practice, many vital aspects of community life are beyond the direct reach of government—for example, religion, the press, and, until recently at any rate, many phases of educational and cultural activity. The separation of powers under the Constitution serves the end of democracy by limiting the roles of the several branches of government and protecting the citizen, and the various parts of the state itself, against encroachments from any source.

The power of constitutional review, to be exercised by some part of the government, is implicit in the conception of a written constitution delegating limited powers. A written constitution would promote discord rather than order in society if there were no accepted authority to construe it, at the least in cases of conflicting action by different branches of government or of constitutionally unauthorized governmental action against individuals. The limitation and separation of powers, if they are to survive, require a procedure for independent mediation and construction to reconcile the inevitable disputes over the boundaries of constitutional power which arise in the process of government. British Dominions operating under written constitutions have had to face the task pretty much as we have, and they have solved it in similar ways. Like institutions have developed in other federal systems.

As far as the American Constitution is concerned, there can be little real doubt that the courts were intended from the beginning to have the power they have exercised. The *Federalist* papers are unequivocal; the Debates as clear as debates normally are. The power of judicial review was commonly exercised by the courts of the states, and the people were accustomed to judicial construction of the authority derived from colonial charters.[2] Constitutional interpretation by the courts, Hamilton said, does not

> by any means suppose a superiority of the judicial to the legislative power. It only supposes that the power of the people is superior to both; and that where the will of the legislature, declared in its statutes, stands in opposition to that of the people, declared in the Constitution, the judges ought to be governed by the latter rather than the former. They ought to regulate their decisions by the fundamental laws, rather than by those which are not fundamental.[3]

Hamilton's statement is sometimes criticized as a verbal legalism.[4] But it has an advantage too. For much of the discussion has complicated the problem without clarifying it. Both judges and their critics have wrapped themselves so successfully in the difficulties of particular cases that they have been able to evade the ultimate issue posed in the *Federalist* papers.

Whether another method of enforcing the Constitution could have been devised, the short answer is that no such method has developed. The argument over the constitutionality of judicial review has long since been settled by history. The power and duty of the Supreme Court to declare statutes of executive action unconstitutional in appropriate cases is part of the living

Constitution. "The course of constitutional history," Mr. Justice Frankfurter recently remarked, has cast responsibilities upon the Supreme Court which it would be "stultification" for it to evade.[5] The Court's power has been exercised differently at different times: sometimes with reckless and doctrinaire enthusiasm; sometimes with great deference to the status and responsibilities of other branches of the government; sometimes with a degree of weakness and timidity that comes close to the betrayal of trust. But the power exists, as an integral part of the process of American government. The Court has the duty of interpreting the Constitution in many of its most important aspects, and especially in those which concern the relations of the individual and the state. The political proposition underlying the survival of the power is that there are some phases of American life which should be beyond the reach of any majority, save by constitutional amendment. In Mr. Justice Jackson's phrase, "One's right to life, liberty, and property, to free speech, a free press, freedom of worship and assembly, and other fundamental rights may not be submitted to vote; they depend on the outcome of no elections."[6] Whether or not this was the intention of the Founding Fathers, the unwritten Constitution is unmistakable.

If one may use a personal definition of the crucial word, this way of policing the Constitution is not undemocratic. True, it employs appointed officials, to whom large powers are irrevocably delegated. But democracies need not elect all the officers who exercise crucial authority in the name of the voters. Admirals and generals can win or lose wars in the exercise of their discretion. The independence of judges in the administration of justice has been the pride of communities which aspire to be free. Members of the Federal Reserve Board have the lawful power to plunge the country into depression or inflation. The list could readily be extended. Government by referendum or town meeting is not the only possible form of democracy. The task of democracy is not to have the people vote directly on every issue, but to assure their ultimate responsibility for the acts of their representatives, elected or appointed. For judges deciding ordinary litigation, the ultimate responsibility of the electorate has a special meaning. It is a responsibility for the quality of the judges and for the substance of their instructions, never a responsibility for their decisions in particular cases. It is hardly characteristic of law in democratic society to encourage bills of attainder or to allow appeals from the courts, in particular cases, to legislatures or to mobs. Where the judges are carrying out the function of constitutional review, the final responsibility of the people is appropriately guaranteed by the provisions for amending the Constitution itself and by the benign influence of time, which changes the personnel of courts. Given the possibility of constitutional amendment, there is nothing undemocratic in having responsible and independent judges act as important constitutional mediators. Within the narrow limits of their capacity to act, their great task is to help maintain a pluralist equilibrium in society. They can do much to keep it from being dominated by the states or the federal government, by Congress or the president, by the purse or the sword.

In the execution of this crucial but delicate function, constitutional review by the judiciary has an advantage thoroughly recognized in both theory and practice. The power of the courts, however final, can only be asserted in the course of litigation. Advisory opinions are forbidden, and reefs of self-limitation have grown up around the doctrine that the courts will determine constitutional questions only in cases of actual controversy, when no lesser ground of decision is available and when the complaining party would be directly and personally injured by the assertion of the power deemed unconstitutional. Thus the check of judicial review upon the elected branches of government must be a mild one, limited not only by the detachment, integrity, and good sense of the Justices, but by the structural boundaries implicit in the fact that the power is entrusted to the courts. Judicial review is inherently adapted to preserving broad and flexible lines of constitutional growth, not to operating as a continuously active factor in legislative or executive decisions.

The division and separation of governmental powers within the American federal system provides the community with ample power to act, without compromising its pluralist structure. The Constitution formalizes the principle that a wide dispersal of authority among the institutions of society is the safest foundation for social freedom. It was accepted from the beginning that the judiciary would be one of the chief agencies for enforcing the restraints of the Constitution. In a letter to Madison, Jefferson remarked of the Bill of Rights:

> In the arguments in favor of a declaration of rights, you omit one which has great weight with me; the legal check which it puts into the hands of the judiciary. This is a body, which, if rendered independent and kept strictly to their own department, merits great confidence for their learning and integrity. In fact, what degree of confidence would be too much, for a body composed of such men as Wythe, Blair and Pendleton? On characters like these, the *"civium ardor prava pubentium"* would make no impression.[7]

Jefferson, indeed, went further. He regretted the absence in the Constitution of a direct veto power over legislation entrusted to the judiciary, and wished that no legislation could take effect for a year after its final enactment.[8] Within such constitutional limits, Jefferson believed, American society could best achieve its goal of responsible self-government. "I have no fear," he wrote, "but that the result of our experiment will be, that men may be trusted to govern themselves without a master."[9]

Democracy is a slippery term. I shall make no effort at a formal definition here. Certainly as a matter of historical fact some societies with parliamentary governments have been and are "democratic" by standards which Americans would accept, although it is worth noting that almost all of them employ second chambers, with powers at least of delay, and indirect devices for assuring continuity in the event of a parliamentary collapse, either through the crown or some equivalent institution, like the presidency in France. But it would be scholastic pedantry to define democracy in such a way as to deny the title of "democrat" to Jefferson, Madison, Lincoln, Brandeis, and others who have found the American constitutional system, including its tradition of judicial review, well adapted to the needs of a free society.[10] As Mr. Justice Brandeis said,

> the doctrine of the separation of powers was adopted by the Convention of 1787, not to promote efficiency but to preclude the exercise of arbitrary power. The purpose was, not to avoid friction, but, by means of the inevitable friction incident to the distribution of governmental powers among three departments, to save the people from autocracy.[11]

It is error to insist that no society is democratic unless it has a government of unlimited powers, and that no government is democratic unless its legislature has unlimited powers. Constitutional review by an independent judiciary is a tool of proven use in the American quest for an open society of widely dispersed powers. In a vast country, of mixed population, with widely different regional problems, such an organization of society is the surest base for the hopes of democracy.[12]

NOTES

1. Many writers have distinguished the authority of the Supreme Court to deny effect to an unconstitutional act of the Congress or the president from its duty under Article VI to declare unconstitutional provisions of state constitutions or statutes, although Article VI declares even federal statutes to be "the supreme Law of the Land" only when made in pursuance of the Constitution. Holmes, "Law and the Court" in *Collected Legal Papers* 291, 295–296 (1920); Jackson, *The Struggle for Judicial Supremacy* 15 et seq. (1941); Thayer, "The Origin and Scope of the American Doctrine of Constitutional Law" in *Legal Essays* 1, 35–41 (1908); Thayer, *John Marshall* 61–65 (1901); Haines, *The American Doctrine of Judicial Supremacy* 131–135, 511–512 (2d ed. 1932).
2. The evidence is reviewed in Thayer, "The Origin and Scope of the American Doctrine of Constitutional Law" in *Legal Essays* 1, 3–7 (1908); Beard, *The Supreme Court and the Constitution* (1912); and Haines, op. cit. supra note 2, at 44–59, 88–121. A useful bibliography appears in Dodd, *Cases on Constitutional Law* 8–18 (3d ed. 1941).
3. *The Federalist*, No. 78 at 506 (Modern Library ed. 1937).
4. See Thayer, *John Marshall* 96 (1901); Thayer, "The Origin and Scope of the American Doctrine of Constitutional Law" in *Legal Essays* 1, 12–15 (1908); Haines, op. cit. supra note 2, at 518–527.

5. Rochin v. California, 342 U.S. 165, 173 (1952).

6. West Virginia State Board of Educ. v. Barnette, 319 U.S. 624, 638 (1943).

7. Jefferson, *Life and Selected Writings* 462 (Modern Library ed. 1944). This passage, Griswold comments, "suggests that while [Jefferson] relied on the Court to safeguard the Bill of Rights, he was also counting on the bill to ensure a long-run democratic tendency on the part of the Court. History has borne out the acumen of this thought. . . . The Court's vested responsibility for our civil liberties has kept it anchored to democratic fundamentals through all kinds of political weather." A. W. Griswold, "Jefferson's Republic—The Rediscovery of Democratic Philosophy," *Fortune* 130 (April 1950). Later in life, of course, Jefferson strongly differed with many of the decisions and opinions of the Supreme Court and expressed his disagreement in terms which sometimes seemed to repudiate the constitutionality of judicial review itself.

8. Jefferson, *Life and Selected Writings* 437, 441, 460 (Modern Library ed. 1944).

9. *The Writings of Thomas Jefferson* 151 (Lipscomb and Bergh ed. 1904).

10. See, e.g., Lincoln, "First Inaugural Address" in *Messages and Papers of the Presidents* 5–12 (Richardson ed, 1897); Wilson, *Constitutional Government in the United States* c. (1911).

11. Myers v. United States, 272 U.S. 52, 293 (1926) (dissenting opinion).

12. See Cardozo, *The Nature of the Judicial Process* 92–94 (1921).

QUESTIONS FOR DISCUSSION

1.1 Aren't all officers of the federal government sworn to uphold the Constitution? Why should judges be given the unique responsibility of protecting Constitutional values?

1.2 What, according to Robert Bork, is the best protection against judicial review becoming judicial supremacy?

1.3 Justice Harlan Fiske Stone wrote, "The only check upon our own exercise of power is our own sense of self-restraint." Is this, indeed, the only check of the power of judicial review?

Chapter
2

Should the Federal Government Provide Greater Assistance to the States?

INTRODUCTION

In the early 1990s many state governments suffered a loss of tax revenue and were faced with the necessity of reducing services and programs. The 1980s witnessed a reduction of federal assistance to the states, with such programs as revenue sharing (direct federal funding for the states) being phased out completely. At the same time Congress passed numerous mandated programs such as the Americans with Disabilities Act, which required state government to provide equal access to services, buildings, and transportation systems for the disabled without providing the funding. Federally mandated programs such as Medicaid, which subsidizes health care for the poor, cost the states about $38 billion in 1992. Such federally required health care programs consumed almost 14 percent of all state budgets in 1990. Critics of these programs claimed that the sovereign states were turning into administrative units of the federal government, corrupting the original intent of the Constitution.

What then is the proper role of federal government? In one of the following articles, Raymond Flynn, the mayor of Boston, argues that cities have the lion's share of our social problems—crime, homelessness, drug abuse, poverty—while the federal government has the lion's share of the tax revenues. He recommends a major national effort to reduce the burden of these problems that the cities and states must carry. He advocates a national health care program, a national youth service corps, and a massive program to build low-cost single-family homes.

Stephen Moore argues that the states cannot blame the federal government for their financial woes. He blames their own profligate spending habits, fed by the 1980s boom, in which governors expanded state programs in corrections, education, health care, and welfare. In the field of education Moore believes that the money has largely purchased an enlarged bureaucracy. Rather than focus upon increasing state services or gaining more federal funds, Moore would concentrate upon economic growth, cutting state income taxes, reducing state programs, and privatizing programs.

This is not simply a debate over states' rights, but over state responsibilities and the role of government in general. Is the path to prosperity and social justice to be found through government or should government—state and federal—leave most of these responsibilities to the private sector?

Operation "Domestic Order"
Devising a "Fair Federalism"

Raymond L. Flynn

Why do mayors like myself look to the White House and Congress for leadership in addressing urban problems? First, because the kinds of problems being addressed here are not local but national in their origin and scope, and in their effects on the national well-being. For one example: No one city, nor all of them together, brought about the recession; neither singly nor in concert can they reverse it. Yet the effects of recession hit hardest and most directly on poor people, and most low-income Americans live in the cities. The problems were bad enough *before* the recession began. Now their effects are visibly spreading beyond the core cities.

Second, we look to Washington because Washington is where the money is. The federal government has used its preemptive powers to capture the lion's share of governmental revenues. But it's not a mistake or an accident that the national government stands first in line where taxes are concerned. Federal functions (foreign relations, national defense, interstate commerce and transit, etc.) are inherently costly. Moreover, only the federal government is able to spread the burdens of taxation equitably over all strata of society and all corners of the land.

The problem is that Washington not only collects the most money but decides where it is to be spent—and sometimes, as over the past decade and more, neither prudently nor productively. Thus, mayors like myself are not running to the federal trough to get help for problems of our own making. (Every year in recent times my own city has balanced its budget and achieved higher bond ratings; here and across the country, citizen satisfaction with *municipal* government is relatively high.) Rather we are asking national policy-makers to open their eyes to the debilitating effects of federal funding decisions on our cities—which contribute at least their fair share of federal revenues—and the concomitant effects on the nation.

Consider the situation I know best. During the past decade, Boston, like many cities, lost hundreds of millions of dollars in federal funds for housing, health care, job training, and community development. Yearly federal assistance to Boston was slashed from $150 million to $64 million—this in the very period when the plagues of homelessness, AIDS, and crack addiction were reaching crisis proportions. For a while, and in some regions of the country, state governments were flush with revenues and able to cushion some of the blow caused by the national government's retreat from the cities. But now most states are facing fiscal crises and budget deficits, and can no longer provide an additional safety net. With old problems festering, new ones appearing, and both kinds made worse by recession, cities face the impact of state cutbacks added to federal indifference.

That is why we need federal leadership to rebuild our cities. So far, we are not getting it. In his annual address, the president did not describe the real state of the union. He did talk about bailing out the banking industry and he once more pursued his personal holy grail, a cut in the capital gains tax; we heard nothing about jobs for the jobless, homes for the homeless, about fighting poverty and seriously promoting economic recovery. Mr. Bush's budget proposal continues a decade of federal withdrawal from concern for the cities and their people. Meantime, by adopting new budget-making rules in the name of fighting the deficit, the Congress has tied itself into procedural knots that all but preclude even the most obviously prudent and cost-effective new initiatives to deal with even the most demanding of our many crises.

Perhaps we shouldn't be surprised. Officials in Washington met last summer to consider proposals for a new antipoverty effort, but they concluded that it was either too expensive or too controversial. One Bush administration official was quoted as saying that their decision was to "keep playing with the same toys. But let's paint them a little shinier."

This is a recipe for disaster. Our cities are a tinderbox, waiting to explode. For example:

- Last year the United States, and most major cities, had the highest number of murders ever recorded. A growing number of young people are involved in gangs and the underground economy of drugs. Homicide is now the leading cause of death among young black males.
- Demand for emergency shelter and soup kitchens has climbed steadily for a decade, according to annual surveys by the U.S. Conference of Mayors. Families with children are the fastest rising segment of Americans who are hungry and homeless.
- Racially motivated incidents of crime and violence are on the rise. As the recession deepens, the competition for scarce resources (including jobs) tightens, prejudice and bigotry could increase.

Let's be clear: We are fighting this war against drugs, violence, and crime today because the federal government—both the White House and Congress—abandoned the war on poverty. Mistakes were made in that war. Some causes of poverty were not addressed. Some approaches were oversold and/or inadequately monitored. But progress was made, and there was promise of more when the costs of that other war (in Southeast Asia) and, later, the rhetoric of supply-side ideologues brought about wholesale retreat. Poverty has been declared a nonproblem, when in fact it is the root and ground of the other conditions that threaten us. More than 33 million Americans—one out of seven—live below the poverty line. The figure for children is yet more alarming: One of every four lives in poverty (among blacks, one of every two). Compared with a decade ago, today's poor are poorer, and likely to be poor for longer periods. More people today are likely to earn their poverty on the job—the "working poor." More and more poor people are concentrated in our cities, while more of the new jobs are located in the suburbs, inaccessible by public transportation.

During this decade of increased destitution, a small number of wealthy Americans became even richer. The richest 1 percent of all Americans (those with average incomes of $549,000) now receive nearly as much income, after taxes, as the bottom 40 percent combined. The average income of those at the very top rose $236,000 during the decade—an increase of 75 percent—while the poorest one-fifth of the population saw its income drop by 3.8 percent. A major factor behind this widening gulf is a dramatic increase in capital gains income received by the wealthiest Americans, according to the Center on Budget and Policy Priorities. Last year alone, they received an average of $175,000 in capital gains income alone—$92,000 more than they received in 1980, after adjusting for inflation. Indeed, the share of national income going to those in the middle is now lower than at any time since World War II. Moreover, as we enter a recession, this disparity between wealthy and other Americans is getting worse.

These economic trends and federal policies are reflected in Americans' daily lives and living conditions.

- The nation's infant mortality rate—10 deaths per 1000 live births—ranks nineteenth in the world, behind those reported by Japan, Hong Kong, and New Zealand. Worse, the infant mortality rate among black Americans (17.6) and within our major cities (for example, 19.7 in Detroit, 19.3 in Washington, D.C., 19.2 in Baltimore, 17.7 in Memphis, 17.3 in Philadelphia, and 16.6 in Chicago) rivals that in many third-world countries.
- About one-fourth of young Americans fail to finish high school. In basic competencies—reading and math, for example—American students (including high school graduates) are far behind their counterparts in other industrial nations. The U.S. ranks nineteenth in teacher/student ratios in public elementary and secondary schools.
- Apart from those who live on the streets or in shelters, millions of Americans live doubled-up or tripled-up in overcrowded apartments, or pay more than they can reasonably afford for substandard housing. Some 85 percent of low-income renters—almost 6 million households—are paying at least 30 percent of their income for housing. Two-thirds of the poor pay at least half of their limited incomes just to keep a roof over their families' heads. Yet fewer than one-third of America's poor receive any kind of housing subsidy. As a result, millions of Americans are just one rent increase, layoff, illness, or other emergency away from becoming homeless. Meanwhile, during the past decade, the homeownership rate steadily declined, especially for young families.

We deserve an America that is at least as strong domestically as it is militarily. What good is a strong defense budget if we don't have a strong America to defend? Persistent poverty is not only a tragic waste of human talent, but also a drain on our nation's productivity. If we are to compete successfully in the new world economy, we must guarantee that our work force is trained, that our research and development dollars strengthen the civilian economy, and that our communities are livable.

The United States has the resources to guarantee every American a decent standard of living. What's needed is the national leadership to forge a progressive domestic agenda for economic recovery and social justice, and recognition by the people as well as the leaders that we cannot fight a war against poverty with an all-volunteer army. In his State of the Union address, President Bush said: "If you've got a hammer, find a nail." But nails cost money, and so do bricks and two-by-fours and windowpanes, not to speak of mortgages. Nevertheless, Mr. Bush's budget proposal includes even further housing cuts.

The president's call to conscience is welcome—but we are going to have to invest resources if we are to improve the nation's productivity and meet new economic competition. Just as the 1980s was a decade of disinvest-ment—a massive federal retreat from our cities—so must the 1990s be a de-cade of reinvestment. A post–Gulf War economic recovery plan cannot be just a couple of tax breaks and then, hope for the best. We must develop a strategic economic recovery plan for the 1990s that directly addresses the specific needs of America's poor, its working families, and its cities.

Let me suggest for key components of a domestic economic recovery and so-cial justice agenda.

1. *Invest in Jobs.* We must put Americans back to work by investing in jobs. There is no better antipoverty program than the dignity of a steady pay-check and a decent job. The federal government must take the lead in prim-ing the pump for economic recovery.

There is plenty of work to do. The United States has fallen far behind Japan and Western Europe in its investment in public infrastructure. In the 1980s, public investment in the United States fell to half of the 1970s rate, and one-quarter of that during the 1950s and 1960s. We see the results in our communities every day. Now we must start repairing our crumbling infra-structure of bridges, roads, and sewers; improve our mass transit system, in-cluding a high-speed rail system between New England and Washington; clean up our physical environment, such as our polluted harbors and rivers; and build affordable housing, by embarking on a large-scale program that of-fers a significant role to community-based nonprofit builders.

A recent report by the Economic Policy Institute (EPI) showed that such public investment would improve the overall economy by stimulating private investment, raising private sector productivity, increasing corporate profits, and spurring overall growth. EPI found that a dollar spent today on public infrastructure investment produces from two to five times more payoff in GNP growth than a dollar spent on tax cuts or deficit reduction.

A program to construct 1 million single-family homes and apartments a year would generate 1.3 million jobs, $34 billion in wages, and $14 billion in additional federal, state, and local tax revenues—and have significant ripple effects to promote economy recovery.

We must also retool our research-and-development priorities, putting our people and brainpower to work improving our civilian productivity with at least the same commitment that goes into inventing new weapons systems. We particularly underutilize our nation's colleges and universities—especially by neglecting federal investment in research linked to economic progress. Our major international competitors all devote significantly more resources toward civilian R&D, stimulating new businesses and technologies, and then helping to market them in the global economy.

2. *Invest in People.* The economy of the 1990s will rest on human re-sources. People and their skills will be the true sources of wealth and com-

petitiveness in the knowledge-driven global economy of the 1990s and beyond. Our education, job training, and human services efforts—all necessary to provide our work force with the skills needed if the United States is to compete in the new global economy—lag far behind those of our competitors. For example, federal funds for job training were more than cut in half during the past decade; hopes that the private sector would fill the gap were not realized.

We must view the physical and social well-being of our population as a long-term investment. We cannot expect a quick fix to a problem that has been evolving for many years. For example:

- Make Head Start—a proven cost-effective winner in the antipoverty effort—available to every three- and four-year-old child. Kids that participate in Head Start are more likely to do well in school, stay in school, finish school, and do well later in life, producing great benefits not only for themselves and their families but for their communities and their country. But only about one-quarter of all eligible children can participate because Washington doesn't provide funding. That is shortsighted and it shortchanges our children.

- Enact a national health care program. The United States is one of only two major industrial nations (the other is South Africa) without one. In Canada, for example, access is universal, spending per capita is less, and providers operate with much less paperwork and red tape than their counterparts in this country. Many poor Americans cannot afford to go off welfare because they and their kids would lose medical benefits. We can start by guaranteeing affordable health care for every pregnant woman and every child and by significantly expanding the preventative WIC nutrition program for women and kids. It makes human and fiscal sense; experience shows that an additional dollar spent on prenatal care saves about $3.38 as a result of the reduced rate of low-birthweight babies.

- Retool our job training efforts to provide all Americans with the skills they need so that the United States can build the world's foremost work force. That means reaching all young people—in or out of school—with first-class training, while guaranteeing them a decent job upon completion of the training. It also means extending and increasing unemployment benefits to laid-off workers while they are retrained. And it means providing all employers with incentives to invest in ongoing training and education for their work force at all levels.

- Create a national youth service corps that gives high school graduates an opportunity to devote two years to community service—working in our urban neighborhoods and rural areas—for which they'd earn a full college scholarship.

3. *Credit Where It's Due.* We have to relieve the current credit crunch that is starving our economy of much-needed investment capital to finance job-creating projects and rebuild our urban neighborhoods. In the past, federal policy—for example, tax incentives for corporate relocation, highway building, and the siting of military installations and contracts—promoted the flight of jobs and investment from our cities to sprawling suburbs and even overseas. Today, we need a national policy that encourages investment in cities to help them compete in the global economy. Federal tax policy should stimulate productive investment, not wasteful speculation. Tax incentives to private business should be coupled with public capital and job training in our inner cities to promote economic development. We should also revise federal laws to provide incentives for public and private pension funds to invest in economic development and affordable housing. Recent studies report that our pension funds are joining many American corporations in heading overseas. It's time to bring them home—and put the pensions of American workers to work for American jobs.

Likewise, the federal government needs to get lenders back in the business of financing job-creating investment and homeownership, not junk bonds and corporate take-overs. One way is for the federal government to insure deposits when funds are used for these specific purposes, but not to insure them for the kind of real estate and corporate speculation that swept the 1980s and helped bring us the current economic crisis.

Federal bank regulators must also enforce the Community Reinvestment Act, which requires lenders to meet the credit needs of low-income and minority neighborhoods. In Boston, we recently used the leverage of CRA—first enacted in 1977 to limit banks' "redlining" practices—to push local banks to create a $400 million community reinvestment program.

4. *Fair Federalism.* Washington must help ease the staggering financial burden facing cities. Cities house most of America's poor people and are expected to provide them—as well as other city residents—with decent schools, health care, police and fire protection, parks and recreation programs, and other public services. But, as Helen Ladd and John Yinger demonstrated in their recent book *America's Ailing Cities* (Johns Hopkins), our large cities simply lack the resources—the tax base—to do the job. Some cities are on the verge of bankruptcy and many cities are currently laying off teachers, police, and firefighters, shutting down schools, hospitals, and recreation programs, and are barely able to perform such housekeeping tasks as filling potholes and plowing snow.

During the 1980s, Washington shifted most of the burden of caring for the poor to cities and states—a scheme one observer has called "fend-for-yourself federalism." But poverty is a national problem, exacerbated by federal policies or inattention. We need a partnership between Washington and the cities—fair federalism.

The *Real* Story Behind State Governments' Financial Crises

Stephen Moore

For most of the last decade, while the Federal government wallowed in red ink, America's state governments widely were being praised as both paragons of fiscal responsibility and innovative laboratories of democracy. Largely thanks to the surging national economy, the 1980s were years when most states were able to please special-interest groups and taxpayers. While vastly expanding their budgets for existing agencies and launching popular and expensive state-funded programs in new policy areas, state lawmakers still managed to meet the bottom-line requirement of a balanced budget each year.

Now, the tab for that spending spree finally is coming due. With as many as 35 states facing substantial deficits, the financial outlook in state capitals may be more gloomy today than at any time since the depression. Aggregate state budget reserves have dwindled to an anemic 1.5 percent of expenditures—their lowest level in memory and less than one-third of the 5 percent reserve level considered fiscally prudent. (Figure 2.1).

The budget deterioration is most acute in the states east of the Mississippi River, particularly in the Northeast, but recently it has surfaced in southern and some western states as well. California, Connecticut, Florida, Massachusetts, Michigan, New Jersey, New York, Rhode Island, Texas, and Virginia each must erase deficit spending of $1 billion or more this year. Governors Mario Cuomo of New York and Pete Wilson of California face the biggest challenges—both must close a staggering two-year shortfall of $6 billion to $10 billion.

The root cause of the budget crisis almost universally has been misdiagnosed by state legislators, economic analysts, and the media. Most blame a variety of economic, political, and fiscal factors all beyond the states' direct control. These include a national economic recession that has drained the states of revenues, citizen resistance in the 1980s to new state taxes, steep declines in federal aid during the 1980s, new spending mandated by Washington, and court-imposed spending requirements for education and corrections.

Although each of these may be partially responsible for the record red ink, they are of minor significance compared with the primary culprit—a decade of runaway state government expenditures. According to Bureau of the Census data, state spending between 1982 and 1989 grew at an annual rate of

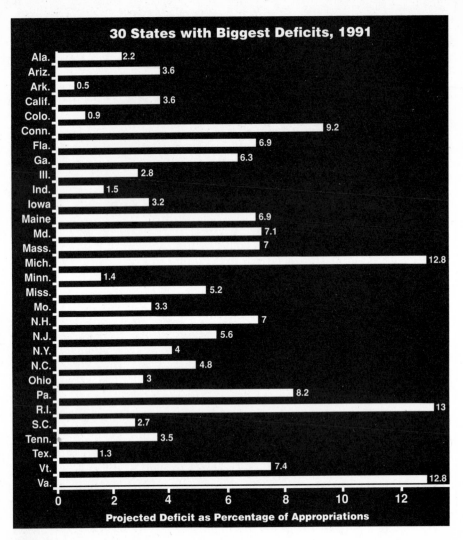

Figure 2.1

8.5 percent, roughly twice the inflation rate. Double-digit yearly percentage expenditure growth became the norm for state-funded programs, such as education, health care, welfare, and corrections. The number of state public employees grew by more than 500,000 in the 1980s and has reached an all-time high of roughly 150 employees per 10,000 residents.

Even in the midst of the current budget crisis, the spending binge continues. In 1990, the states increased expenditures on primary education by 10 percent, higher education by 9.5 percent, corrections by 17 percent, and Medicaid by 18 percent.

The aggregate state spending trends tell only a portion of the story. They do not explain the differing fiscal fortunes of the states—for example, why Massachusetts and New York are nearly insolvent today while Montana and Oregon are enjoying healthy surpluses.

Close examination of the fiscal behavior of the individual states during the 1980s reveals that the villain is uncontrolled expenditures. With few exceptions, those with the most severe deficits saw their economies and tax revenues grow rapidly over the past decade, but allowed spending to grow even faster. For the nation as a whole, state expenditures rose by 104 percent between 1980 and 1989. In some states, however, the increase was dramatically greater than that. In California, it grew by 119 percent; Connecticut, 174 percent; Florida, 169 percent; Massachusetts, 134 percent; and Virginia, 119 percent. In the nearly bankrupt states of the Northeast as a whole, it rose by 129 percent.

Although the amount of state taxes paid per person almost doubled, from $658 to $1,150, between 1980 and 1989, governors and legislators are demanding more revenues to cover their deficits. In 1990, they enacted $11 billion in new taxes, making it the single worst year for state taxpayers ever, according to the National Association of State Budget Officers. With deficits continuing to mount, almost two-thirds of the legislatures again are pressing taxpayers for more funds. Only a handful of new-breed, fiscally conservative governors—including Lawton Chiles of Florida, John Engler of Michigan, William Weld of Massachusetts, and Douglas Wilder of Virginia—have resisted the relentless crusade for new taxes and are cutting spending.

Notwithstanding the efforts of such governors, a distressingly familiar fiscal pattern has taken shape in the halls of state governments over the course of the past decade. Tax receipts and spending rose sharply during the economic expansion, and mountainous deficits have arrived during the current recession. That situation has prompted resistance to spending restraint and persistent calls for tax increases by powerful special-interest groups—teachers' unions, government employees, contractors, hospitals, welfare providers, etcetera—to balance the budget without service disruptions. Meanwhile, state taxpayers continue to get squeezed.

In short, the fiscal policies of the state governments in the 1990s have come to closely resemble those of Washington. Governor Weld's observation that the Massachusetts legislature lost its capacity to "just say no" to special interests easily could describe the culture of spending that now prevails in almost all of the capitals. State lawmakers should recognize from the experience of the federal government that they are sliding down a slippery slope leading to fiscal disaster, not fiscal balance.

The surge in red ink that has brought many state governments to the brink of bankruptcy would have been unimaginable a few years ago. Riding on a crest of prosperity, the states enjoyed sizable surpluses in the 1980s even as they pumped up spending. Since those boom years, aggregate state budget reserves plummeted from 4.8 percent of expenditures in 1989 to 3.3 percent in 1990 to 1.5 percent in 1991. Many states today are in the precarious fiscal situation of having almost no cash reserves to deal with even a mild budgetary contingency. New York and Massachusetts already have had their bond ratings lowered several times, which raises their cost of borrowing funds, and other states with dwindling financial reserves face the same prospect.

The genesis of budget deficits is no mystery. For most states, the 1980s were years of vast government program expansion. Bureau of the Census data reveal that, between 1980 and 1989, their combined expenditures went from $258 billion to $525 billion. That represented a nominal increase of 8.5 percent per year and an annual rise of 3.5 percent above inflation.

Much of the increase has occurred in four areas: education, health care, welfare, and corrections. Meanwhile, capital expenditures—for roads, bridges, environmental facilities, and other infrastructure—have declined slightly as a percentage of state budgets. The 1980s also were a period in which many revenue-rich states ventured into new areas of publicly provided services, such as day care, economic development, tourism, cultural and arts programs, mental health, and job training. During the "Massachusetts Miracle" years of the mid-1980s, for example, the state paid a subsidy of over $8,500 per student attending the state arts school; was the only state to reimburse patients for all 32 optional Medicare services—including chiropractic treatment; and purchased a $35,000 modern art sculpture to place in front of a prison.

One consequence of the build-up in spending has been a substantial bureaucratization of government. Even though polls indicate that most Americans do not believe they are receiving significantly better services from the states than they have in the past, the number of employees as a percentage of the population roughly has doubled since 1960.

SOARING TAXES

An analysis by the National Conference of State Legislatures suggests that 20–35 states were looking to raise taxes in 1991 or 1992 to meet budget shortfalls. This comes on the heels of a record $11 billion in new state taxes implemented in 1990. New Jersey Gov. James Florio rammed a $2.8 billion tax package through the legislature, the largest state hike in U.S. history. California voters approved Proposition 111, doubling the state gasoline tax from 9 to 18 cents per gallon, to pay for new roads. This tax will raise $18 billion over 10 years. Massachusetts approved $1.2 billion in new income, sales, and motor fuel taxes. New York raised $938 million in miscellaneous taxes. Such tax actions have created a taxpayer backlash in many states. In five, tax-raising governors—Republicans and Democrats alike—were chased from office by an irate electorate in the 1990 elections.

Undaunted, most legislatures pushed forward with tax plans in 1991, including:

- Introduction of a personal income tax in Connecticut, New Hampshire, Tennessee, and Texas.
- An income tax rate hike and a base broadening in California, Maryland, Mississippi, New York, Rhode Island, and Vermont.
- Higher or broadened sales taxes in Arkansas, California, Connecticut, Georgia, Kansas, Maine, Maryland, Mississippi, New York, North Carolina, Oregon, South Carolina, South Dakota, and Vermont.
- A gasoline tax hike in Idaho, Maryland, New Mexico, New York, and Rhode Island.
- New or higher cigarette and/or liquor taxes in California, Iowa, Minnesota, Nevada, Pennsylvania, Texas, and Vermont.
- Higher corporate taxes in Georgia, Nevada, New Hampshire, New York, Pennsylvania, and Rhode Island.

The supposed justification for such new and increased taxes is that state treasuries have been depleted of revenues because of the recession and the residual effects of the citizens' tax revolt of the late 1970s. For most states, however, nothing could be further from the truth. Per capita state tax burdens have been climbing steadily since 1960 and nearly have doubled since 1980.

According to a report by the Tax Foundation, taxes consume 34 cents of every dollar of earnings today. It calculates that the average family of four with two wage earners and a total income of $46,000 pays $17,139 in taxes, of which $4,775 are state and local taxes.

One reasonably might expect that the states with the most rapid economic growth in the 1980s and correspondingly large tax revenue windfalls from that growth would be in the best fiscal health today. In most cases, precisely the opposite is true. The states with fast revenue growth in the 1980s and the heaviest current tax burden tend to be those experiencing crippling deficits, not healthy surpluses.

That point is underscored by examining the fiscal experience of the 10 states facing deficits of $500 million or more: California, Connecticut, Florida, Georgia, Massachusetts, Michigan, New Jersey, New York, Pennsylvania, and Virginia. Eight of them enjoyed revenue growth above the national average in the 1980s—Michigan and Pennsylvania were the two exceptions. The heavily taxed states, not the lightly taxed ones, are burdened with big budget deficits today. Clearly, high taxes are no assurance of a balanced budget.

The rapid budget deterioration of the eight northeastern states—Connecticut, Maine, Massachusetts, New Hampshire, New Jersey, New York,

Rhode Island, and Vermont—is a case study in how rising taxes can be a double-edged sword for state governments. Thanks to rapid economic growth, their tax revenues grew 20 percent faster than did those of all other states from 1980 to 1988. Yet, despite their faster revenue growth, those 8 states now have negative budget reserves of two percent, while the other 42 have positive balances.

Why are the northeastern states awash in red ink? Their plight can be summarized concisely: Rapid revenue growth invited unbridled spending expansion on programs that cannot be cut back painlessly. Between 1980 and 1989, outlays escalated by 173 percent in Connecticut, 137 percent in Massachusetts, 145 percent in New Jersey, and 115 percent in New York and Maine.

Even normally fiscally conservative New Hampshire joined the public-sector feeding frenzy; its expenditures rose by 111 percent in the 1980s. "We did a lot of good things in the years we had the money," explains New Hampshire State Representative Donna P. Sytek, the Republican chairman of the House Ways and Means Committee. "But now all these programs are perceived as essential, and we cannot take them away without a lot of screams from the public." The experience of New Hampshire and the rest of the nearly bankrupt New England states suggests that tax hikes are a recipe not for fiscal balance, but for uncontrollable expenditures.

COMMON MYTHS ABOUT STATE BUDGET SHORTFALLS

For understandable reasons, most state officials refuse to acknowledge that a breakdown in fiscal discipline in the 1980s is at the root of their financial crisis today. Rather, they blame a combination of other factors, such as the national economic recession, declining federal aid, and the citizen tax revolts of the past decade. However, such complaints are based on myth, not reality.

Myth no. 1: The states sharply have cut back spending in response to growing deficits. Many governors and state legislators insist that, in response to dwindling budget reserves and a sputtering economy, they have been forced to cut back vital services. Thus, they allegedly have no alternative but to turn to new revenues as the only way to balance the budget. The truth is that the fiscal distress signals that began to appear in 1989 have not deterred an ongoing growth of expenditures, which have continued to grow faster than inflation in all but a very few states. Aggregate expenditures grew by 8.7 percent in 1989, 7.7 percent in 1990, and 6.5 percent in 1991—a rate of spending that is 2.7 percent above the inflation rate. That is not a dramatic rate of spending—especially in relation to the explosive growth of the middle and late 1980s—but neither is it a sign of austerity.

One encouraging budget development is that, out of economic necessity, many of the northeastern states—other than Connecticut and Maine—have begun to restrain their spending. For instance, outlays since 1989 have climbed only 8 percent in Massachusetts and 5 percent in New Jersey and New York.

On the other hand, a new disturbing trend is that the South has become the region of massive state spending growth. The fiscal policies of the southern states have become almost mirror images of those witnessed in the Northeast in the 1980s, and they are producing the same unhappy results. Florida, Georgia, Kentucky, North Carolina, and Texas all have seen their operating budgets grow by roughly 20 percent or more in just two years.

Myth no. 2: Reductions in federal aid during the 1980s have caused state budget deficits. While federal aid dropped from about 25 percent of state budgets in 1980 to less than 20 percent in 1991, that was mainly due to the states' rapidly increasing their own funding of new programs, rather than to any reduction in federal aid.

Although federal aid to states and cities in total dollars was cut back severely in the early 1980s, such payments have climbed steadily from $108 billion to $159 billion since 1987. Today's state budget deficits hardly can be blamed on the Reagan and Carter reductions in federal aid that occurred 10 budget cycles ago. Indeed, the states' fiscal performance of the last dozen years bears little or no relationship to fluctuations in federal aid.

Actually, federal aid has been more of a curse than a blessing. Because federal grant programs typically require state matching funds, such payments can increase, rather than decrease, the states' own-source tax burdens and spending. Lured by what appears to be free federal money, they often are induced to use a portion of their own tax revenue for projects they never would undertake on their own.

The states do have a legitimate gripe with federally mandated spending—on such areas as Medicaid, welfare, corrections, highways, and the environment—which can consume as much as 60 percent of a state's annual budget. As onerous and unjustified as they are, it is doubtful that policies handed down from Washington can account for all, or even a substantial amount, of the states' budgetary red ink. If increased mandates or reductions in federal aid are responsible for the decline in fiscal health, how have such states as Idaho, Montana, and Wisconsin managed to avoid the budget deficits that have plagued others? Presumably, they have suffered from the same Washington-imposed payment reductions and spending requirements. The fact that the states' budgetary circumstances vary dramatically from region to region and state to state suggests that the unique fiscal behavior of the individual states, not national factors such as federal aid, is the primary explanation for the deficits.

Myth no. 3: State spending on education must rise to make up for a decade of neglect. More than a dozen states either have raised or are planning new taxes to comply with court-ordered "school finance equalization" requirements. California, Kentucky, Montana, New Jersey, and Texas are a few of the states that already have raised taxes in response to those court decisions. Typically, the judges in such cases have empowered themselves to require the legislature to equalize per-student spending on education within the state. For the education establishment, "equalization" has become a buzzword for more money.

Those cases have reinforced two false impressions: that the states are neglecting education and that a larger commitment of state tax dollars to the nation's schools will increase the educational performance of America's children. State and local spending on education rose from $89 billion to $188 billion between 1980 and 1989. Given falling enrollment, such expenditures might have been expected to ease during that period.

Moreover, an increasing portion of those education dollars has come from the states, not local school districts, where money is better spent. Before 1970, funding for primary and secondary schools came almost exclusively from local property taxes, with only a small fraction originating from state government. Today, almost half of all education funds come from the states.

Pumping more state tax dollars into the schools is likely to yield disappointing results in improving education. There is nearly unanimous agreement among researchers that, above a minimum level, government spending on education is unrelated to test scores and other measures of education performance. South Dakota is a case in point. It ranks forty-seventh in per student state expenditures for education, but fifth in the nation in SAT scores and in the top 10 in most other rankings of educational performance.

Myth no. 4: States should raise income taxes to make tax codes fairer. As it is in Washington, so-called tax fairness is now the rage in the nation's state capitals. A well-publicized 1991 document from the Citizens for Tax Justice suggests that "virtually every state taxes its poor and middle income families at rates significantly higher than those faced by the richest families." The group's prescription: States should make their income tax systems more progressive.

The popular perception is that the states' tax structures grew more unfair in the 1980s. The reality is that income taxes, which have become increasingly progressive and fall most heavily on the rich, have been the fastest growing revenue source for state governments. The percentage of total state taxes derived from income tax receipts today is twice as high as it was in the mid-1960s.

The states could not possibly choose a more economically destructive way to raise revenues than through personal and corporate income taxes. In 1982, the Joint Economic Committee of the U.S. Congress compared the tax policies of the 16 states with the fastest-growing incomes and the slowest-growing incomes between 1970 and 1979. The results demonstrated that income growth in a state is inversely related to the level of state and local tax burdens, changes in such tax burdens, the amount of income taxes levied, and the progressivity of the income tax rates.

The study concluded:

> The evidence is strong that tax and expenditure policies of state and local governments are important in explaining variations in economic growth between states—far more important than other factors frequently cited such as climate, energy costs, the impact of federal fiscal policies, etc. It is clear that high rates of taxation lower the rate of economic growth, and that states that lower their tax burdens are rewarded with an enhancement in their economic growth. Income taxes levied on individuals and corporations are particularly detrimental to growth, more so than consumption-based taxes or user charges that do not reduce incentives to work or form capital. Progressive taxation not only lowers the rate of economic growth compared with proportional or regressive taxation, but in the process hurts the very persons that progressive taxes are designed to help: the poor.

TAX HIKES' DIRE CONSEQUENCES

The recent experiences of the individual states confirm that conclusion. Iowa, for instance, is suffering from one of the Midwest's highest income taxes. A 1987 study by the Iowa Tax Education Foundation, *The Iowa Exodus: Why Are People Leaving the State?*, included interviews with 251 former Iowans who had moved out during the 1980s. The study found that the state's very high income tax rates were a major factor in explaining the migration.

New Jersey instituted a $2.8 billion tax increase in 1990. Although it featured substantial increases in excise taxes (including a boost in the sales tax from 6 to 7 percent), the major change was in personal income tax rates. Gov. Florio doubled the top marginal rate to 7 percent for individuals earning more than $75,000, one of the highest top rates in the nation. New Jersey's program is being viewed as a national experiment on the effects of new taxes on a state's economic pulse. An initial analysis by the New Jersey–based consulting firm Polyconomics predicts a severe economic recession in the state, with growth as much as 3 percent lower than it would otherwise have been by 1992:

> State tax revenues could decline by approximately five to 10 percent by 1992 with property tax revenues of local governments possibly declining by as much as 20 to 30 percent. Net relocation of corporate offices to the state will turn negative, eliminating about half the demand for mid-range ($250,000 to $500,000) homes, and about two-thirds of the demand for new office space. . . . A vicious cycle of declining property values and declining tax reve-

nues, combined with higher property tax revenue requirements, will throw many New Jersey communities into fiscal crisis.

Already, some of those dire predictions are proving highly accurate. Real estate values in New Jersey have dropped substantially, unemployment has climbed from below to above the national average, and business bankruptcies nearly doubled in 1990.

A study for the Texas Public Policy Foundation by economist Thomas Dye finds that state income taxes have had two primary effects, both undesirable. First, they have slowed the rate of income growth in states that have adopted them. Second, they have led to an acceleration in state spending in those states. Dye investigated the economic and fiscal changes in the eight states that most recently enacted an income tax and concluded:

> Dramatic rises in state government spending were recorded in six of the eight states that adopted an income tax. Of course, state spending rose before and after adoption of an income tax. But the rate of increase following adoption of an income tax was significantly higher than the rate of increase prior to doing so. Each of these six states began spending significantly more than preadoption forecasts.

> In six of the eight states, personal income growth slowed significantly following enactment. Personal income continued to grow in these states, but the rate of increase was significantly lower following adoption of income taxation.

In sum, state income taxes would seem to have little to commend them. State-by-state evidence suggests that governors and legislators should resist increases in personal income tax rates in redesigning their tax codes. Indeed, a pro-growth fiscal strategy would involve making substantial reductions in those tax rates.

With each passing month, the fiscal outlook for America's state governments grows more bleak. Predictably, the preferred method of reversing the tide of red ink in state capitals is to raise taxes. Advertised spending reductions often are fictitious, built from highly inflated budgetary baselines.

The reality of the fiscal policies of the states varies widely from the rhetoric. Those that insist spending has been cut to the bone are many of the very states that expanded their budgets by more than 50 percent in real dollars during the past decade. The ones that argue that the bureaucracy has been pruned are the same states which have allowed the number of workers on their payrolls relative to the number of private-sector workers supporting their salaries to climb to an all-time high. Moreover, the states that claim Washington has left them high and dry are receiving $150 billion in federal aid this year, an all-time record in real dollars.

State lawmakers now have two options. The first is to close the budget gaps through tax hikes. New Jersey's Florio spearheaded that approach in 1990 and is now one of the most unpopular politicians in America. The alternative path is being tested by three first-term governors: Democrat Doug Wilder of Virginia and Republicans John Engler of Michigan and William Weld of Massachusetts. They propose to erase the sizable deficits they inherited from their predecessors through spending cutbacks alone and not a penny of new taxes. It is too early to predict whether their programs can succeed politically. However, their fiscal blueprint does offer a ray of hope that the tax-and-spend cycle finally can be disrupted and that balanced budgets once again will become standard operating procedure in state capitals.

QUESTIONS FOR DISCUSSION

2.1 Is it true that state and local governments are closer to the people and, thus, more accountable to the public?

2.2 Should the Congress be able to pass legislation mandating state policies and services without providing any of the funds?

2.3 Does it make sense to federalize certain programs, health and welfare for example, and leave others, education for example, entirely to state and local governments?

Chapter
3

Should Private Consensual Adult Sexual Behavior Be Protected by the Constitution?

INTRODUCTION

The Supreme Court announced in *Bowers* v. *Hardwick* (1986) that the Constitution did not prevent states from outlawing homosexual sodomy. One spokesman of a gay rights group denounced this decision as the moral equivalent of the *Dred Scott* opinion. Some predicted a wave of homophobia and feared that law enforcement officials would have a new hunting license to torment gays. In fact, *Bowers* changed very little. Sodomy laws have been on the books for hundreds of years, and they are rarely, if ever, enforced. The importance of the case was not in its immediate social consequences, but in its constitutional meaning. This involves the right to privacy—its contours and standing in the Constitution—and the role of the Supreme Court as the final arbiter of our social values.

The right to privacy is not mentioned explicitly in the Constitution. There are, however, privacy elements in some provisions of the Bill of Rights. The Fourth Amendment protects people from unreasonable searches and seizures, while the Fifth Amendment guarantees the right against self-incrimination. It was not until *Griswold* v. *Conn.* (1965) that the Court acknowledged an independent right to privacy, overturning a Connecticut law banning the sale of birth-control devices and information. In that case Justice William O. Douglas declared that the right to privacy was found in the "penumbras [shadows] of the Bill of Rights."

In *Roe* v. *Wade* (1973), the Court expanded the right to privacy and recognized a woman's right to terminate her pregnancy—a decision that must rank as one of the Court's most controversial. Later, in *Bowers* the Court was asked to expand the right to privacy to include private consensual homosexual sodomy. Given the direction the Court had chartered in *Roe*, this did not seem to be an unreasonable expectation. If a woman's decision to abort her pregnancy was considered largely beyond the reach of the state, why not the private acts of two adult homosexuals?

However, in *Bowers*, the conservatives were in the majority. Justice Byron White, writing for the majority in the excerpted opinion that follows, stated that the right to privacy is restricted to matters involving family, marriage, and procreation. Such rights are "deeply rooted in the nation's history and tradition." Laws against homosexual sodomy, he asserted, "have ancient roots."

Justice Harry Blackmun, who wrote the majority opinion in *Roe*, dissented in *Bowers* (excerpted in the following). He argued that the right to privacy goes beyond the boundary of family life and involves "the fundamental interest all individuals have in controlling the nature of their intimate associations with others." In Blackmun's words, the case was not about the "fundamental right to engage in homosexual sodomy," but, rather, about "the right to be let alone."

Majority Opinion
Bowers v. *Hardwick* (1986)

Justice Byron White

Justice White delivered the opinion of the Court.

In August 1982, respondent Hardwick (hereafter respondent) was charged with violating the Georgia statute criminalizing sodomy by committing that act with another adult male in the bedroom of respondent's home. After a preliminary hearing, the District Attorney decided not to present the matter to the grand jury unless further evidence developed.

Respondent then brought suit in the Federal District Court, challenging the constitutionality of the statute insofar as it criminalized consensual
sodomy. He asserted that he was a practicing homosexual, that the Georgia
sodomy statute, as administered by the defendants, placed him in imminent
danger of arrest, and that the statute for several reasons violates the federal
Constitution. The District Court granted the defendants' motion to dismiss
for failure to state a claim, relying on *Doe* v. *Commonwealth's Attorney for
the City of Richmond*, which this Court summarily affirmed.

A divided panel of the Court of Appeals for the Eleventh Circuit reversed. The court first held that, because *Doe* was distinguishable and in any
event had been undermined by later decisions, our summary affirmance in
that case did not require affirmance of the District Court. Relying on our
decisions in *Griswold* v. *Connecticut* (1965); *Eisenstadt* v. *Baird* (1972); *Stanley* v. *Georgia* (1969); and *Roe* v. *Wade* (1973), the court went on to hold that
the Georgia statute violated respondent's fundamental rights because his homosexual activity is a private and intimate association that is beyond the
reach of state regulation by reason of the Ninth Amendment and the Due
Process Clause of the Fourteenth Amendment. The case was remanded for
trial, at which, to prevail, the State would have to prove that the statute is
supported by a compelling interest and is the most narrowly drawn means of
achieving that end.

[1] Because other Courts of Appeals have arrived at judgments contrary
to that of the Eleventh Circuit in this case, we granted the Attorney General's petition for certiorari questioning the holding that the sodomy statute violates the fundamental rights of homosexuals. We agree with petitioner that
the Court of Appeals erred, and hence reverse its judgment.

[2] This case does not require a judgment on whether laws against
sodomy between consenting adults in general, or between homosexuals in
particular, are wise or desirable. It raises no question about the right or
propriety of state legislative decisions to repeal their laws that criminalize
homosexual sodomy, or of state-court decisions invalidating those laws on
state constitutional grounds. The issue presented is whether the federal
Constitution confers a fundamental right upon homosexuals to engage in sodomy and hence invalidates the laws of the many States that still make such
conduct illegal and have done so for a very long time. The case also calls for
some judgment about the limits of the Court's role in carrying out its constitutional mandate.

We first register our disagreement with the Court of Appeals and with
respondent that the Court's prior cases have construed the Constitution to
confer a right of privacy that extends to homosexual sodomy and for all in-
tents and purposes have decided this case. The reach of this line of cases was
sketched in *Carey* v. *Population Services International* (1977). *Pierce* v.
Society of Sisters (1925), and *Meyer* v. *Nebraska* (1923), were described as

dealing with child rearing and education; *Prince* v. *Massachusetts* (1944), with family relationships; *Skinner* v. *Oklahoma ex rel. Williamson* (1942), with procreation; *Loving* v. *Virginia* (1967), with marriage; *Griswold* v. *Connecticut, supra,* and *Eisenstadt* v. *Baird, supra,* with contraception; and *Roe* v. *Wade* (1973), with abortion. The latter three cases were interpreted as construing the Due Process Clause of the Fourteenth Amendment to confer a fundamental right to decide whether or not to beget or bear a child. *Carey* v. *Population Services International, supra,* 431 U.S., at 688–689, 97 S.Ct., at 2017–2018.

Accepting the decisions in these cases and the above description of them, we think it evident that none of the rights announced in those cases bears any resemblance to the claimed constitutional right of homosexuals to engage in acts of sodomy that is asserted in this case. No connection between family, marriage, or procreation on the one hand and homosexual activity on the other has been demonstrated, either by the Court of Appeals or by respondent. Moreover, any claim that these cases nevertheless stand for the proposition that any kind of private sexual conduct between consenting adults is constitutionally insulated from state proscription is unsupportable. Indeed, the Court's opinion in *Carey* twice asserted that the privacy rights, which the *Griswold* line of cases found to be one of the protections provided by the Due Process Clause, did not reach so far.

Precedent aside, however, respondent would have us announce, as the Court of Appeals did, a fundamental right to engage in homosexual sodomy. This we are quite unwilling to do. It is true that despite the language of the Due Process Clauses of the Fifth and Fourteenth Amendments, which appears to focus only on the processes by which life, liberty, or property is taken, the cases are legion in which those Clauses have been interpreted to have substantive content, subsuming rights that to a great extent are immune from federal or state regulation or proscription. Among such cases are those recognizing rights that have little or no textual support in the constitutional language. *Meyer, Prince,* and *Pierce* fall in this category, as do the privacy cases from *Griswold* to *Carey.*

Striving to assure itself and the public that announcing rights not readily identifiable in the Constitution's text involves much more than the imposition of the Justices' own choice of values on the states and the federal Government, the Court has sought to identify the nature of the rights qualifying for heightened judicial protection. In *Palko* v. *Connecticut* (1937), it was said that this category includes those fundamental liberties that are "implicit in the concept of ordered liberty," such that "neither liberty nor justice would exist if [they] were sacrificed." A different description of fundamental liberties appeared in *Moore* v. *East Cleveland,* 431 U.S. 494, 503, 97 S.Ct. 1932, 1937, 52 L.Ed.2d 531 (1977) (opinion of Powell, J.), where they are characterized as those liberties that are "deeply rooted in this Nation's history and tradition." *Id.*, at 503, 97 S.Ct., at 1938 (Powell, J.). See also *Griswold* v. *Connecticut*, 381 U.S., at 506, 85 S.Ct., at 1693.

It is obvious to us that neither of these formulations would extend a fundamental right to homosexuals to engage in acts of consensual sodomy. Proscriptions against that conduct have ancient roots. See generally, Survey on the Constitutional Right to Privacy in the Context of Homosexual Activity, 40 U.Miami L.Rev. 521, 525 (1986). Sodomy was a criminal offense at common law and was forbidden by the laws of the original 13 States when they ratified the Bill of Rights. In 1868, when the Fourteenth Amendment was ratified, all but 5 of the 37 States in the Union had criminal sodomy laws. In fact, until 1961, all 50 states outlawed sodomy, and today, 24 states and the District of Columbia continue to provide criminal penalties for sodomy performed in private and between consenting adults. See Survey, U.Miami L.Rev., *supra*, at 524, n. 9. Against this background, to claim that a right to engage in such conduct is "deeply rooted in this Nation's history and tradition" or "implicit in the concept of ordered liberty" is, at best, facetious.

[3] Nor are we inclined to take a more expansive view of our authority to discover new fundamental rights imbedded in the Due Process Clause. The Court is most vulnerable and comes nearest to illegitimacy when it deals with judge-made constitutional law having little or no cognizable roots in the language or design of the Constitution. That this is so was painfully demonstrated by the face-off between the Executive and the Court in the 1930s, which resulted in the repudiation of much of the substantive gloss that the Court had placed on the Due Process Clauses of the Fifth and Fourteenth Amendments. There should be, therefore, great resistance to expand the substantive reach of those Clauses, particularly if it requires redefining the category of rights deemed to be fundamental. Otherwise, the Judiciary necessarily takes to itself further authority to govern the country without express constitutional authority. The claimed right pressed on us today falls far short of overcoming this resistance.

Respondent, however, asserts that the result should be different where the homosexual conduct occurs in the privacy of the home. He relies on *Stanley* v. *Georgia*, 394 U.S. 557, 89 S.Ct. 1243, 22 L.Ed.2d 542 (1969), where the Court held that the First Amendment prevents conviction for possessing and reading obscene material in the privacy of one's home: "If the First Amendment means anything, it means that a State has no business telling a man, sitting alone in his house, what books he may read or what films he may watch." *Id.*, at 565, 89 S.Ct., at 1248.

Stanley did protect conduct that would not have been protected outside the home, and it partially prevented the enforcement of state obscenity laws; but the decision was firmly grounded in the First Amendment. The right pressed upon us here has no similar support in the text of the Constitution, and it does not qualify for recognition under the prevailing principles for construing the Fourteenth Amendment. Its limits are also difficult to discern. Plainly enough, otherwise illegal conduct is not always immunized whenever it occurs in the home. Victimless crimes, such as the possession and use of illegal drugs, do not escape the law where they are committed at home. *Stanley* itself recognized that its holding offered no protection for the possession in the home of drugs, firearms, or stolen goods. *Id.*, at 568, n. 11, 89 S.Ct., at 1249, n. 11. And if respondent's submission is limited to the voluntary sexual conduct between consenting adults, it would be difficult, except by fiat, to limit the claimed right to homosexual conduct while leaving exposed to prosecution adultery, incest, and other sexual crimes even though they are committed in the home. We are unwilling to start down that road.

[4] Even if the conduct at issue here is not a fundamental right, respondent asserts that there must be a rational basis for the law and that there is none in this case other than the presumed belief of a majority of the electorate in Georgia that homosexual sodomy is immoral and unacceptable. This is said to be an inadequate rationale to support the law. The law, however, is constantly based on notions of morality, and if all laws representing essentially moral choices are to be invalidated under the Due Process Clause, the courts will be very busy indeed. Even respondent makes no such claim, but insists that majority sentiments about the morality of homosexuality should be declared inadequate. We do not agree, and are unpersuaded that the sodomy laws of some 25 States should be invalidated on this basis.

Accordingly, the judgment of the Court of Appeals is
Reversed.

Dissenting Opinion

Justice Harry Blackmun

Justice Blackmun, with whom Justice Brennan, Justice Marshall, and Justice Stevens join, dissenting.

This case is no more about "a fundamental right to engage in homosexual sodomy," as the Court purports to declare, *ante*, at 2844, than *Stanley* v. *Georgia* (1969), was about a fundamental right to watch obscene movies, or

Katz v. *United States* (1967), was about a fundamental right to place interstate bets from a telephone booth. Rather, this case is about "the most compresive of rights and the right most valued by civilized men," namely, "the right to be let alone." *Olmstead* v. *United States* (1928) (Brandeis, J., dissenting).

The statute at issue, Ga.Code Ann. § 16–6–2 (1984), denies individuals the right to decide for themselves whether to engage in particular forms of private, consensual sexual activity. The Court concludes that § 16–6–2 is valid essentially because "the laws of . . . many States . . . still make such conduct illegal and have done so for a very long time." *Ante*, at 2843. But the fact that the moral judgments expressed by statutes like § 16–6–2 may be " 'natural and familiar . . . ought not to conclude our judgment upon the question whether statutes embodying them conflict with the Constitution of the United States.' " *Roe* v. *Wade*, 35 L. Ed.2d 147 (1973), quoting *Lochner* v. *New York* (1905) (Holmes, J., dissenting). Like Justice Holmes, I believe that "[i]t is revolting to have no better reason for a rule of law than that so it was laid down in the time of Henry IV. It is still more revolting if the grounds upon which it was laid down have vanished long since, and the rule simply persists from blind imitation of the past." Holmes, The Path of the Law, 10 Harv. L. Rev. 457, 469 (1897). I believe we must analyze Hardwick's claim in the light of the values that underlie the constitutional right to privacy. If that right means anything, it means that, before Georgia can prosecute its citizens for making choices about the most intimate aspects of their lives, it must do more than assert that the choice they have made is an " 'abominable crime not fit to be named among Christians.' " *Herring* v. *State* (1904).

I

In its haste to reverse the Court of Appeals and hold that the Constitution does not "confe[r] a fundamental right upon homosexuals to engage in sodomy," *ante*, at 2843, the Court relegates the actual statute being challenged to a footnote and ignores the procedural posture of the case before it. A fair reading of the statute and of the complaint clearly reveals that the majority has distorted the question this case presents.

First, the Court's almost obsessive focus on homosexual activity is particularly hard to justify in light of the broad language Georgia has used. Unlike the Court, the Georgia Legislature has not proceeded on the assumption that homosexuals are so different from other citizens that their lives may be controlled in a way that would not be tolerated if it limited the choices of those other citizens. Cf. *ante*, at 2842, n. 2. Rather, Georgia has provided that "[a] person commits the offense of sodomy when he performs or submits to any sexual act involving the sex organs of one person and the mouth or anus of another." Ga. Code Ann. § 16–6–2(a) (1984). The sex or status of the persons who engage in the act is irrelevant as a matter of state law. In fact, to the extent I can discern a legislative purpose for Georgia's 1968 enactment of § 16–6–2, that purpose seems to have been to broaden the coverage of the law to reach heterosexual as well as homosexual activity. I therefore see no basis for the Court's decision to treat this case as an "as applied" challenge to § 16–6–2, see *ante*, at 2842, no. 2, or for Georgia's attempt, both in its brief and at oral argument, to defend § 16–6–2 solely on the grounds that it prohibits homosexual activity. Michael Hardwick's standing may rest in significant part on Georgia's apparent willingness to enforce against homosexuals a law it seems not to have any desire to enforce against heterosexuals. But his claim that § 16-6-2 involves an unconstitutional intrusion into his privacy and his right of intimate association does not depend in any way on his sexual orientation.

Second, I disagree with the Court's refusal to consider whether § 16–6–2 runs afoul of the Eighth or Ninth Amendments or the Equal Protection Clause of the Fourteenth Amendment. Respondent's complaint expressly invoked the Ninth Amendment, and he relied heavily before this Court on *Griswold* v. *Connecticut* (1965), which identifies that Amendment as one of the specific constitutional provisions giving "life and substance" to our understanding of privacy. More importantly, the procedural posture of the case requires that we affirm the Court of Appeals' judgment if there is *any* ground on which respondent may be entitled to relief. This case is before us on petitioner's motion to dismiss for failure to state a claim, 17. It is a well-settled principle of law that "a complaint should not be dismissed merely because a plaintiff's allegations do not support the particular legal theory he advances, for the court is under a duty to examine the complaint to determine if the allegations provide for relief on any possible theory." Thus, even if respondent did not advance claims based on the Eighth or Ninth Amendments, or on the Equal Protection Clause, his complaint should not be dismissed if any of those provisions could entitle him to relief. I need not reach either the Eighth Amendment or the Equal Protection Clause issues because I believe that Hardwick has stated a cognizable claim that § 16–6–2 interferes with constitutionally protected interests in privacy and freedom of intimate association. But neither the Eighth Amendment nor the Equal Protection Clause is so clearly irrelevant that a claim resting on either provision should be peremptorily dismissed. The Court's cramped reading of the issue before it makes for a short opinion, but it does little to make for a persuasive one.

II

"Our cases long have recognized that the Constitution embodies a promise that a certain private sphere of individual liberty will be kept largely beyond the reach of government." *Thornburgh* v. *American College of Obstetricians & Gynecologists* (1986). In construing the right to privacy, the Court has proceeded along two somewhat distinct, albeit complementary, lines. First, it has recognized a privacy interest with reference to certain *decisions* that are properly for the individual to make. Second, it has recognized a privacy interest with reference to certain *places* without regard for the particular activities in which the individuals who occupy them are engaged. The case before us implicates both the decisional and the spatial aspects of the right to privacy.

A

The Court concludes today that none of our prior cases dealing with various decisions that individuals are entitled to make free of governmental interference "bears any resemblance to the claimed constitutional right of homosexuals to engage in acts of sodomy that is asserted in this case." *Ante,* at 2844. While it is true that these cases may be characterized by their connection to protection of the family, see *Roberts* v. *United States Jaycees* (1984), the Court's conclusion that they extend no further than this boundary ignores the warning in *Moore* v. *East Cleveland* (1977) (plurality opinion), against "clos[ing] our eyes to the basic reasons why certain rights associated with the family have been accorded shelter under the Fourteenth Amendment's Due Process Clause." We protect those rights not because they contribute, in some direct and material way, to the general public welfare, but because they form so central a part of an individual's life. "[T]he concept of privacy embodies the 'moral fact that a person belongs to himself and not others nor to society as a whole.' " *Thornburgh* v. *American College of Obstetricians & Gynecologists* (Stevens, J., concurring). And so we protect the decision whether to marry precisely because marriage "is an association that promotes a way of life, not causes; a harmony in living, not political faiths; a bilateral loyalty, not commercial or social projects." *Griswold* v. *Connecticut.* We protect the decision whether to have a child because parenthood alters so dramatically an individual's self-definition, not because of demographic considerations or the Bible's command to be fruitful and multiply. Cf. *Thornburgh* v. *American College of Obstetricians & Gynecologists, supra* (Stevens, J., concurring). And we protect the family because it contributes so powerfully to the happiness of individuals, not because of a preference for stereotypical households. Cf. *Moore* v. *East Cleveland* 1939 (plurality opinion). The Court recognized in *Roberts* that the "ability independently to define one's identity that is central to any concept of liberty" cannot truly be exercised in a vacuum; we all depend on the "emotional enrichment from close ties with others." *Ibid.*

Only the most willful blindness could obscure the fact that sexual intimacy is "a sensitive, key relationship of human existence, central to family life, community welfare, and the development of human personality," *Paris*

Adult Theatre I v. *Slaton*; see also *Carey* v. *Population Services International* (1977). The fact that individuals define themselves in a significant way through their intimate sexual relationships with others suggests, in a Nation as diverse as ours, that there may be many "right" ways of conducting those relationships, and that much of the richness of a relationship will come from the freedom an individual has to *choose* the form and nature of these intensely personal bonds.

In a variety of circumstances we have recognized that a necessary corollary of giving individuals freedom to choose how to conduct their lives is acceptance of the fact that different individuals will make different choices. For example, in holding that the clearly important state interest in public education should give way to a competing claim by the Amish to the effect that extended formal schooling threatened their way of life, the Court declared: "There can be no assumption that today's majority is 'right' and the Amish and others like them are 'wrong.' A way of life that is odd or even erratic but interferes with no rights or interests of others is not to be condemned because it is different." *Wisconsin* v. *Yoder* (1972). The Court claims that its decision today merely refuses to recognize a fundamental right to engage in homosexual sodomy; what the Court really has refused to recognize is the fundamental interest all individuals have in controlling the nature of their intimate associations with others.

QUESTIONS FOR DISCUSSION

3.1 The law which was challenged in *Bowers* outlawed both homosexual and heterosexual sodomy. Yet, Justice White chose to focus upon homosexual sodomy and said nothing about laws barring heterosexual sodomy. Should privacy rights extend to one but not the other? Is this a consistent argument?

3.2 Strict constructionists are uncomfortable with the right to privacy because it cannot be located in the text of the Constitution. They feel that the limits and parameters of such rights are vague since they have little constitutional history. Once the Court discovers such rights, the strict constructionists worry that it will roam broadly in defining them and will venture in the area of policy-making. Is this a valid concern? How then would the right to privacy be protected?

3.3 If Justice Blackmun is correct that the right to privacy includes "the right to be let alone," should the Court also protect so-called victimless crimes such as gambling, prostitution, and drug use?

Chapter
4

Does Affirmative Action Help Minorities?

INTRODUCTION

At the root of the affirmative action debate are two competing concepts of justice. One emphasizes individual fairness and merit, and the other stresses equality and social justice. The former focuses upon an individual's right to be evaluated on his or her abilities alone and envisions a color-blind society. The latter stresses society's obligation to compensate women and minorities for past injustices.

Affirmative action has no one clear definition beyond the general understanding that it requires employers and schools to go further than non-discrimination in making opportunities available to women and minorities. Supporters feel that habits of racial and sexual discrimination die hard and that only positive results can erase a legacy of racism and sexism. They do not feel that people who come from victimized groups can be expected to compete immediately on a level playing field. Critics argue that affirmative action has become a matter of statistical goals and quotas that violate the principle of color-blindedness. They also feel that affirmative action programs place a stigma on minority accomplishments and serve to enflame race relations.

Affirmative action has become increasingly controversial. To some it is a matter of racial justice, and, to others, it involves reverse discrimination. Civil rights leaders consider it the keystone of their programs, while many white males consider themselves to be its victims. What was once a strong consensus for civil rights has been weakened.

In the following selections, Herman Schwartz, an advocate of affirmative action, argues that "the use of goals and timetables . . . has helped to make modest improvements" in the conditions of minorities. He claims that race-conscious selections to ensure minority representation in the make-up of police departments is sound public policy. On the other hand, Professor Walter E. Williams, an opponent of affirmative action, claims that racial preferences for black students in college admission only masks the real problem of poor academic preparation and inferior inner-city public schools.

In Defense of Affirmative Action
A Look at Realities, a Reply to Critics

Herman Schwartz

The Reagan administration's assault on the rights of minorities and women has focused on the existing policy of affirmative action. This strategy may be shrewd politics but is mean-spirited morally and insupportable legally.

The attack on affirmative action is only a small part of this administration's campaign against the hard-won rights of blacks, women, and other groups that suffer the inequities of society. Since 1964 this country has developed and refined a body of constitutional, statutory, and regulatory approaches designed to exorcise the existence and effects of the racism and sexism so deeply entrenched in our society. Until 1981 all of our presidents, to a greater or lesser extent, contributed to this effort, even when, like Richard Nixon, they were less than enthusiastic. The Reagan administration has broken with this tradition. President Reagan's spokespeople—Assistant Attorney General for Civil Rights William Bradford Reynolds and Reagan's Civil Rights Commission appointees Clarence Pendleton and Morris Abram—declare their unlimited devotion to fighting discrimination and furthering civil rights, and in Abram's case there is an honorable track record.

But the administration's record has been one of across-the-board hostility to civil rights, and though the politically potent issue of affirmative action may have dominated rhetorically, it actually represents only part of the offensive.

Examples are numerous. The Reagan administration vigorously supported tax exemption for schools that discriminate against blacks. It crusaded for a specific intent rule that would have greatly handicapped both federal enforcement and private plaintiffs in voting rights and housing cases, and grudgingly surrendered on voting rights when Congress overwhelmingly declined to go along. It has consistently been permissive regarding voting law changes that blacks have questioned, as was the case in Louisiana and North Carolina. It has approved previously rejected proposals by Louisiana, Mississippi, and North Carolina regarding compliance with federal court orders to rid their higher education systems of racial discrimination; has held up as a model a school desegregation plan it negotiated in Bakersfield, California, which the *New York Times* called a "blueprint for evasion and for continuing the administration's lax approach to school desegregation"; and has intervened against black plaintiffs in school desegregation cases, with Mr. Reynolds in a South Carolina case instructing his trial attorneys to make "those bastards . . . jump through every hoop."

Judicial and other appointments have gone overwhelmingly to white males, even in the heavily black District of Columbia, where only 3 of 14 judges appointed by Reagan have been members of racial minorities.

Where women are concerned, the administration has urged sharp limitations on the nondiscrimination obligations of educational institutions receiving federal money, has opposed the Equal Rights Amendment, and has opposed equal pay for equal work. It has also refused to follow a congressional mandate that the Department of Justice intervene frequently on behalf of retarded, mentally disturbed, and other children and adults institutionalized in intolerable conditions. Neither has it enforced §504 of the Disabled Persons Civil Rights Act, which outlaws discrimination, but instead it has tried to reduce the obligation of federal agencies and others to accommodate the handicapped.

All these acts and policies are in addition to the administration's position on goals and timetables and in most cases represent a 180-degree shift from the position of all prior administrations. Most revealing of this shift is the administration's corruption of the United States Commission on Civil Rights, transforming it from an independent conscience of the national community, committed to advancing civil rights and free from political interference, to an arm of the administration committed to promoting antiminority, antiwomen, and antihandicapped policies.

All this is perhaps not surprising, given a president who as a governor and an opinion leader had opposed every major civil rights law enacted by

Congress in the last 20 years, though now Mr. Reynolds has only praise for these same statutes, which he claims mandate "race neutrality."

Affirmative action has been defined as "a public or private program designed to equalize hiring and admission opportunities for historically disadvantaged groups by taking into consideration those very characteristics which have been used to deny them equal treatment."[1] The controversy swirls primarily around the use of numerical goals and timetables for hiring or promotion, for university admissions, and for other benefits. It is fueled by the powerful strain of individualism that runs through American history and belief.

It is a hard issue, about which reasonable people can differ. Insofar as affirmative action is designed to compensate the disadvantaged for past racism, sexism, and other discrimination, many understandably believe that today's majority should not have to pay for their ancestors' sins. But somehow we must undo the cruel consequences of the racism and sexism that still plague us, both for the sake of the victims and to end the enormous human waste that costs society so much. Civil Rights Commission Chairman Pendleton has conceded that discrimination is not only still with us but is, as he put it, "rampant." As recently as January 1984, the dean of faculty at Amherst College wrote in the *New York Times:*

> In my contacts with a considerable range of academic institutions, I have become aware of pervasive residues of racism and sexism, even among those whose intentions and conscious beliefs are entirely nondiscriminatory. Indeed, I believe most of us are afflicted with such residues. Beyond the wrongs of the past are the wrongs of the present. Most discriminatory habits in academia are nonactionable; affirmative action goals are our only instrument for focusing sustained attention.

The plight of black America not only remains grave, but in many respects, it is getting worse. The black unemployment rate—21 percent in early 1983—is double that for whites and the gap continues to increase. For black 20- to 24-year-old males, the rate—an awful 30 percent—is almost triple that for whites; for black teenagers the rate approaches 50 percent. More than half of all black children under three years of age live in homes below the poverty line. The gap between white and black family income, which prior to the 1970s had narrowed a bit, has steadily edged wider, so that black-family income is now only 55 percent of that of whites. Only 3 percent of the nation's lawyers and doctors are black and only 4 percent of its managers, but over 50 percent of its maids and garbage collectors. Black life expectancy is about six years less than that of whites; the black infant mortality rate is nearly double.

Although the situation for women, of all races, is not as bad, the average earnings of women still, at most, are only two-thirds of those of their male counterparts. And the economic condition of black women, who now head 41 percent of the 6.4 million black families, is particularly bad; a recent Wellesley study found that black women are not only suffering in the labor market, but they receive substantially less public assistance and child support than white women. The economic condition of female household heads of any race is just as deplorable: 90 percent of the 8.4 million single-parent homes are headed by women, and more than half are below the poverty line. Bureau of Labor Statistics data reveal that in 1983 women actually earned *less* than two-thirds of their male counterparts' salaries, and black women earned only 84 percent of the white female incomes. In his 1984 State of the Union address, President Reagan claimed dramatic gains for women during the 1983 recovery. A *Washington Post* analysis the next day charitably described his claims as "overstated," noting that the Bureau of Labor Statistics reports (on which the president relied) showed that "there was no breakthrough. The new jobs which the president cited included many in sales and office work, where women have always found work" and are paid little.

We must close these gaps so that we do not remain two nations, divided by race and gender. Although no one strategy can overcome the results of centuries of inequity, the use of goals and timetables in hiring and other benefit distribution programs has helped to make modest improvements. Studies in 1983 show, for example, that from 1974 to 1980 minority employment with employers subject to federal affirmative action requirements rose 20 percent, almost twice the increase elsewhere. Employment of women by covered contractors rose 15 percent, but only 2 percent among others. The number of black police officers nationwide rose from 24,000 in 1970 to 43,500 in 1980; that kind of increase in Detroit produced a sharp decline in citizen hostility toward the police and a concomitant increase in police efficiency. There were also large jumps in minority and female employment among firefighters, and sheet metal and electrical workers.

Few other remedies work as well or as quickly. As the New York City Corporation Counsel told the Supreme Court in the *Fullilove* case about the construction industry (before Mayor Edward Koch decided that affirmative action was an "abomination"), "less drastic means of attempting to eradicate and remedy discrimination have been attempted repeatedly and continuously over the past decade and a half. They have all failed."

What, then, is the basis for the assault on affirmative action?

Apart from the obvious political expediency and ideological reflex of this administration's unvarying conclusion that the "haves" deserve government help and the "have-nots" don't, President Reagan and his allies present two related arguments: (1) hiring and other distributional decisions should be made solely on the basis of individual merit; (2) racial preferences are always evil and will take us back to *Plessy* v. *Ferguson* and worse.

Quoting Dr. Martin Luther King, Jr., Thurgood Marshall, and Roy Wilkins to support the claim that anything other than total race neutrality is "discriminatory," Assistant Attorney General Reynolds warns that race consciousness will "creat[e] . . . a racial spoils system in America," "stifle the creative spirit," erect artificial barriers, and divide the society. It is, he says, unconstitutional, unlawful, and immoral.

Midge Decter, writing in the *Wall Street Journal* a few years ago, sympathized with black and female beneficiaries of affirmative action programs for the "self-doubts" and loss of "self-regard" that she is sure they suffer, "spiritually speaking," for their "unearned special privileges."

Whenever we take race into account to hand out benefits, declares Linda Chavez, the new executive director of the Reagan Civil Rights Commission, we "discriminate," "destroy[ing] the sense of self."

The legal position was stated by Morris Abram, in explaining why the reshaped Commission hastened to do Reagan's bidding at its very first meeting by withdrawing prior Commission approval of goals and timetables:

> I do not need any further study of a principle that comes from the basic bedrock of the Constitution, in which the words say that every person in the land shall be entitled to the equal protection of the law. Equal means equal. Equal does not mean you have separate lists of blacks and whites for promotion, any more than you have separate accommodations for blacks and whites for eating. Nothing will ultimately divide a society more than this kind of preference and this kind of reverse discrimination.[2]

In short, any form of race preference is equivalent to racism.

All of this represents a nadir of "Newspeak," all too appropriate for this administration in Orwell's year. For it has not only persistently fought to curtail minority and women's rights in many contexts, but it has used "separate lists" based on color, sex, and ethnic origin whenever politically or otherwise useful.

For example, does anyone believe that blacks like Civil Rights Commission Chairman Clarence Pendleton or Equal Employment Opportunities Commission Chairman Clarence Thomas were picked because of the color of their *eyes?* Or that Linda Chavez Gersten was made the new executive director for reasons having nothing to do with the fact that her maiden and professional surname is Chavez?

Perhaps the most prominent recent example of affirmative action is President Reagan's selection of Sandra Day O'Connor for the Supreme Court. Obviously, she was on a "separate list," because on any unitary list this obscure lower-court state judge, with no federal experience and no national reputation, would never have come to mind as a plausible choice for the highest court. (Incidentally, despite Ms. Decter's, Mr. Reynold's, and Ms. Chavez's concern about the loss of "self-regard" suffered by beneficiaries of such preferences, "spiritually speaking" Justice O'Connor seems to be bearing her loss and spiritual pain quite easily.) And, like so many other beneficiaries of affirmative action given an opportunity that would otherwise be unavailable, she may perform well.

This is not to say that Reagan should not have chosen a woman. The appointment ended decades of shameful discrimination against women lawyers, discrimination still practiced by Reagan where the lower courts are concerned, since he has appointed very few female federal judges apart from Justice O'Connor—of 123 judgeships, Reagan has appointed no women to the court of appeals and only 10 to the district benches. Of these judgeships, 86 percent went to white males. But the choice of Sandra O'Connor can be explained and justified only by the use of affirmative action and a separate list, not by some notion of neutral "individual merit" on a single list.

But is affirmative action constitutional and legal? Is its legal status, as Mr. Abram claims, so clear by virtue of principles drawn from the "basic bedrock of the Constitution" that no "further study" is necessary?

Yes, but not in the direction that he and this administration want to go. Affirmative action is indisputably constitutional. Not once but many times the Supreme Court has upheld the legality of considering race to remedy the wrongs of prejudice and discrimination. In 1977, for example, in *United Jewish Organizations* v. *Carey*,[3] the Supreme Court upheld a New York statute that "deliberately increased the nonwhite majorities in certain districts in order to enhance the opportunity for election of nonwhite representatives from those districts," even if it disadvantaged certain white Jewish communities. Three members of the Court including Justice Rehnquist explained that "no racial slur or stigma with respect to whites or any other race" was involved. In the *Bakke* case,[4] five members of the Court upheld the constitutionality of a state's favorable consideration of race as a factor in university admissions; four members would have sustained a fixed 16 percent quota. In *United Steelworkers of America* v. *Weber*,[5] a 5:2 majority held that private employers could set up a quota system with separate lists for selecting trainees for a newly created craft program. In *Fullilove* v. *Klutznick*,[6] six members of the Court led by Chief Justice Burger unequivocally upheld a congressional set-aside of 10 percent for minority contractors on federal public works programs.[7]

All members of the present Court except for Justice O'Connor have passed on affirmative action in one or more of these four cases, and each has upheld it at one time or another. Although the decisions have been based on varying grounds, with many differing opinions, the legal consequence is clear: Affirmative action is lawful under both the Constitution and the statutes. To nail the point home, the Court in January 1984 not once but *twice* rejected the Justice Department's effort to get it to reconsider the issue where affirmative action hiring plans are adopted by governmental bodies (the Detroit Police Department and the New York State Corrections system), an issue left open in *Weber*, which had involved a private employer.

The same result obtains on the lower-court levels. Despite the persistent efforts of Reagan's Justice Department, all the courts of appeals have unanimously and repeatedly continued to sustain hiring quotas.

Nor is this anything new. Mr. Reynolds told an audience of prelaw students in January 1984 that the Fourteenth Amendment was intended to bar taking race into account for any purpose at all, and to ensure race neutrality. "That was why we fought the Civil War," he once told the *New York Times*. If so, he knows something that the members of the 1865–1866 Congress, who adopted that amendment and fought the war, did not.

Less than a month after Congress approved the Fourteenth Amendment in 1866 the very same Congress enacted eight laws exclusively for the freedmen, granting preferential benefits regarding land, education, banking facilities, hospitals, and more. No comparable programs existed or were established for whites. And that Congress knew what it was doing. The racial preferences involved in those programs were vigorously debated with a vocal minority led by President Andrew Johnson, who argued that the preferences wrongly discriminated against whites.

All these governmental actions reflect the obvious point that, as Justice Harry Blackmun has said, "in order to get beyond racism, we must first take account of race. There is no other way." Warren Burger, our very conservative chief justice, had made the point even clearer in a prophetic commentary on this administration's efforts to get the courts to ignore race when trying to remedy the ravages of past discrimination. Striking down in 1971 a North Carolina statute that barred considerations of race in school assignments, the chief justice said:

> The statute exploits an apparently neutral form to control school assignments' plans by directing that they be "color blind"; *that requirement, against the background of segregation, would render illusory the promise of Brown.* Just as the race of students must be considered in determining whether a constitutional violation has occurred so also must race be considered in formulating a remedy . . . *[color blindness] would deprive school authorities of the one tool [race consideration] absolutely essential to fulfillment of their constitutional obligation to eliminate existing dual school systems.* [Emphasis added.][8]

So much for "basic bedrock" constitutional principles. But this is hardly surprising from an administration in which a White House spokesman denied that the Justice Department was failing to enforce the law—"unless you call all of the decisions of the Supreme Court the law of the land," he explained.

But what of the morality of affirmative action? Does it amount to discrimination? Is it true, as Brian Weber's lawyer argued before the Supreme

Court, that "you can't avoid discrimination by discriminating"? Will racially influenced hiring take us back to *Plessy* v. *Ferguson*, as Pendleton and Reynolds assert? Were Martin Luther King, Jr., Thurgood Marshall, Roy Wilkins, and other black leaders against it?

Hardly. Indeed, it is hard to contain one's outrage at this perversion of what Dr. King, Justice Marshall, and others have said, at this manipulation of their often sorrow-laden eloquence, in order to deny a handful of jobs, school admissions, and other necessities for a decent life to a few disadvantaged blacks out of the many who still suffer from discrimination and would have few opportunities otherwise.

No one can honestly equate a remedial preference for a disadvantaged (and qualified) minority member with the brutality inflicted on blacks and other minorities by Jim Crow laws and practices. The preference may take away some benefits from some white men, but none of them is being beaten, lynched, denied the right to use a bathroom, a place to sleep or eat, being forced to take the dirtiest jobs or denied any work at all, forced to attend dilapidated and mind-killing schools, subjected to brutally unequal justice, or stigmatized as an inferior being.

Setting aside, after proof of discrimination, a few places a year for qualified minorities out of hundreds and perhaps thousands of employees, as in the Kaiser plant in the *Weber* case, or 16 medical-school places out of 100 as in *Bakke*, or 10 percent of federal public work contracts as in *Fullilove*, or even 50 percent of new hires for a few years as in some employment cases—this has nothing in common with the racism that was inflicted on helpless minorities, and it is a shameful insult to the memory of the tragic victims to lump together the two.

This administration claims that it does favor "affirmative action" of a kind: "Employers should seek out and train minorities," Linda Chavez told a *Washington Post* interviewer. Apart from the preference involved in setting aside money for "seeking out" and "training" minorities (would this include preference in training programs like the *Weber* plan, whose legality Mr. Reynolds said was "wrongly decided"?), the proposed remedy is ineffectual—it just doesn't work. As the "old" Civil Rights Commission had reported, "By the end of the 1960s, enforcement officials realized that discernible indicators of progress were needed." Consequently, "goals and timetables" came into use.[9]

Questions may nevertheless remain. Does affirmative action divide people? Is group thinking immoral? Dangerous? Where does it stop—aren't we all minorities, and aren't we all therefore entitled? If so, won't we wind up with claims totaling 200 percent of the pie? Should a white policeman or firefighter with ten years in the department be laid off when a black or a woman with less seniority is kept because an affirmative action decree is in force? Aren't those denied a job or another opportunity because of an affirmative action program often innocent of any wrong against the preferred group and just as much in need of the opportunities?

The last question is the most troubling. Brian Weber was not a rich man and he had to support a family on a modest salary, just like any black worker. A craft job would have been a significant step up in money, status, and working conditions. And *he* hadn't discriminated against anyone. Why should he pay for Kaiser's wrongs?

A closer look at the *Weber* case brings some other factors to light. Even if there had been no separate list for blacks, Weber would not have gotten the position, for there were too many other whites ahead of him anyway. Moreover, but for the affirmative action plan, there would not have been any craft training program at the plant at all, for *any* whites.

Furthermore, even with the separate list, the number of whites adversely affected was really very small. The Kaiser plan (adopted "voluntarily" to avoid employment discrimination suits by blacks and the loss of federal contracts) contemplated hiring only 3 to 4 minority members a year, out of a craft work force of 275–300 and a total work force of thousands. In the first year of its operation, Kaiser still selected only a handful of blacks, because it also brought in 22 outside craftsmen, of whom only one was black. In the 1980 *Fullilove* case, in which the Supreme Court upheld a 10 percent set-aside of federal public works projects for minority contractors, only 0.25 percent of the total annual expenditure for construction in the United States was involved. In *Bakke*, only 16 places out of 100 at one medical school were set aside for minorities. A new Boston University special admissions program for black medical students will start with three a year, with the hope of rising to ten, increasing the minority enrollment at the school by 2 percent.

The *Weber* case discloses another interesting aspect of affirmative action plans. Because they can adversely affect the careers of majority white males, creative ingenuity is often expended to prevent this from happening. In *Weber*, a new craft program benefiting both whites and blacks was set up. Although white employees and the union had been clamoring for such a program for many years, it wasn't until Kaiser felt it had to adopt an affirmative action program that it granted this request. In the layoff cases, time sharing and other ways of avoiding the dismissals—including raising more money—can be devised. So much for Mr. Reynolds's worries about "stifling the creative spirit."

Strains can and do result, especially if deliberately stirred up. But strain is not inevitable: Broad-ranging goals and timetable programs for women and blacks were instituted in the Bell Telephone Company with no such troubles. The same holds true elsewhere, especially when, as in *Weber*, the program creates new, previously unavailable opportunities for whites. On the other hand, some whites may be upset, even if, as the administration urges, the remedies are limited to specific identifiable victims of discriminatory practices. If a black applicant can prove that an employer wrongly discriminated against him personally, he would be entitled to the seniority and other benefits that he would have had but for the discrimination—with the administration's blessing—and this would give him competitive seniority over some white employees regardless of those employees' innocence. The same thing happens constantly with veterans' and other preferences, and few opponents of affirmative action seem to be upset by that.

Among some Jews, affirmative action brings up bitter memories of ceiling quotas, which kept them out of schools and jobs that could on merit have been theirs. This has produced a serious and nasty split within the civil rights movement. But affirmative action goals and timetables are really quite different. Whereas quotas against Jews, Catholics, and others were ceilings to limit and keep these groups out of schools and jobs, today's "benign preferences" are designed to be floors that let minorities into a few places they would not ordinarily enter, and with relatively little impact on others.

There is also a major confusion, exploited by opponents, resulting from the fact that we are almost all ethnic or religious minorities. Of course we are. And if it were shown that any minority is being victimized by intentional discrimination *and* that the only way to get more of that minority into a relatively representative portion of the work force or school is through an affirmative action plan, then these people would be entitled to such a remedy.

There is really nothing inherently wrong about taking group identity into account, so long as the person selected is qualified, a prerequisite that is an essential element of all affirmative action programs.[10] We do it all the time, with hardly a murmur of protest from anyone. We take group identity into account when we put together political slates, when a university gives preference to applicants from a certain part of the country or to the children of alumni, when Brandeis University restricts itself to Jews in choosing a president (as it did when it chose Morris Abram) or Notre Dame to Roman Catholics or Howard University to blacks, when we give preference to veterans for jobs, promotions, and the like, when the administration finds jobs in government for children of cabinet members. Some of these examples are less laudable than others. But surely none of these seldom criticized practices can be valued above, or has the serious purpose of undoing, the effects of past and present discrimination. In choosing a qualified applicant because of a race preference we merely acknowledge, as Morton Horwitz has pointed out, "the burdens, stigmas, and scars produced by history . . . the injustices heaped on his ancestors and, through them on him. The history and culture of oppression, transmitted through legally anonymous generations, is made antiseptic when each individual is treated as a separate being, disconnected from history."[11]

In some cases, moreover, group-oriented choices are necessary for effective performance of the job. Justice Powell in the *Bakke* case noted the importance of ethnic and other diversity for a university, as a justification for taking race into account as one factor in medical school admissions. He did stress that the choice must be individualized, but his choice of the Harvard program as a model gave away the ball game because of a key part of it (described in the appendix to his opinion but not in the excerpt he chose to quote) is a certain number of minority admissions as a goal.

One area where effective job performance almost mandates such group consideration is precisely the area where the administration has chosen to make its stand against affirmative action in the courts: police departments. The confrontation of an almost all-white police force with an angry, socially depressed minority community has produced violence, police brutality (thoroughly documented by the pre-Reagan Civil Rights Commission), and inefficient police work. Those unhappy conditions were in fact a major reason for extending Title VII of the Civil Rights Act to state and local governments.

Such race-conscious selection within police departments has worked. In Detroit, a largely black city where racial friction between a nearly all-white police force and ghetto dissidents had been epidemic and bloody—one such incident sparked the violence in 1968 that led to the death of 34 people—the police department voluntarily instituted an affirmative action plan that, as the Justice Department itself has admitted, "was expressly made as a response to undeniable past discrimination against blacks that had created a police force that was largely unresponsive to the concerns of a substantial portion of the City's population." Since then racial incidents and police community frictions have declined.[12]

Affirmative action has, of course, not always been completely effective. No policy can be. Certain marginally qualified students have been unable to meet the academic demands of colleges and professional schools. Once these problems emerged, however, many schools set up special remedial programs that, like the Kaiser craft training plan, often benefited needy whites as well. Unfortunately, the Reagan administration's cutbacks on educational programs (for all its talk of support for "affirmative action" in improving education and training) have decimated these programs, with the result that far fewer marginally qualified minority students are being admitted to colleges and professional schools.

The seniority layoff problem is undeniably the most troubling, for in this case people lose jobs they *have*, obviously a more serious matter than not getting a job you want but don't have. But layoffs on the traditional "last in, first out" basis will undo what little progress we have made toward racial equity.[13] And a layoff of whites is far more likely to result in quick rehiring than a layoff of blacks, as Boston and Memphis both showed: When the courts in those cases ordered whites to be laid off, money suddenly materialized and all the laid-off workers were promptly rehired.[14]

Nevertheless, this is the one situation in which the Supreme Court has struck down an affirmative action plan. In the Memphis firefighters' case, the Court ruled that the concern for seniority reflected in Title VII of the Civil Rights Act of 1964 barred federal courts from overriding seniority to maintain gains for minorities from affirmative action plans.[15]

There are indeed problems with affirmative action, but not of the kind or magnitude that Messrs. Reynolds and Abram claim: problems about whether these programs work, whether they impose heavy burdens, how these burdens can be lightened, and the like. They are not the basis for charges that affirmative action is equivalent to racism and for perverting the words of Dr. King and others.

"Equal is equal" proclaims Morris Abram, and that's certainly true. But it is just as true that equal treatment of unequals perpetuates and aggravates inequality. And gross inequality is what we still have today. As William Coleman, secretary of transportation in the Ford administration, put it,

> For black Americans, racial equality is a tradition without a past. Perhaps, one day America will be color-blind. It takes an extraordinary ignorance of actual life in America today to believe that day has come. . . . [For blacks], there is another American "tradition"—one of slavery, segregation, bigotry, and injustice.

One final note. After so many years of invidious, cruel color-consciousness, of devastating "special treatment," and of harmful "group thinking," one cannot avoid suspicion about the sudden demand for color neutrality just as society begins trying to undo the harm wrought by hostile color-consciousness. Skepticism seems especially justified when some of those making the demand have in the past always been indifferent to color-hurt minorities and still oppose the struggle for equal rights in almost every other sphere. This is, after all, an administration that does not include (unless Mr. Abram is considered an administration man) a single person with a record of leadership or even of supporting activity on behalf of civil rights and minority advance. That could not have been said of any previous administration of the past 50 years. It is an administration whose leader, when asked whether he agreed with Senator Jesse Helms that FBI files would show Martin Luther King, Jr. had ties to Communists, replied with a grin, "We'll know in about 35 years, won't we?" Perhaps the most appropriate lesson from all this is what Hamlet learned: "That one may smile, and smile, and be a villain."

NOTES

1. Myrl Duncan, "The Future of Affirmative Action: A Jurisprudential Critique," *Harvard Civil Rights—Civil Liberties Law Review*, 17:503 (1982). Another description is Ann Fagan Ginger's: "Affirmative action means that someone who

has the potential for being a good employee, apprentice, supervisor, or professional, but who lacks the formal, paper qualification customarily required, is nonetheless offered an opportunity to get into the classroom, apprenticeship program, or job, in order to enable the applicant to overcome the effects of past discrimination." Ginger, "Who Needs Affirmative Action," *Harvard Civil Rights—Civil Liberties Law Review, 14* (1979): 265, 268.

2. *New York Times*, January 18, 1984.

3. 430 U.S. [Supreme Court] 144 (1977).

4. University of California v. Bakke, 438 U.S. [Supreme Court] 262 (1978).

5. 443 U.S. [Supreme Court] 199 (1979).

6. 448 U.S. [Supreme Court] 448 (1980).

7. The Reagan administration has nevertheless reduced the number of government contracts going to minority firms by almost 10 percent, reversing a 15-year policy. And in some cases where local governments have adopted minority set-asides, the Justice Department is trying to annul them as unconstitutional, despite the Supreme Court's decision in *Fullilove*.

8. Board of Education v. Swann, 402 U.S. [Supreme Court] 43, 45–46.

9. U.S. Commission on Civil Rights, *Affirmative Action in the 1980s: Dismantling the Process of Discrimination*, November 1981, p. 19.

10. Of the 16 minority admittees in *Bakke*, 15 graduated from the medical school.

11. Morton Horwitz, "The Jurisprudence of Brown and the Dilemmas of Liberalism," *Harvard Civil Rights—Civil Liberties Law Review* 14 (1979): 599, 610.

12. In New Orleans as well, the Justice Department is trying to turn the clock back and get the federal court to reverse itself and strike down goals and timetables for police promotion. The first black policeman in New Orleans was not hired until 1950, and the bathrooms were segregated as late as the mid-1960s. A black policewoman was running the department's community-relations operation but was not promoted to the appropriate rank, and of course was paid far less than a similarly responsible white male. New Orleans agreed to a consent decree with promotional goals, which the Justice Department attacked. When the Equal Employment Opportunity Commission tried to file a brief in support of the New Orleans plan, Justice pressured it into not doing so, even though the brief had already been written and approved. Several civil rights organizations obtained a copy of the brief, which was widely available, and, adopting it as their own, brought it to the attention of the court.

13. The pre-Reagan Civil Rights Commission found that fiscal cutbacks caused by the 1974–1975 recession had a devastating effect on minorities in local government. "The recent recession has had a critical impact on minorities and women. Many had only recently obtained their first promising jobs. Increasing numbers had begun to penetrate employment areas of great importance in our society, such as state and local government. Because they have not had time to acquire adequate seniority, however, minority members and women have been affected disproportionately by the personnel cutbacks occasioned by this recession, and much of their limited progress had thereby been obliterated. In light of dismal predictions of slow economic recovery and continuing high unemployment, this recession threatens to lock these groups into place as a permanent, expendable

economic and social underclass. . . . In New York City, layoffs in mid-1975 of 371 female officers appointed since January 1973 by the New York City Police Department ended their brief tenure with the previously overwhelmingly male police force. Over half of all Hispanic city workers in New York lost their jobs between July 1974 and November 1975." Quoted from the U.S. Commission on Civil Rights, *Last Hired, First Fired: Layoffs and Civil Rights* (Washington, D.C.: Government Printing Office, 1977), pp. 60–61, 25–26.

14. The primary reason that white Boston police with ten years' seniority were laid off was not that blacks were retained but because of the veterans' preference. In Memphis, the laid-off white firefighters didn't have longer service than the blacks retained because of the affirmative action decree; both groups had equal seniority, but the white workers had priority on an *alphabetical* list.

15. Firefighters' Union Local No. 1784 v. Stotts,—U.S. [Supreme Court]—(June 12, 1984). The Court's opinion gratuitously went far beyond the layoff problem, however, and intimated disapproval of court-ordered quotas for hiring or promotion as well. If these intimations become law in a future case, efforts to improve employment opportunities for minorities and women will be devastated. Even without such a decision, the Court's language will probably deter lower courts from entering such decrees until further clarification, and will discourage settlements; also, the Department of Justice immediately announced it would try to reopen and set aside the hundreds of such affirmative action decrees entered since 1969.

Race, Scholarship, and Affirmative Action
Campus Racism

Walter E. Williams

The decade of the 1980s has seen a rise in racial incidents on America's campuses. At Smith College, "NIGGERS, SPICS, AND CHINKS QUIT COMPLAINING OR GET OUT" was painted on a campus building. In a UC Berkeley building "NIPS GO HOME" was scrawled on the wall. The University of Michigan's Ann Arbor campus radio station featured ethnic jokes aimed at blacks. *The Dartmouth Review*, an independent conservative student newspaper, published an article satirizing black language titled, "Dis Sho' Ain't No Jive, Bro." A leaflet opposing Holocaust studies and a swastika painted on a wall were found at Stanford University. At Philadelphia's Temple University, a White

Student's Union was formed. Since 1986, the National Institute against Prejudice and Violence has documented racial incidents on 160 college campuses, including some of the nation's most prestigious. In addition, more and more colleges are becoming the focal point of membership recruitment by the White Aryan Resistance, Skinheads, and the Ku Klux Klan.

Racial incidents have not been a one-sided coin. A black full professor at Dartmouth College frequently uses the term "honky" in his classroom in reference to whites. A black student at Vassar College hurled anti-Semitic insults at a Jewish student which included "dirty Jew," "stupid Jews," and "f—— Jews." At the University of Pennsylvania campus, three black non-students crushed the skull of an Oriental student. On the campuses of Drexel University and the University of Pennsylvania, black nonstudents have been alleged to systematically seek out white students to extort and rob.

Civil-rights advocates, affirmative-action officials, and politicians see the increase in campus racial incidents as the result of an "atmosphere" created by the Reagan administration. Their reasoning is that by its attacks on affirmative action, the administration created a perception of a tolerance for racism. To counteract this "atmosphere," there have been calls for more affirmative-action recruitment programs, mandated Black Studies classes as part of the college curriculum, more "cultural diversity," and more resources devoted to race relations.

Here we might explore the opposite line of causation and ask instead, what role has current campus racial policy played in the build-up of resentment and bitterness, and the consequent rise in campus racial incidents?

Affirmative action in recruitment makes the assumption, implicit or explicit, that a pool of black academic talent exists and that the paucity of blacks enrolled in the nation's colleges, medical schools, and law schools is a result of racial discrimination in admissions. Whether colleges currently engage in discriminatory policies against blacks is a matter for speculation; however, the question of just how large is the pool of black academic talent that meets standard college admissions criteria is not.

Black students score well below the national average on every measure of academic achievement. In 1983, fewer than 4,200 black college-bound high-school graduates, out of 75,400, had grade-point averages of 3.75 (B+) or better, compared to 7,858 out of 36,048 Asians, and 115,722 out of 701,345 whites. That means that 5.5 percent of black college-bound seniors earned B+ averages, compared to nearly 22 percent for Asians and 16.5 percent for whites.

Standard Achievement Test (SAT) scores tell an even more dismal story about college preparation. In 1983, across the nation, 66 out of 71,137 black college-bound seniors (less than a tenth of 1 percent) achieved 699, out of a possible 800, on the verbal portion of the SAT, and fewer than a thousand achieved scores of 600 or higher. On the mathematics portion of the SAT, 205 blacks had scores over 699 and fewer than 1,700 achieved scores of 600 or higher.

Of the roughly 35,200 Asians taking the test, 496 scored over 699 on the verbal portion (1.4 percent) and 3,015 on the mathematics. Of the roughly 963,000 whites taking the test, 9,028 scored over 699 on the verbal (just under 1 percent) and 31,704 scored over 699 on the mathematics.

An important debate wages over just what SAT scores measure and predict, and how reliably they do so. Regardless of the outcome of the debate, the tests do say something about academic achievement in the tested material. Black performance on them has important implications concerning the availability of academically qualified black students for college recruitment.

At some of the nation's most prestigious schools, the SAT scores of the student body are as follows: At Amherst, 66 percent of the students score above 600 on the verbal and 83 percent above 600 on the mathematics; at Bryn Mawr, 70 percent above 600 on the verbal and 70 percent over 600 on the mathematics; at Haverford, 67 and 86 percent; at MIT, 72 and 97 percent. The median student SAT scores for the verbal and mathematics portions are 600 at Brown, Columbia, Cornell, Dartmouth, Duke, Georgetown, Harvard, Oberlin, Princeton, Williams, Yale, and other colleges ranked as most competitive. Student SAT scores at schools ranked very competitive, such as Franklin and Marshall, Lafayette, Brandeis, and Lehigh, range in the high 500s and low 600s.

The black scores on the SAT, compared with the SAT performance of the general student body at the most prestigious schools, suggests that even if these schools made every heroic recruitment effort, it would be impossible to find much more than a tiny handful of blacks who would match the academic characteristics of these schools' average student. In 1983, there were 570 blacks who had combined SAT verbal and mathematics scores above 1,200, compared to 60,400 whites who did. That means, given the paucity of well-qualified blacks, that less-elite schools, among the nation's more than three thousand institutions of higher learning, are quickly left drawing from the lower end of the pool of college-bound black students.

At the graduate-school level, the academic tale is even more gruesome. The Graduate Record Examination (GRE) is used as part of the admissions process by most graduate schools. It has three parts: verbal, quantitative, and analytical. In 1983, the mean national GRE scores were 499 on the verbal, 516 on the quantitative, and 522 on the analytical. Black mean scores were well below the national means: 370 on the verbal, 363 on the quantitative, and 363 on the analytical, which translates into a 129-point deficit on the verbal, 153 on the quantitative, and 159 on the analytical. Black performance on the GRE is lower than that of any other ethnic group reported taking the test (American Indians, Mexican-Americans, Asians, Puerto Ricans, Latin Americans, and whites).

Poor black performance on standardized tests is frequently dismissed as owing to cultural bias of the test. If the charge of cultural bias has merit in the first place, in the sense that a culture-free test could be devised, one would expect cultural bias to be exhibited most strongly on the verbal portion of the test, where there are questions of reading comprehension, language, and literature. A much better performance relative to the national mean would be expected on those parts of the test where cultural bias is minimized—that is, mathematics and analytic reasoning. As it turns out, blacks are closer to the national norm on the verbal portion of the GRE and furthest behind on the quantitative and analytical portions.

The Asian population is more culturally distinct than other reported groups taking the GRE. However, the mean Asian score on the verbal portion of the GRE is 479, just 20 points below the national mean and 109 points higher than blacks. On the quantitative portion of the GRE, Asians' mean score is 575, outscoring the nation by 59 points. On the analytical portion, the Asian mean score is 522, identical with the national mean. Therefore, we might ask: If the examination is culturally biased, how is it that people of a culture far more alien to the American culture score close to the national mean?

Black performance on the GRE also allows us a preliminary assessment of what goes on while blacks are undergraduates. When blacks enter college as freshmen, their SAT scores as a percentage of the national norm are about 80 percent. After four years of college, those who take the GRE achieve scores that are only 71 percent of the national norm. Whatever the caveats regarding what tests measure, an unambiguous conclusion is that the achievement deficit of blacks does not diminish during four years of undergraduate training.

The fact that the black achievement deficit does not diminish demands more investigation into the possible reasons. Maybe there is nothing that can be done in the space of four or five years of college to significantly repair pre-college damage. Maybe the pattern of courses chosen by black students are not the most effective in terms of remediation. In any case, much more needs to be done to search for answers to these important questions.

Colleges and universities, under many sources of pressure, have sought to increase their enrollment of black students. If colleges adhered to rigid academic guidelines for admission, most would be frustrated in these efforts. Therefore, academic standards must be compromised. That is, colleges and universities must have one standard for admittance for whites and a lower one for blacks.

Whatever justification may be given for such a practice, it cannot help but build resentment, bitterness, and a sense of unfair play among whites, as it has already in matters of hiring, promotions, and layoffs. Official policy calling for unequal treatment by race is morally offensive whether it is applied to favor blacks or applied to favor whites.

Recently, charges have surfaced about discrimination against Asian-Americans at some of the nation's most prestigious colleges, like UCLA, Harvard, Berkeley, and Brown. In 1982, Asians admitted to Harvard had a combined SAT score of 1,467, compared to a combined SAT score of 1,355 for whites. On the average, an Asian had to score over 100 points higher to be admitted than a white. At Brown, between 1983 and 1987, the Asian admittance rate declined, while Asian academic performance (SAT scores and grade-point averages) increased.

Jack Bunzel reports in *The Public Interest* (Fall 1988) that "virtually all American-Indians, Hispanics, and blacks who apply to Berkeley, and meet the minimum UC requirements, are admitted [though it is possible to meet those requirements with a GPA of 2.78]. . . . white or Asian students are rarely accepted by Berkeley without a GPA of at least 3.7 or 3.8" According to Bunzel, for an Asian to have a 50 percent chance of admission to Berkeley, he needs to have an Academic Index score of 7000, while a score of 4800 is enough for a black.

The other side of the admittance issue is the graduation issue. According to Bunzel, UC Berkeley figures show that 66 percent of white students and 61 percent of Asian students graduate within five years. Only 41 percent of Hispanics and 27 percent of blacks graduate in five years. These facts show that affirmative-action programs in college recruitment do not come close to being even a zero-sum game where blacks benefit at the expense of Asians. It is more like a negative-sum game, where everybody is worse off. In other words, Berkeley's affirmative-action program leads to the rejection of Asian and white students with a higher probability of graduation in favor of black and Hispanic students with a significantly lower probability of graduation. Thus, white and Asian students are being sacrificed to the benefit of no one.

This kind of affirmative action is not only inept social policy, it produces personal tragedy. Bunzel relates a story told by Donald H. Werner, headmaster of Westminster School:

> UC Berkeley made decisions on two of its students this past year, both Californians. Student A was ranked in the top third of his class, student B in the bottom third. Student A had College Board scores totaling 1,290; student B's scores totaled 890. Student A had a good record of citizenship; student B was expelled last winter for breaking a series of major school rules. Student A was white; student B was black. Berkeley refused student A and accepted student B.

The use of dual standards by college administrators, in an effort to produce "diversity" in the student body, is widespread. Whatever noble goals foster dual standards, one of their side effects is that of producing racial animosity and resentment. It is easy to understand, though not to justify, how individuals who may never have harbored feelings of racial resentment can come to resent blacks, Hispanics, and other "protected" groups.

Blacks have difficult experiences on campus: high chances of being on academic probation and feelings of alienation from the larger community, which may be manifested in self-segregation, and dropping out of college. Today, there is little evidence of acts of official college racial discrimination against blacks. The bulk of black problems stem from poor academic preparation for college. Continually focusing on affirmative-action programs at the college level, while ignoring the massive educational fraud taking place at the primary and secondary schools blacks attend, means that campus problems will exist in perpetuity. It means most blacks will always need special admission privileges.

Today, many major cities have black mayors, large black representation on the city councils, and many black teachers and principals; in some large cities the superintendent of schools is black. That means blacks have many more policy choices than they had in the past. In the name of future generations of blacks, it is high time that responsible black people stop worrying about what whites are doing to blacks and begin to focus on what blacks are doing to blacks.

QUESTIONS FOR DISCUSSION

4.1 Is there a distinction between the use of racial quotas for desegregating public schools and their use in determining admission to colleges and universities?

4.2 Is there a difference between granting a preference to racial minorities in college or professional school admission and granting a preference to children of college alumni?

4.3 Can you establish a level playing field without taking into consideration a group's history of exclusion and economic deprivation?

4.4 Does affirmative action legitimize the concept of group rights as opposed to individual rights? And does that do damage to our traditional concept of rights under the Constitution?

Chapter 5

How Deep Is the Split in the Conservative Movement?

Neoconservatives versus Paleoconservatives

INTRODUCTION

American conservatism, relegated to the fringes of American politics in the 1950s and 1960s, became a sprawling, complex, and mainstream political movement in the 1980s. Its intellectual leaders, such as William F. Buckley, who felt alienated from the centrist Republican administrations of Eisenhower, Nixon, and Ford, had considerable influence in the Reagan administration. Much of what held the movement together was a passionate opposition to communism and a strident support for pursuit of the Cold War. When the Soviet empire collapsed with such suddenness in the late 1980s and early 1990s, anticommunism evaporated as the glue that held the conservative movement together.

Conservatives felt, no matter what, that Ronald Reagan was one of them, and they tolerated his compromises. George Bush, who called Reagan's supply side economic proposals "voodoo economics," in the 1980 primaries, was never considered a bona fide conservative. When he broke his pledge of "no new taxes" in 1990 and signed a civil rights bill in 1991 he had once denounced as a "quota" bill, conservatives broke ranks. Some rallied around Pat Buchanan, a conservative journalist and one-time assistant in the Reagan White House. Buchanan not only denounced Bush's compromises on taxes and civil rights, but he called for an America First foreign policy, which shunned foreign aid and free trade. He also called for a dismantling of the welfare state. His cause warmed the hearts of the *paleoconservatives*, whose views descended from the old anti–New Deal, pro-isolationist right of the 1930s.

While the paleoconservatives harbored deep suspicions of George Bush, their deepest hostilities were directed toward the *neoconservatives*. These were a feisty group of intellectuals such as Irving Kristol, Norman Podhoretz, and Jeane Kirkpatrick, who abandoned liberalism in the 1970s and grew suspicious of governmental schemes to solve our social problems. The neoconservatives, in contrast to the paleoconservatives, are staunch internationalists and cheered President Bush's leadership before and during the Gulf War. The neoconservatives have not lost their concern for the poor and are smitten with an approach to the problems of poverty, which deemphasizes bureaucracy and stresses the importance of individual responsibility. They support such proposals as school vouchers, welfare as workfare, and tenant ownership and management of public housing.

The paleoconservatives desire to reduce the welfare state and reinvest authority in the church and the family. They have little interest in the ideas of the neoconservatives, which they see as the back door to the welfare state.

In the following selection, Dan Himmelfarb, arguing from a neoconservative point of view, claims that neoconservatives are in "the tradition of liberal-democratic modernity, the tradition of Montesquieu, Madison, and Tocqueville." Paleoconservatism, which locates its roots in the medieval and ancient worlds, is, according to Himmelfarb, "fundamentally extra-American."

Paul Gottfried, an outspoken paleoconservative, explains in his essay the depth of the conservative split and the impact of Pat Buchanan's presidential candidacy on the conservative movement.

Conservative Splits

Dan Himmelfarb

In his contribution to a symposium on "The State of Conservatism" in the Spring 1986 issue of the *Intercollegiate Review*, the Old Right historian and editor Paul Gottfried noted that neoconservatives "have always been open in expressing their contempt for the Old Right." Whether or not this claim is valid—and there is reason to question its validity, inasmuch as a central theme of neoconservative thought is that the enemies are now on the Left—the converse seems to be true: Criticism of neoconservatism has come to be an increasingly conspicuous feature of Old Right writings.

The general complaint is that neoconservatives exert disproportionate influence within the "conservative intellectual movement," that neoconservatism is now regarded as roughly equivalent to—rather than merely a species of—"American conservatism." Thus Clyde Wilson, in the *Intercollegiate Review* symposium, wrote (of the Old Right) that "we have simply been crowded out by overwhelming numbers. . . . Our estate has been taken over by an impostor, just as we were about to inherit." And Stephen J. Tonsor took the following well-publicized swipe at neoconservatives at a Philadelphia Society meeting: "It is splendid when the town whore gets religion and joins the church. Now and then she makes a good choir director, but when she begins to tell the minister what he ought to say in his Sunday sermons, matters have been carried too far."

The tension between neoconservatism and what has come to be called paleoconservatism (i.e., the Old Right) is one of the major themes of *The Conservative Movement*, a slim book by Paul Gottfried and Old Right editor Thomas Fleming,[1] which serves, essentially, as a postscript to George H. Nash's excellent history, *The Conservative Intellectual Movement in America* (1976). While the authors of *The Conservative Movement* are considerably more evenhanded and less polemical in their treatment of neoconservatism than previous Old Right observers have been, Gottfried and Fleming's attitude toward neoconservatism remains unmistakably—albeit subtly—critical.

Why the conflict? What is (are) the difference(s) between neoconservatism and paleoconservatism? Are these differences superficial or fundamental?

There are several prevailing explanations for the split between neo- and paleoconservatives. Some are more convincing than others. None is entirely satisfactory.

One explanation holds that it is not so much the neoconservatives' conservatism that is new as their conversion to it. That is to say, neoconservatives and paleoconservatives differ only with respect to their past: As opposed to the neoconservatives, who moved—or "progressed," as some would say—from socialism to anti-Communist liberalism to conservatism, the paleoconservatives have spent their entire lives on the right half of the political spectrum. At present, according to this explanation, there is no significant difference between the two groups. Thus Nathan Glazer's definition of a neoconservative: "someone who wasn't a conservative."

While this account may apply to the neoconservative "elders"—Irving Kristol, Norman Podhoretz, and Hilton Kramer, for example—it cannot explain why younger editors and writers, who have never embraced any ideology of the Left, choose to think of themselves as neoconservatives rather than simply as conservatives. The existence of second-generation neoconserva-tives suggests that it is possible to have been a neoconservative all of one's life—or at least since political consciousness began.

A second explanation stresses the link between neoconservatism and so-cial science—or more specifically, sociology, the discipline of choice for, among others, Nathan Glazer, Peter L. Berger, and Seymour Martin Lipset. (Daniel Bell, another sociologist who is regularly identified with neoconser-vatism, continues to spurn the label.) Paleoconservatives, in contrast, are generally suspicious of social science: They eschew "tinkering," and reject the view of society as a set of "problems" for which there are discoverable "solutions." Thus Gottfried and Fleming distinguish between the paleo-conservatives, whose "hearts [are] in literature and theology," and the neo-conservatives, who "revel in statistics and computerized information." Paleoconservatives, add the authors, "rarely sought the kind of statistical confirmation that neoconservative academics produce for their positions."

While it is true that neoconservatives tend to be more respectful than paleoconservatives of the social-scientific method, the connection between neoconservatism and social science is often exaggerated—perhaps because of a tendency to equate neoconservative thought with the contents of the *Public Interest*. While it is fair to describe the *Public Interest*, with its tables, graphs, and regression analyses, as a social-science journal, such a description is inappropriate for *Commentary*, which regularly publishes es-says on history, religion, and literature, among other topics outside the bounds of social science. Still less is there anything social-scientific about the *New Criterion*.

Insofar as neoconservatives do take social science seriously, moreover, their approach tends to be skeptical: Neoconservative social scientists have consistently argued that a large part of the solution to social problems lies in the restoration of tradition, authority, and restraint. Thus Nathan Glazer, writing in these pages in 1971,[2] argued that "the breakdown of traditional modes of behavior is the chief cause of our social problems," and prescribed "hesitation in the development of social policies that sanction the abandon-ment of traditional practices" and "the creation and building of new tradi-tions." And James Q. Wilson, contributing an essay on "Private Virtue and Public Policy" to the twentieth-anniversary issue of the *Public Interest* (Fall 1985), wrote: "In almost every area of important public concern, we are seek-ing to induce persons to act virtuously, whether as schoolchildren, applicants for public assistance, would-be lawbreakers, or voters and public officials." Neoconservative social science is not, in the language of Max Weber, *wertfrei* (value-free), nor is it necessarily inconsistent with the paleoconservative (i.e., non-social-scientific) approach to social problems.

A third explanation emphasizes the "Jewish" character of neoconservatism. Thus Gottfried and Fleming: "Among the factors that led . . . many . . .

neoconservatives to disengage from the Left, their Jewishness was certainly significant." (Stephen Tonsor has stated that "neoconservatism is culturally unthinkable aside from the history of the Jewish intellectual in the twentieth century.") According to this explanation, there is something inherently Jewish about neoconservatism, while paleoconservatism is thought to be intrinsically Christian (usually specifically Catholic). Or, stated differently (and more bluntly): Paleoconservatism is the conservatism of Christians, neoconservatism the conservatism of Jews.

While it is fair to argue that Judaism is a "significant" aspect of neoconservatism, it is probably an exaggeration to say that neoconservatism is "unthinkable" apart from it. The anti-Israel sentiment, to say nothing of anti-Semitism, that has become increasingly prominent in certain Left-liberal circles in the last twenty years, has indeed been an important influence on many who have broken with the Left. But this is by no means the only feature of Left liberalism that neoconservatives find objectionable; the contemporary Left's anti-Americanism, for example, is a quality that has led Gentiles as well as Jews to repudiate the Left. Brigitte and Peter Berger (both Lutherans) have observed, in these pages,[3] that "many more non-Jews identify with neoconservatism than is often supposed." And whatever causes Michael Novak (a lay Catholic theologian) and Richard John Neuhaus (a Lutheran pastor) to feel more comfortable with the neoconservative than with the paleoconservative label, it is certainly not Judaism.

A fourth explanation suggests that the distinction between neo- and paleoconservatism is a matter of placement on the political spectrum: Neoconservatives are thought to be "to the left" of paleoconservatives. Gottfried and Fleming, for example, see neoconservatives as "political centrists who deplore the lack of moderation on both sides of the spectrum," and add that "neoconservatives, who may have learned from Arthur Schlesinger's book by that title the value of claiming to be the vital center, never abandon, at least rhetorically, the *juste milieu.*" The view of neoconservatives as center-rightists is accurate in many respects—particularly with regard to the welfare state. Gottfried and Fleming are certainly correct when they observe that neoconservatism "is not entirely incompatible with modern state planning," and that "almost all neoconservatives . . . remain qualified defenders of the welfare state." And their distinction between the neoconservatives' plans to "trim" the welfare state and the paleoconservatives' desire to "dismantle" it is an important one.

Neoconservatives also tend to be "to the left" of paleoconservatives socially and culturally. In the preface to *The Conservative Movement,* the authors write that "one conclusion that may be drawn from this book" is that an "emphasis on progress" is a "distinctive feature of the contemporary American Right"—that is, an American Right that has come increasingly under the influence of neoconservatism. Most of the (neoconservative) contributors to the November 1985 *Commentary* symposium,[4] as Gottfried and Fleming observe, wrote favorably about recent improvements in the areas of civil rights and economic well-being. Against neoconservatives, who emphasize social and material progress, paleoconservatives tend to see moral degeneration—itself a product of secularization—as the distinguishing characteristic of American life in the second half of the twentieth century.

There is also the matter of party identification. It is probably safe to say that virtually all paleoconservatives are registered Republicans. As for neoconservatives, though the dominant branch of the Democratic party currently embraces the very ideas and policies against which they have rebelled, many neoconservatives still do not feel entirely comfortable with the Republican party—if only from an emotional or psychological standpoint. While it is likely that Robert Nisbet was exaggerating when he wrote (in the Fall 1985 *Public Interest*) that "probably only a small fraction of those who had been most prominent in the *Public Interest* and in *Commentary* voted for Reagan" in 1980 and 1984, it remains true that many—perhaps most—of the older neoconservatives, and more than a few of the younger ones, continue to think of themselves as Democrats, even while distancing themselves from the policies and candidates of the Democratic party. (Nathan Glazer, two years after his confession of his conversion to conservatism,[5] endorsed the candidacy of George McGovern, himself a founding father of the left wing of the Democratic Party.[6])

With regard to domestic policy, then, it is fair to say that neoconservatism is a center-right tendency, and that paleoconservatism is "to its right." It would be difficult to support a similar claim, however, with regard to foreign policy. If movement from left to right on the foreign-policy spectrum represents a movement from less anti-Communism to more, a case can be made for locating neoconservatives "to the right" of paleoconservatives. For in contrast to neoconservatism, a prominent feature of which is an unapologetic and unyielding anti-Communism, paleoconservatism, as Gottfried and Fleming acknowledge, "for all its professed anti-Communism, retains some of its old isolationist spirit." In foreign policy it is the paleoconservatives, not the neoconservatives, who are the "moderates."

The difference between paleoconservatives and neoconservatives, in sum, is thought to be a difference of chronology (old-timers vs. Johnnies-come-lately); a difference in attitude toward social science (hostility vs. sympathy); a difference of religion (Christianity vs. Judaism); or a difference in location on the political spectrum (right vs. center-right). Each of these explanations is only partially correct. There is another, better way of explaining the tension between the two conservatisms—namely, as a tension between two distinct philosophical traditions.

Reflecting on the definition of a neoconservative, Irving Kristol has written that "the political tradition . . . which neoconservatives wish to renew and revive . . . is the political tradition associated with the birth of modern liberal society—a society distinguished from all others by representative government and a predominantly free-market economy."[7] Stephen Tonsor, seeking to distinguish "real" conservatism from neoconservatism, has argued that "conservatism has its roots in a much older tradition. Its world view is Roman or Anglo-Catholic; its political philosophy, Aristotelian and Thomist; its concerns, moral and ethical; its culture, that of Christian humanism."

The fundamental difference between neoconservatism and paleoconservatism is this: Neoconservatives belong to the tradition of liberal-democratic modernity, the tradition of Montesquieu, Madison, and Tocqueville; paleoconservatives are the heirs to the Christian and aristocratic Middle Ages, to Augustine, Aquinas, and Hooker. The principles of neoconservatism are individual liberty, self-government, and equality of opportunity; those of paleoconservatism are religious—particularly Christian—belief, hierarchy, and prescription.

Insofar as the principles that neoconservatives embrace are rather explicitly American—they are conspicuously embodied in the Declaration of Independence, for example—and insofar as these are not the principles with which paleoconservatives feel most comfortable, it is fair to say that paleoconservatism is fundamentally extra-American. That is to say, it stands outside the American liberal tradition. Thus Gottfried and Fleming, acknowledging the premodern—indeed, antimodern—character of paleoconservatism, locate its roots in "a civilization that went back beyond the American past, into the medieval and ancient worlds."

This philosophical division underlies the many instances in which neoconservatives and paleoconservatives disagree even while agreeing, in which they agree on what but not on why. Take the Founding Fathers, for example, of whom conservatives of every stripe tend to be respectful, if not reverent. For neoconservatives the Founders are liberals in the best sense: They are champions of individual rights, popular government, spiritual equality, and cultural and religious pluralism. Paleoconservatives, in contrast, place the Founders in the Christian tradition; they regard them as defenders of the "religious heritage" of Western civilization.

Thus, in the seminal work of paleoconservatism, *The Conservative Mind* (1953), Old Right elder Russell Kirk's treatment of the Founding Fathers consists of a chapter on John Adams, by all estimates the most Burkean of the Founders. The lead author of *The Federalist*, James Madison, himself less respectful than Adams of predemocratic ages, does not appear in Kirk's 450-page book: The index skips from James Mackintosh to Sir Henry Maine. Kirk devotes four pages to democratic capitalism (which "demolished conservative ramparts"). And as for the influence of John Locke, Kirk has written (in *National Review*) that "Richard Hooker, directly or indirectly, had far more to do with the fundamental opinions of the Founding Fathers than did Locke."

Or take anti-communism, generally regarded as a common denominator of the different brands of conservatism. Neoconservatives are anti-Communist because communism is the enemy of freedom and democracy, paleoconservatives because it is the enemy of religion, tradition, and hierarchy. For neoconservatives the relevant distinction between East and West is not the distinction between atheism and belief (as it is for paleoconservatives), nor is it the distinction between socialism and capitalism (as it is for certain libertarians). The fundamental difference, rather, is that between totalitarianism and freedom. Thus neoconservatives reject communism in favor of some version of liberal-democratic capitalism, while paleoconservatives reject it in favor of what Gottfried and Fleming call "historic nationalities." (What is meant by "historic nationality" is not entirely clear, though presumably it implies some variety of monarchy, theocracy, or other traditionalist societal arrangement.) Paleoconservatives are critical of neoconservative anti-communism, which Gottfried and Fleming identify with "global democratic revolution." This vision of global democracy is "secularist" and "politically and sexually egalitarian," and thus "as far removed from a traditionalist world view as from Marxist-Leninism."[8]

This philosophical division also explains the difference between neo- and paleoconservatives in their attitude toward liberalism (in the original sense of that term) and its underlying ideals. Take equality. Neoconservatives contrast equality of opportunity, a central tenet of liberalism, with equality of result, which they regard as an essentially discriminatory and coercive, and therefore illiberal, doctrine. Paleoconservatives are less apt to draw this distinction: They are suspicious of any principle bearing the name equality. Thus neoconservatives, by and large, are favorably disposed toward the civil-rights movement of the 1960s, but are critical of affirmative action, particularly when that term implies the use of quotas. In supporting the former and opposing the latter, neoconservatives are being entirely consistent—that is, consistently liberal: In contrast to the civil-rights movement, whose goals were a color-blind society and an end to legal discrimination, affirmative action requires a race-conscious society and a new form of legal discrimination.

Which is not to say that the paleoconservative view of equality is necessarily inconsistent. While neoconservatives regard affirmative action as a *perversion* of the ideals of the civil-rights movement, paleoconservatives see it as an *extension:* Both the civil-rights movement and affirmative action have egalitarian goals; both are objectionable. Or as Gottfried and Fleming put it: "Unlike the neoconservatives, [the Old Right] remains irreconcilably opposed to . . . the principle of social equality." Thus neoconservatives tend to be respectful of Martin Luther King, Jr., whom they regard as a champion of liberal ideals, but not of Jesse Jackson, for example, whose ideas they regard as illiberal. Paleoconservatives, in contrast, for whom the relevant feature of each man is his egalitarianism (broadly defined), are respectful of neither. (Gottfried and Fleming think President Reagan's declaring King's birthday a national holiday represents a betrayal.)

If neoconservatives are defenders of the American liberal tradition, they are clearly not liberals in the sense in which that term is generally used today. For neoconservatives there are two kinds of liberals: genuine and counterfeit. The latter are men and women of the Left, who, in the last 25 years, have usurped the liberal label, leaving real liberals to be designated neoconservatives. These so-called liberals are illiberal in many respects: Insofar as they support quotas in employment and education, they reject the liberal ideal of a society indifferent to race, gender, and ethnicity; insofar as they are inhospitable to certain views (particularly on college campuses), they show contempt for the liberal ideals of free speech and toleration of unpopular, heretical, or minority opinion; and, most important, insofar as they regard communism as a lesser threat than anti-communism, they betray an indifference to large scale tyranny, the opposition to which once served as the very definition of liberalism.

Paleoconservatives, in contrast, do not distinguish between good liberals and bad; for them the phrases "great liberal tradition" and "liberal in the best sense" are merely oxymorons. Paleoconservatives regard liberalism—in all its forms—as intrinsically flawed, primarily because it is a secular and egalitarian tendency, insufficiently respectful of tradition. Thus, while neoconservatives draw a distinction between the liberalism of Franklin Roosevelt, Harry Truman, and John F. Kennedy, on the one hand, a liberalism representing a double commitment to progressivism in domestic policy and vigorous anti-communism in foreign policy, and the anti-anti-Communist liberalism of George McGovern and his heirs, on the other, paleoconservatives see not disjunction but continuity.

A central theme of *The Conservative Movement* is that American conservatism, under the influence of neoconservatism, has, in the last two decades, moved "left." (The authors, for example, write that the emergence of neoconservatism has had the effect of "shift[ing] the parameters of conservative respectability toward the center.") Rather than arguing that American conservatism has moved left, however, it might be more accurate to say that half of American liberalism moved left and half—that is, the neoconservatives—stayed put. Or as Gottfried and Fleming themselves put it: "Neoconservatism . . . arose in reaction to what was regarded as a betrayal of purpose. . . . Democrats and young radicals [had] corrupted the great liberal tradition." In fact, "neoconservatism" is probably a misnomer—and doubly so: It is not particularly new, and it is not necessarily conservative (at least not in the classical or medieval sense). Perhaps "paleoliberalism" would be a better term.

And just as the eighteenth- and nineteenth-century liberals opposed the Tories and *ancien régime* to their right, and the French Revolutionists and socialists to their left, so too does neoconservatism stand in opposition to both (Old) Right and (New) Left. At this point in history the fundamental challenge to liberal democracy—both externally, in the form of Communist totalitarianism, and internally, in the form of an anti-anti-Communist academic/intellectual community—comes from the Left. Thus liberal democrats (a.k.a. neoconservatives) must devote their energy to countering attacks from this quarter. In different historical circumstances, however, in which the challenge came from the opposite flank, it is entirely conceivable that the friends of liberal democracy would make ready to do battle with the Right. In this regard, it might be helpful to think not of conservatives and liberals, but of liberal democrats and their opponents, on both Left and Right.

An implicit thesis of *The Conservative Movement*—and an explicit thesis of previous essays by Old Right authors—is that neoconservatism is not an authentic conservatism, that it is insufficiently distinguishable from welfare-state liberalism. (Gottfried himself has written, in the *Intercollegiate Review* symposium, that one of the "common mistakes among interpreters of the current American Right" is "treating neoconservatives as genuine conservatives.") Yet neoconservatives might make a similar claim with respect to paleoconservatives. For if conservatism implies "presentism," if it means a defense of existing institutions, then there is reason to question the authenticity of a self-proclaimed American conservatism that readily identifies itself as a medieval tendency.

Indeed, it might with some justification be argued that it is neoconservatism, and not paleoconservatism, that is both genuinely American and genuinely conservative. In a brilliant 1957 essay in the *American Political Science Review*, Samuel P. Huntington, implicitly adopting the thesis of Louis Hartz's *The Liberal Tradition in America* (1955), argued that American conservatives must be liberals, that antiliberal American conservatism is an anachronism. "American institutions . . . ," wrote Huntington, "are liberal, popular, and democratic. They can best be defended by those who believe in liberalism, popular control, and democratic government. Just as aristocrats were the conservatives in Prussia in 1820 and slaveowners were the conservatives in the South in 1850, so the liberals must be the conservatives in America today."

Whether or not one is "truly" a conservative, however, ought not to be a matter of fundamental importance. More significant than what one is called is what one believes: Labels matter less than principles. Thus liberal democrats should be willing to regard as friends those who are generally sympathetic to the principles of liberal democracy, regardless of what these individuals are called (or call themselves). And, conversely, liberal democrats should hesitate to regard as friends those who, irrespective of how they are labeled, are uncomfortable with, suspicious of, or hostile toward liberal-democratic ideals.

NOTES

1. Twayne Publishers, 140 pp., $18.95.
2. "The Limits of Social Policy," September 1971.
3. "Our Conservatism and Theirs," October 1986.
4. "How Has the United States Met Its Major Challenges Since 1945?"
5. "On Being Deradicalized," *Commentary*, October 1970.
6. "McGovern and the Jews: A Debate" (with Milton Himmelfarb), *Commentary*, September 1972.
7. "What is a Liberal—Who is a Conservative?: A Symposium," *Commentary*, September 1976.
8. The authors' claim that neoconservative anti-Communism rests on the "stated or implicit assumption that American democracy with its mixed economy is the supreme human good" is at best only half right. Certainly neoconservatives prefer liberal democracy to both Communist and traditionalist societies. Few neoconservatives would agree, however, that democratic capitalism is—or, indeed, that *any* political or economic system can be—the "supreme human good." And insofar as neoconservatives embrace liberal democracy, they do so not so much because it is best as because it is least bad: With Churchill, they regard democracy as the worst political system, except for any other.

The Coming Conservative Crack-Up

Paul Gottfried

The paleoconservatives may in fact be doing a public service by representing what Clinton Rossiter called in looking at the postwar Right, "the thankless persuasion." After all, they do carry on their work in the face of growing obstacles. Nonetheless, it is doubtful that others will rush to take their places on the ramparts when this generation of paleoconservatives passes from the scene. Without some prospect for victory, or at least for redressing the disparity in power between the two sides, the struggle already begins to seem pointless.

Many Old Right scholars have expressed eagerness to return to universities, where identification with the neoconservative Right has been a considerable liability. Others have intimated that they are less offended by the intelligent Left than by the self-promoting Right and would like nothing better than to explore the possibilities, not of alliances but of cooperative associations. For some time now, scholars in Southern studies (history, sociology, and literature) on Right and Left have been working together to improve the standards of their disciplines, and similar developments may be expected in other fields. A surprising number of paleoconservatives read *The Progressive, The Nation*, and *The Utne Reader*, and find these journals no more alien or irritating than *National Review.* Leftists, we are told, have the courage of their convictions, no matter how bizarre those convictions might seem; the same cannot be said for conservatives. Many on the Old Right have gone so far as to repudiate the conservative label altogether and prefer to call themselves reactionaries or nationalists or libertarians, anything to avoid a term that they see as tainted with cowardice and opportunism.

In the fall of 1991 the neoconservatives suffered noticeable reversals of fortune. During October of last year Elliot Abrams, former assistant secretary of state and one of the most vocally ideological neoconservatives in the Reagan administration, pleaded guilty in a federal court to having deceived Congress about aid to Contra rebels in Nicaragua. Abrams had been open and even vehement about seeking to commit the United States to the global democratic agenda, and his downfall left his paleoconservative as well as leftist critics at least quietly satisfied. The continued endorsement of Abrams and his doctrinal goals in the *Wall Street Journal* (October 9, 1991) revealed a certain desperation combined with neoconservative militancy. Also in October, in the wake of worsening financial problems at *National Review* leading to the removal of its publisher, it was learned that the magazine's editor, John O'Sullivan, had turned down a commissioned review by the paleoconservative warhorse M. E. Bradford. The cancelled piece contained unkind comments about Abraham Lincoln, and O'Sullivan was clearly concerned about offending his neoconservative editors and sponsors. Attacks against O'Sullivan then surfaced in the usually neoconservative *Washington Times*, where columnist Samuel T. Francis was given a free hand. Inconsistencies were found to be present in the accounts that *National Review* was then circulating about why its editors had bumped Bradford's reviews; letters, also published in the *Washington Times*, detailed the cancellation of other commissioned essays by *National Review* editors that failed to take the neoconservative line.

The ascent of David Duke as a Southern politician may also be seen as assisting the paleocons. Unlike the neoconservatives and the movement-conservative Washington foundations, paleoconservatives have warned against fawning on the civil rights establishment. John O'Sullivan was correct in the pointed observation he made in his letter of October 17, 1991, to the *Washington Times*, that the paleoconservatives blend "old theories" with "newer and less conservative stress on recruiting the discontented and alienated in American society against institutions which are now seen as irredeemably corrupt." And while the Heritage Foundation boasts of its bridge-building to black, Hispanic, and feminist spokespersons and while the neoconservative D'Souza calls for affirmative action to "lower class" blacks, the paleoconservatives continue to preach war against the managerial welfare state. Like the French Communists of the interwar years, the paleoconservatives advocate a *politique du pire*. That which shakes loose the Washington power structure and its handpicked conservative opposition is what this Right most readily supports. To whatever extent Duke represents a populist indignation that the neoconservative and Washington conservative powerbrokers cannot satisfy while enjoying the good will of the Washington media, the Louisiana politician is serving paleoconservative ends. As Evans and Novak point out about Duke's constituency, "These citizens are not Klansmen or Nazis. They do not resemble the hate-filled crowds George Wallace attracted 20 years ago. They are alienated from the political system that has given them David Duke as the only means to redress their grievances." Paleoconservatives recognize this fact and hope to exploit it, however much they also try to dissociate themselves from Duke's past unsavory associations or from his defeat in Louisiana in November 1991. But the rebirth in the South of right-wing populism—in a less dramatic form in Mississippi's gubernatorial race than in neighboring Louisiana—has not, at least thus far, put wind back into the paleoconservatives' sails. No substantial money has been rechanneled from the neoconservative philanthropic empire, and the major media continue to deal with the neoconservatives as the only respectable opposition.

Another issue that paleoconservatives have tried to exploit in their war with neoconservatives and the Washington conservative establishment is the abandonment of the electoral Right in pursuit of nonexistent constituencies. For example, the close identification of the Weyrich and Feulner operations with the Zionist Right has not resulted in substantial Jewish movement into the conservative camp. And those who have criticized the establishment Right's unswerving identification with Israeli hawks have often been labeled as anti-Semites even by other conservatives. Even less productive to date has been the work of Heritage Foundation's New Majority Project, which aims at bringing primarily blacks into the conservative mainstream. Aside from endorsing black capitalism and enterprise zones, both to be advanced through government fiscal policies, Heritage also stood firmly behind Clarence Thomas during his congressional hearings in the fall of 1991. Despite stated reservations on the Right about Thomas's own judicial activist views and his reduction of natural law to an ill-defined belief in equality, Washington movement conservatives went to his aid as soon as he was nominated to the Supreme Court. One reason was that Thomas's presence on the Supreme Court as a "black conservative," it was hoped, would spur the growth of a black conservative electorate. This obviously has not occurred despite the widespread support for Thomas among blacks polled during his confirmation hearings before the Senate. One Harris poll conducted in October and November 1991 nonetheless concludes that movement conservative efforts to drive a wedge between black voters and their left-liberal civil rights leadership have utterly failed: "Black support for the NAACP stands at 13-1 positive, for the Leadership Conference on Civil Rights at 11-1, for Jesse Jackson at 9-1 and for the Black Congressional Caucus at 8-1. All these ratios are almost precisely the same as they were in the 1970s and in the 1960s." Echoing a theme framed by the paleoconservatives, Earl Graves, publisher of *Black Enterprise* magazine, notes that "black conservatives are the new fantom army." Paleoconservatives were among the early critics of this unsuccessful opening from the Right to black electorates. Yet they have been in no position to change this strategy, having neither the foundations nor the money nor the media access to effect strategic changes in Republican electoral politics.

Paleocons have, however, been prominent in organizing the America First Committee, which prepared the way for the announcement in November 1991 of a presidential bid by Patrick J. Buchanan. Two problems seem inherent in this candidacy, neither of which bodes well for the paleoconservatives. One, Buchanan has already suffered devastating assaults from both the neoconservatives and like-minded liberals for the views he expressed on the American Zionist lobby. While the charges against him were certainly not proved beyond doubt, even the suspicion of anti-Semitism, taken as insensitivity to Jewish concerns, can be politically destructive. Buchanan has entered the race after trading dangerous insults, which can—and may already have—hurt his presidential ambitions. His challenge to an incumbent Republican president, moreover, will damage his standing among Republican loyalists, to whom he has hitherto appealed precisely as one of them. While in the past Buchanan and his paleoconservative allies were identified, for the most part, as loyal Republicans, they could be depicted hereafter as ideologically driven spoilers.

Then, too, if Buchanan's campaign is to go anywhere, it must have behind it Washington-New York conservatives and neoconservative mouthpieces like the *Wall Street Journal*. This can only happen if Buchanan accepts new counsels: that is, abandons the media-weak paleoconservatives for their rivals, who have access to newspapers and TV. Outside of the "respectable" conservative camp, controlled by the neoconservatives and the Washington foundations, Buchanan will not fare well in any presidential campaign. Once in that camp, however, he will lose his freedom of action and be pushed into adopting views similar to those of Kemp and Bennett. He may become another version of a familiar political type, the socially compassionate and minority-conscious pro-growth conservative who enjoys media approval but no real electoral base. He will also have to wait his turn among other neo-conservatives who have closer ties to their sponsors and seem less apt to offend AIPAC, including Vice President Dan Quayle.

Paleoconservatives and paleolibertarians are correct to insist that they alone have a genealogical claim to be on the American Right. What should be asked is whether the future will contain a Right at all, apart from celebrants of a global age or lobbyists to whom the term "right-wing" has been applied in accordance with changing journalistic criteria. Right and Left are designations that came into use in the modern West in response to particular upheavals. They may already be destined to pass, like so much else in a specifically Western society. The historical specificity that the paleoconservatives cherish can no longer be reconciled with the globalist ideals of our intellectual and business elites. But if there is one virtue shared by all authentic men of the Right, it is the combination of short-term pessimism with long-term optimism. No social order can endure for much longer than a few centuries, and the rise and fall of civilizations cannot be halted by propaganda, no matter how generously funded by foundation grants. America will one day be "one with Nineveh and Tyre," and all the particularities that conservatives have striven to maintain will disappear. But the more general principles for which they struggled, if they are (as conservatives believe) an enduring part of a natural order ordained in Heaven, will always reappear, when circumstances favorable to civilization return, like desert flowers after rain.

QUESTIONS FOR DISCUSSION

5.1 Is there a genuine American conservatism, given our lack of a prerevolutionary tradition—a landed gentry, an established church, and a titled nobility. Are all Americans, by their own history, liberal democrats?

5.2 Can the neoconservatives with their affinity to the liberalism of Franklin Roosevelt, Harry Truman, and John Kennedy be truly placed in the conservative tradition?

5.3 Where would the Reagan and Bush administrations be placed in all this debate?

Chapter 6

Is the Younger Generation Indifferent to Politics?

INTRODUCTION

A 1990 Times Mirror study discovered that young Americans between the ages of 18 and 29 are less informed and less involved in national and international affairs than any other generation of Americans over the past half-century. In the years from 1941 to 1975, young people followed world and national events as closely as their parents did. Since 1975, in the aftermath of Vietnam and Watergate, Americans under 25 have become increasingly less knowledgeable about current events.

The study showed that younger people are less likely to read a newspaper, watch TV news, or listen to the news on the radio than older Americans. When young Americans do tune in a news program, it is more likely to be *A Current Affair* than *The MacNeil/Lehrer News Hour*. This indifference to hard news is also manifest in voting behavior. In 1988 only 36 percent of Americans aged 18–24 voted, in contrast to 65 percent of Americans 25 or older. In every election since 1972 the percentage of voting participants among younger voters (under 25) has declined.

Why such indifference? We have witnessed in the late 1980s and early 1990s some of the most dramatic and exhilarating events of the twentieth century—the end of the Cold War, the fall of the Soviet Union, the sudden and dramatic American victory in the Gulf War. With the Cable News Network and its global satellite communication, events have never been more immediate.

In the following selections Curtis Gans wrestles with the question of *Why Young People Don't Vote*. He focuses on the education system, which, he feels, has failed to stress public service and social obligations; and on the advent of TV, which, Gans claims, "translates people from participants and stockholders in our society to spectators and consumers." Gans wants to find a way to make political education as "visually exciting as TV."

Harry C. Boyte argues that civic education should emphasize community service and issues that have relevance to young people, such as racial conflict among teens and relations between school officials and students. Political education must provide hands-on experience, so Boyte claims, "to practice political skills like strategic thinking, bargaining, negotiating, listening, argument, problem-solving and evaluation."

Why Young People Don't Vote

Curtis Gans

Young people vote less than any other group in the United States. When we enfranchised young people between the ages of 18 and 21, we enfranchised the first group *not* to increase its rate of participation in the years following enfranchisement. Blacks consistently increased their participation so that they are within five percentage points of whites. Women consistently increased their participation until they now vote at a higher rate than men. But since we enfranchised youth, their level of participation has not gone up.

We don't know why young people vote, but we do know a good deal about why adults vote—or don't vote. I am going to discuss the general problem of nonvoting and relate youth to it.

Three weeks before the 1986 election, I was in Chicago, and a week later, I was in New York. When I looked in the streets, there were no placards, bumper stickers, buttons, people hawking literature, or signs that one of our two most important elections was about to take place.

The major news magazines, for the two weeks prior to and the week of the election, had nothing on their covers to suggest that an election was about to take place. Two television networks announced that they would not give full coverage to the election on election night but would put on more lucrative commercial programming. Even National Public Radio was putting election news on its final cycle.

Neither political party offered one issue, theme, or purpose for voting Republican or Democrat. The only evidence that there was a campaign going on was the nastiness of 30-second commercials on television, except for the last week, in which the president, speaking to groups of largely ineligible students, urged people to win again "for the Gipper," and to reject the Carter administration, six years long gone.

Is it any wonder that the United States has the lowest rate of voter turnout of any democracy in the world in its presidential elections, with the occasional exception of Switzerland and India, and the lowest of any nation in the world in its congressional elections? In the last two decades, fully 20 million people have dropped out of the political process. The rate of youth participation shows that they are not being replaced.

If we have a 16.6 percent rate of youth participation, what is our future in terms of leadership, societal cohesion, and involvement? A high degree of inattention is an invitation to demagoguery and abuse. If people do not participate in the political system, then there is the danger of people participating outside of the political system to bring change. There are a number of opportunities for us to reverse this trend.

The first is values. My parents came from a generation largely shaped by the depression. They had a principal value of creating a society in which their children would have better lives. The next generation translated that vision, in a comparatively affluent society, to making society better. We committed ourselves, in one way or another, to a degree of public service for the betterment of society for future generations. I have a terrible sense that the generation that is growing up now is looking at personal betterment, not the betterment of the future.

In that sense, former Secretary of Education William Bennett is right— somewhere in the educational process, we have to inculcate values larger than the self. That applies to home and school.

The second problem/opportunity is advocacy. For 30 years, from the New Deal to the early 1960s, we had a national consensus that narrowed public debate. It was built around the Great Depression and World War II. The first part of the consensus was Keynesian economics and economic pump-priming for growth. The second was the New Deal, which was essentially a series of attacks on specific problems—create an agency, attack a problem. The third was global containment, first of Hitler, and then of communism.

Both parties accepted this consensus, differing only in how the goals were to be achieved. Republicans wanted to go slow in adding new social programs. Democrats wanted them to proliferate. Republicans wanted our containment to be more militaristic; Democrats wanted it to be more ideological and economic.

Then, in the sixties, three things happened. First, we had stagflation. The paradigm of Keynes came apart. Second, we found that social programs often conflicted with each other. As we built highways, we strangled cities. As we pushed for industrial growth, we polluted the air and created acid rain. Could you deal with everything as an isolated series of problems, or did you have to look at the undetermined effects of dealing with the problems in isolation? Third, the big object lessons of the war in Vietnam were the limits of American power to contain or control the world globally and the need to redefine a set of vital interests that were more narrow and more manageable.

I think we solved none of these problems. The problem we face now is that there is no consensus of values that speaks to both the needs and feelings of the American people. We could turn voting participation around if we simply had a candidate who advocated what people perceived as their needs, and then was able to deliver, once elected.

The third part of the problem/opportunity has to do with both governments and political parties. Political parties were extraordinarily important in separating the wheat from the chaff on issues, training leadership, and exerting some discipline in the way candidates performed once in office. They could deliver. That delivery mechanism has broken down for lots of different reasons.

First was the progressive movement around the turn of the century, which took the nomination process out of the hands of the leaders and put it into the hands of the people. Second was the New Deal, which took the hiring power away from local organizations and gave it to the federal government. Third was the advent of television, and campaigning by television, which essentially made the party irrelevant. You now hire a media advisor to run a campaign.

So the parties are infinitely weaker. They are also misaligned. What we have right now on the Republican side is essentially right-wing populism and big-business greed. On the Democratic side is a cacophony of interests that adds up to mush. People don't think they face a real choice. In fact, they have choices—the parties are different—but not real choices in terms of the world that a large percentage of people see.

The fourth problem/opportunity is the existence of issues that don't seem to be solved. Commuter traffic is worse than ever. Family farmers feel equally threatened by whatever administration is in power. For flyers, the products of deregulation seem to be delays and cancelled flights, and for those flying to or from smaller towns, infinitely increased costs.

In many instances, the political process seems to be frustrating majority rule. Between 60 and 70 percent of the American people opposed what we were doing in Nicaragua in the last six or seven years, and yet the government would not act to stop it. There's an example also on the conservative side. At least 70 percent of the American people want at least a moment of silence in the schools, but they haven't been able to get it.

In the sixties and seventies, events had important impacts on participation. The first was the development of the birth control pill, which I consider the most salutary for participation, because it essentially liberated women to have greater control over their bodies and to take a much more active role in both the economic and political life of our society.

The second was the advent of television as a central factor in our lives. There is probably no more deleterious aspect of our society. Television translates people from participants and stockholders in our society to spectators and consumers. We get news on TV in one-minute or half-minute blips. Without a sense of context, it is very hard to make historical judgments. We expect our politics to deliver solutions quickly. People are shot into the firmament, like Jimmy Carter, and, before we have had a chance to evaluate the down side, swept to a nomination. Through television, political campaigns come down to a battle of 30-second commercials.

As I suggested earlier, education can help us do something to end the downward spiral. We ought to deal nationally with parents on the TV viewing habits of their children, but for the majority of young people in this country, TV will continue to act as a baby-sitter. And their perceptions and experiences are going to be shaped by television.

Somehow we have to find tools to make teaching about our political process as visually exciting as TV. Seventy percent of the young people in America are probably not going to do the type of disciplined reading necessary to learn about issues, so we better find other ways, through the media, to make participation work.

Teachers can deal with values and advocacy. They can try to develop ways for young people to learn how to work in concert in a political context. I don't think you can get young people to deal with the broad, intractable range of problems we face, but one of the things you can do in working with young people, since the central issue in voting is the feeling of efficacy, is to find ways that they can define things that they care about and that they can work to change on a much more local level. In that experience and satisfaction, they might find some efficacy and some reason for participation.

At root, my feeling has always been that voting is a religious act. Participation occurs despite the fact that we know most elections are not decided by our one vote. The critical problem is that the religion is gone; the will is gone. This is not a problem that will be answered in a year. If you want to get into the area of participation, and particularly youth participation, you better be in it for the long haul because the problem is not small, nor should we think small.

Turning on Youth to Politics

Harry C. Boyte

Studies by the Times Mirror Center ("The Age of Indifference") and others purport to reveal that today's teenagers and young adults view politics with nearly universal hatred and express apathy toward public affairs generally. A little more probing uncovers a more complex set of attitudes. Allan Moyle's film *Pump Up the Volume*, based in part on workshops with teenagers in New York, reveals a generation not so much apathetic as disgusted with adult hypocrisy, furious at adults' apparent inaction on mounting social problems, cynical about 1960s-style protest and uncertain about what else there is to do. But it is clear enough that civics classes, weekend senior trips to Washington, and simple exhortations to be "good citizens"—the stuff of political education for earlier generations—are not going to do much to interest young people in the political world.

Into this breach has come youth community service. Its advocates claim that voluntary service prepares a self-centered, materialistic generation for citizenship through cultivating a civic concern for others. Thus, one recent major report on young people, the Grant Commission's 1988 study, "Youth and America's Future," argued that "if the service commitment begins early enough and continues into adulthood, participatory citizenship would become . . . 'habits of the heart,' family and community traditions of local political participation that sustain a person, a community and a nation." The term "community service" is generally used to refer to individual voluntary efforts: tutoring; working in food shelters, adult literacy programs, nursing homes, or hospitals; programs like Big Brothers/Big Sisters of America. It is a growing movement.

A handful of Ivy League college and university presidents organized the Campus Compact in November 1985 to stimulate voluntary community service. By 1987, 259 campuses were involved. The city of Detroit passed a requirement of 200 hours of community service for graduation from high school; Atlanta issued a 75-hour minimum requirement "in an effort to enhance students' understanding of the obligations of a good citizen." Springfield, Massachusetts, made service part of the curriculum from kindergarten through high school. In Washington a bipartisan consensus, stretching from Edward Kennedy to George Bush, passed the Community Service Act of 1990, which provides a mechanism for federal funding of community service projects through public schools and volunteer organizations.

Community service can make important contributions to education through exposure to other cultures, experiential learning and personal growth. In reality, however, service does little to interest students in politics or teach citizenship.

Service is like a generational ink-blot test: How one views it depends on one's politically formative experiences. Older adults across the political spectrum believe that service involvements will revive the kind of political idealism that puts aside self-interest in the pursuit of a larger cause or the common good. Such hopes grow from memories of the idealistic ambience of their own youth. For the right, community service recalls the unambiguous patriotism of the 1950s, when the "Free World" battled countries behind the "Iron Curtain" and the United States was the unique repository of moral rectitude. For the left, community service aims at restoring the idealism of civil rights and antiwar protesters who went into nonviolent combat against segregationists in the South or military recruiters on campus. William F. Buckley and Jesse Jackson may disagree about which ideals community service should cultivate, but both see service as a way of generating altruistic concern.

Community service has a different meaning for young people, however. Steven Conn, a recent college graduate, summarized his generation's views in an open-letter response to Buckley's call for national service: "Many of us in the twentysomething crowd feel we are being bequeathed a colossal mess."

Today's youth see service as an *alternative* to moralized politics and citizenship as normally understood by left or right. Service involvements offer opportunities for real-life experiences that are down-to-earth, serious, and immediately relevant to people's lives. This appeals to young people who have grown cynical about hortatory political rhetoric of any sort.

While college presidents were forming Campus Compact and school systems were instituting service requirements, young adults were creating their own service movement. The most dramatic story is that of the Campus Outreach Opportunity League (COOL), launched in 1984 by a group of recent college graduates to provide encouragement and technical assistance for youth-initiated service programs. When co-founder Wayne Meisel began a 1500-mile trek starting in Maine and ending up in Washington, D.C., to help spark community service projects on campuses, he found little volunteer activity of any kind. Six years later, COOL was at the center of a vital and expanding national network, with 600 campuses involved and almost 1500 students attending its annual conference last year at UCLA.

Far from seeing its purpose as reviving youthful citizenship or political idealism, COOL was from the beginning overtly apolitical. Indeed, it billed itself as an explicit alternative to the political wars on campus between right and left. Meisel depicted the service movement as aimed at the "silent majority" on campuses, between "knee-jerk liberals" on the left and "jerks" on the right.

To younger Americans, repudiation of self-interest sounds disingenuous in a world that trumpets the life styles of the rich and famous and praises the virtues of free enterprise. From its inception COOL stressed benefits that students receive from service involvements. "Self-interest, readily understood, is a win-win deal," said Meisel. "This whole movement is about linking complementary needs." Behind such sentiments lies a palpable hunger for community on the part of a generation that has seen the family disintegrate and the neighborhoods torn apart by racial discord. Volunteers focus on concrete tasks, disavowing sweeping political or social reconstruction. "I do community service for myself," said one woman at a North Carolina college who began a mentoring program for pregnant teens. "I have a passion for it. I can't save the world."

However, the absence of a broader vocabulary of politics that draws attention to the public realm has problematic consequences. Most service programs include little learning or discussion about the policy dimensions of the "issues" (such as poverty, homelessness, drug use, illiteracy) that students wrestle with through person-to-person effort. Volunteers—usually middle-class and generally white—rarely have occasion to reflect on the complex dynamics of power, race, and class that are created when young people go out to "serve" in low-income areas.

Moreover, absent a vocabulary of public politics, community service adopts the therapeutic language of personal development that now pervades society. From TV talk shows to Congressional debates, terms and concepts like accountability, respect for public contribution, negotiation, and recognition of honest differences have been replaced by a therapeutic vocabulary of personal intimacy. This has strengths within communities of friendship. But it assumes sameness—"we all have the same feelings under the skin, after all"—and blurs racial, ethnic, economic, and religious differences. It also obscures questions of power and accountability. Marion Barry appealed for personal sympathy when questioned about drug abuse; Senator David Durenberger told voters in Minnesota that he felt cut off from his friends in the Senate as a result of exposure of his misdeeds.

In community service, a similar emphasis on feelings and personal expressiveness is at work. In high schools, for example, most curriculums for community service stress personal growth. A representative listing of the learning objectives in youth service elaborates goals like "self-esteem," "a sense of personal worth," "self-understanding," "independence," "personal belief in the ability to make a difference," "consciousness about one's personal values," "openness to new experiences," "capacity to persevere in difficult tasks," "exploration of new identities and unfamiliar roles" and "skills in caring for others." Politics was entirely absent. Campus service projects are similarly suffused with a personalized language. Campus programs have

names like GIVE; Project LOVE; Si, Se Puede ("Yes, You Can," a high
school program at Phillips Academy in Andover, Massachusetts); and HOT
(Helping Others Today). COOL's logo consists of hands reaching out to mend
torn hearts.

There are signs of growing restiveness with such excessively apolitical
language. In *Pump Up the Volume* Christian Slater, playing a high school student who creates an underground radio persona named Harry Hard-On, ex-
poses the psychobabble of the guidance counselor and his "full array of
counseling resources" as a cover for the school administration's heavy-
handedness, deceit, and incompetence. In COOL, behind the posture of
apoliticism there has been a slow process of political self-definition for a generation distinguishing itself from the 1960s and convinced it does not need
much more "consciousness raising." Since they entered school, teenagers and
young adults have heard from parents and teachers—1960s veterans, after
all—an unremitting litany of problems, crises, and disasters facing American
society, from poverty to pollution, from racism to falling S.A.T. scores. What
they haven't heard is what is actually being done to solve those problems.
The real-world experience of dealing with diverse environments has
prompted within COOL a desire for practical knowledge about what can be
done. Over the past year, the organization has begun to develop curricular
materials addressing questions of policy, power and politics.

A different way to teach politics is essential if we want to encourage
teens and young adults to assume the full responsibilities of citizenship, that
is, a significant role in public affairs. Partly, this means retrieving older definitions. The word "politics" comes from the Greek *politikos*, meaning "of a
citizen." A citizen-centered politics re-creates the concept of a public realm,
different from private life, in which diverse groups learn to work together
effectively to address public problems, whether or not they like one another
personally or agree on other issues. Politics, to be meaningful, also requires
an *experience of power.*

Project Public Life at the University of Minnesota's Hubert Humphrey
Institute of Public Affairs, which has worked with COOL in developing materials and training for groups to use in political debates and education, has
found that teenagers also respond well to a "problem-solving politics" in
which they take on roles as important actors. The Public Achievement program of Project Public Life, co-sponsored with St. Paul Mayor Jim Scheibel,
Minnesota 4-H, and others, is based on a pedagogy in which young people
define their own goals and have the space to work on them. Issues sometimes
resemble those dealt with by community service, such as concern about the
environment. More often, Public Achievement's emphasis on teens' identification of issues in which they have a direct stake leads to projects that explicitly raise questions of power and that address problems close to home,
like day care for unwed mothers, relations between school officials and

students, and racial conflict among teens. Public Achievement regularly brings together different teams of teenagers in public environments where they learn how to work practically across racial and class lines.

Participants clearly distinguish this experience from community service and other conventional educational activities. "I thought politics meant politicians lying on TV," says one student. "I hated it. Now we've lived out a whole new meaning of politics." Another student, Mary Brennan, from St. Bernard school, says, "It feels good to be able to show what you can do without the shelter of adults. I learned I have a lot of talents that I haven't been using."

Young people come into the world with no special knowledge about politics; political skills and arts are learned, like basketball or music. The goal of civic education should be to provide young people with hands-on public experience, with opportunities to practice political skills like strategic thinking, bargaining, negotiation, listening, argument, problem solving, and evaluation. It should teach both the rewards and the effectiveness of politics. This also requires a process of systematic reflection on the nature of public life and key political concepts like power, accountability, and interests.

Such an approach is a significant shift from conventional community service. Service as practiced today is important, but its language of caring and community is no antidote for youthful cynicism about politics, and its predominantly one-on-one character leaves little room for political learning.

As this generation defines itself politically, it is likely to focus less on altruism, protest, or flag-waving than on finding practical answers to the critical problems of the nation. We badly need this kind of pragmatic populism, in which citizens have more power, authority, and responsibility than they do as sentimentalized "points of light." The end of the Gulf War has left America with an even larger mess, which only politically active citizens can solve.

QUESTIONS FOR DISCUSSION

6.1 Does the instant and close coverage by satellite television of world events such as the Gulf War and fall of the Soviet Union involve people more directly or does it emphasize their role as mere spectators?

6.2 Is Boyte right in arguing that political education needs to focus upon practical problem-solving skills such as negotiation and bargaining and immediate issues such as racial conflict in the school in order to give young people a sense of political efficacy?

6.3 Does contemporary youth culture with its emphasis upon the visual and the flashy deaden the interest of young people in the complexities of contemporary politics?

Chapter
7

Are PACs a Threat to Our Political System?

INTRODUCTION

For many, political action committees (PACs) are the bane of American politics. They are considered the repositories of special interest money that feed politicians the vast sums they need to run expensive, high-tech, modern campaigns and keep themselves in office. In return for this largess, politicians provide these special interest groups with access to their offices not available to ordinary citizens. PAC money usually gravitates to incumbents who are in a position to help their particular cause, and, consequently, incumbents in Congress have become increasingly difficult to dislodge.

PACs are designed to channel campaign money from an interest group to political candidates sympathetic to their cause. PACs can be organized by corporations, labor unions, trade associations, ideological groups, individual politicians, agriculture cooperatives, and professional associations. The Federal Election Act of 1974 set a $1000 limit on individual contributions to candidates and a $5000 limit on contributions from groups, such as PACs. By the late 1980s there were over 4200 PACs spending over $150 million annually on federal campaigns.

PACs do have their defenders, who argue that they increase funding for campaigns and, thus, the information available to voters; that they rechannel money that has been put into campaigns so that voters can see the relationship between lobbies and members of Congress more clearly; and that they allow unions to offset the power of wealthy corporate chieftains who have always been important individual contributors. Some argue that PACs only represent the pluralism of American politics and that no one PAC or group of PACs can dominate congressional actions. Labor PACs and corporate PACs, liberal PACs and conservative PACs, industry PACs and environmental PACs often serve as a counterbalance to each other.

In the following account, David Corn accounts the ways PAC money has influenced the behavior of four individual senators. Corn argues that these senators introduced relatively technical amendments alleviating the impact of government regulations on industries from whom they received substantial PAC money. "As long as members of Congress need to turn to well-heeled individuals, corporations, trade associations, labor unions and other special interests to finance their runs for office, the favors will fly and the taxpayer will pick up the tab."

If PACs were to be eliminated, what would take their place? Government financing raises concerns about favoritism to the two major parties and about government policing of the political process itself. A return to individual contributions could bring back the bad old days of fat cat contributors having excessive influence over government policy.

In opposing a bill to limit the amount of money PACs can give to a congressional race, Senator Phil Gramm (R-Tex.) argues that, "those who scream the loudest about political action committees are the very special groups that lost power to political action committees . . . They are the groups that once exercised power, the political parties, the powerbrokers who operated from smoke-filled rooms, the media." Senator Gramm claims that PACs have helped to strengthen democracy by opening up the political arena to more competitors and by allowing people who are not media personalities to raise money and run for office.

The biggest obstacle to changing the present law may be the Congress itself, whose members gain election through the present system and, despite certain protestations, are quite comfortable with it.

Shilling in the Senate

David Corn

The amendment concerned the testing of prospective pesticides, and the language seemed altogether innocuous. "Whatever tests . . . are required by more than one state or federal agency, such tests . . . shall be coordinated and synchronized among the agencies so as to avoid unnecessary repetition and redundancy." Who could be in favor of unnecessary redundancy?

But Senator Rudy Boschwitz, who was pushing the amendment to the Federal Insecticide, Fungicide and Rodenticide Act at a session of the Senate Agriculture Committee last year, was not acting solely in the name of efficiency. Boschwitz was shilling for a very special interest: small manufacturers of pesticides. And he was doing so in the fashion that occurs in Congress daily: maneuvering at a "mark-up," the underreported committee meetings where legislation gets modified.

North Carolina's Jesse Helms and tobacco, Connecticut's Christopher Dodd and insurance, West Virginia's Robert Byrd and coal—these are well-known partnerships. But many less visible joint enterprises exist in both houses of Congress, engaged in by both liberals and conservatives. I have selected Boschwitz and three of his colleagues—Bennett Johnston, Orrin Hatch, and Alan Cranston—as four not-too-extraordinary examples of how the system operates. They may not necessarily be the worst offenders; such an honor is difficult to award, given the number of contenders. These are just tales of business as usual, which is what makes them alarming.

Boschwitz claimed his pesticide amendment would help small firms develop new products and save consumers from bearing the "inordinate costs," via higher prices, of too much product testing. But to those familiar with pesticide law the amendment had another intent: to subvert the efforts of individual states that write pesticide regulations stiffer than the Federal requirements. Most of the committee saw through Boschwitz. His fellow Republican Pete Wilson put it bluntly: "I think [the amendment] is frankly an effort to achieve a uniformity [of pesticide testing] for the convenience of manufacturers." In fact, prior to the session, the amendment had been widely referred to as the "CSMA amendment," after the Chemical Specialties Manufacturers Association, a trade group representing firms that manufacture home-use pesticides.

Some CSMA members are based in Minnesota, the state Boschwitz represents. Would that justify supporting a bill that would weaken pesticide regulation nationwide? The *Minneapolis Star Tribune* didn't see a home-state interest and chastised Boschwitz for pushing the amendment. But there was another local connection. A key lobbyist for the provision was Jon Grunseth, vice president of the Minneapolis-based Economics Laboratory, which owns ChemLawn and is part of CSMA. Grunseth, whose wife is a major Republican fundraiser in Minnesota, is himself a player in Republican politics and is considering running for governor. Moreover, the political action committees of CSMA members gave Boschwitz at least $30,000 when he ran for reelection in 1984.

At the end of the debate on the amendment, when it became clear that Boschwitz could not persuade a majority of the committee, CSMA representatives were willing to throw in the towel, according to Janet Hathaway, an attorney for the Natural Resources Defense Council, who was at the session. But Boschwitz, to the surprise of some present, pressed for a vote. "CSMA didn't communicate [its willingness to surrender] to Boschwitz," Hathaway recalls. "It's a little embarrassing to pass a note to the Senator saying 'CSMA says to give up.' " The committee rejected his amendment, 14 to 4.

On March 24, Bennett Johnston, the powerful chair of the Senate Energy and Natural Resources Committee, must have realized that a pet project of his was sunk. That was the day that the Exxon Valdez struck a reef and dumped 10 million gallons of crude oil into Prince William Sound. Only nine days earlier, Johnston, a Louisiana Democrat, had carefully navigated through his committee a bill to open the coastal plain of the Arctic National Wildlife Refuge in Alaska to oil and gas drilling.

For the past two years, Johnston has tried to deliver a piece of the wildlife refuge, the nation's sole unspoiled Arctic ecosystem, to the oil industry. But Johnston could not sell the measure to his fellow Democrats. When the committee voted on his bill in February 1988, eight of the ten Democrats refused to support the chair. The bill, however, squeaked out of committee on an 11-to-8 vote; but it didn't move on the Senate floor. This year it was a top priority of Johnston, until the oil spill. He then deep-sixed the measure, explaining it would be "politically foolish" to push it.

Johnston's affection for big energy goes well beyond oil. In 1986 he successfully pushed a bill that favored privately owned utilities over public utilities in federal licensing involving hydroelectric power. Last year he fought back proposed legislation that would make contractors at Department of Energy–owned nuclear facilities—including General Electric, Rockwell, and Westinghouse—liable for accidents caused by their own gross negligence. Johnston has now revived a bill that would save the nuclear industry billions of dollars.

In 1969 the government began enriching uranium for the burgeoning commercial nuclear power industry. The 1954 Atomic Energy Act requires the Department of Energy to price its enrichment services so that it recovers the program's cost. But the General Accounting Office reported in 1987 that the DOE, as of 1986, had not recovered $8.8 billion; that sum may now have risen to more than $10 billion. The utilities claim this debt is solely the result of accounting trickery. Last year, Johnston was one of the proponents of a measure that would restructure the uranium industry and set the amount of unrecovered costs at about $364 million, a figure acceptable to the utilities. In 1988 he succeeded in ushering the bill through the Senate but it died in the House.

On a complex issue such as this, there may be room for honest disagreement; but the room would have to be quite large to accommodate the range between $364 million and $10 billion. Johnston argues that maintaining a healthy nuclear industry is in the national interest. It certainly is in his interest. His finance reports overflow with money from a host of energy concerns. When he was running for reelection in 1983 and 1984, he received more than $121,000 from energy PACs and at least $84,000 from individuals who work in the business. Last year, he earned $8,000 in honorariums from G.E., Chevron, and electric utilities.

Johnston has taken special-interest campaign financing to creative heights via his own Pelican PAC, established in 1987 and named after the Louisiana state bird. As detailed by *Congressional Quarterly*, this PAC has been managed by a small group of former Johnston aides who now lobby for big energy interests. Many of its funds came from individuals who worked for energy companies, according to Federal Election Commission records. Two of the prime movers behind Pelican, both former Johnston aides, are Robert Szabo, who has lobbied for electric utilities, the Uranium Producers of America, and the corporation that owns the drilling rights in the Arctic refuge; and Charles McBride, who has lobbied for the American Nuclear Energy Council and nuclear utilities. Pelican's mission was to raise money that Johnston, then contending for the majority leader's job in the Senate, could funnel to the senatorial campaigns of other Democrats. Johnston doled out over $200,000 in 1987 and 1988, but his largesse failed to win him the votes he needed from his colleagues.

Asked about the propriety of his Pelican scheme, Johnston said, "I'm very much playing by the rules." He's right. By Washington rules, there is nothing wrong when a senator recruits aides turned lobbyists to hit up special interests—whose profits the senator can greatly affect—to finance an effort to obtain the top Senate leadership post.

Orrin Hatch is the ranking Republican on the Senate Labor and Human Resources Committee, which oversees health legislation. He is also the beneficiary of great wads of cash from health-related industry, whose interests frequently come before his committee. For example, in the years before Hatch's 1988 reelection he took in more than $30,000 from company officials and PACs of Eli Lilly, Bristol-Myers, and Pfizer.

Last year the House passed the Medical Device Improvements Act, which was intended to better regulate such items as pacemakers, incubators, and X-ray machines. The bill was the product of extensive negotiations between congressional staff and the Health Industry Manufacturers Association, according to congressional sources and Jerry Connor, a former lobbyist for HIMA. Consumer advocates felt that the bill did not go far enough, but it did tighten a loophole that had allowed medical device manufacturers to escape federal review of many new products.

Three medical device companies and HIMA members—Pfizer, Bristol-Myers, and Eli Lilly—bolted and vowed to sink the bill in Senate. They found an ally in Hatch. He and Representative John Dingell, chair of the House Energy and Commerce Committee, which had responsibility for the medical device bill, began negotiating. Hatch provided Dingell with a list of several proposed changes in the legislation, most of which appeared reasonable to the House side and did not seem, at first blush, to be linked to Pfizer, which had taken the lead in opposing the bill.

But Hatch's list included a measure that previously had been introduced on its own as a bill by Senator Howell Heflin and Representative Dan Glickman. This proposal would prevent foreign citizens from using U.S. courts to sue American manufacturers of defective products. Pfizer had a well-publicized and pressing interest in the measure due to trouble it had with its Bjork-Shiley heart valve. Between 1979 and 1986, 85,000 valves had been implanted in patients, about half of whom were foreigners; as of June 1988 the valve had been linked to 123 deaths. At that time at least 40 foreign citizens were suing Pfizer in California.

The Pfizer bailout provision Hatch proposed adding to the medical device bill fell outside the scope of Dingell's committee, so that Dingell could not have attached it to the medical device bill whether he wanted to or not. Though Hatch failed to deliver this favor to Pfizer, he did succeed in blocking the medical device bill in the Senate, where it expired when Congress adjourned last year. A Hatch spokesperson maintains that the senator was not acting at the behest of Pfizer but on behalf of a number of senators who had various objections to the House bill. But, according to a congressional aide, Pfizer was boasting that Hatch had killed the bill for the company.

Hatch's labors might end up backfiring. This year the House is expected to start all over on a new medical devices bill. "The companies may regret what happened," Connor says, noting that the House might be tempted to pass a tougher measure. Hearings are planned for later this year. The word, says Connor, is that at least one Pfizer product will be featured prominently at the session.

On March 27, 1987, Senator Pete Domenici, a Republican from New Mexico, took to the Senate floor to offer Amendment 59 to the Competitive Equality Banking Act, a major piece of financial legislation. Domenici's measure was quite simple. It would limit the amount of junk bonds a state-chartered and federally insured savings and loan institution could hold in its portfolio. Domenici noted that limits already applied to federally chartered S&Ls and that it seemed unreasonable to allow state-chartered thrifts to engage in high-risk investment yet receive the same insurance. The amendment did not please junk-bond peddlers with Drexel Burnham, Lambert or the state-regulated S&Ls in California that hold a lot of these bonds; both forces lobbied against the provision.

Several senators spoke out against Domenici's amendment, among them Alan Cranston, the Democratic liberal from California. For Cranston, the majority whip and a member of the Banking Committee, this must have been a special moment. He was helping two of his good friends—the S&L industry and Drexel—at the same time. To Cranston's reelection campaign of 1986, Drexel executives and the firms, PAC contributed at least $42,800, and thrift industry PACs, $47,000. With Cranston and others in opposition, Domenici's endeavor failed.

If you're looking for senators who front for industry, one Federal Elections Commission official says, check out the Banking Committee. This is where the titanic forces of the U.S. economy do battle. Insurance interests oppose banks eager to get into the insurance field. The securities industry tries to keep banks from underwriting securities. Major financial firms seek to get a piece of banking. Thrifts vie for less regulation and greater powers. Each bloc has its champions. Cranston, according to former committee aides, usually does double time, helping both S&Ls and the financial services industry. Once, says a committee source, a Cranston aide submitted amendments to a banking bill without the Senator's having read them. They were put in at the request of a trade association of financial services firms.

Cranston consistently has fought efforts to strengthen the capital-reserve standards for S&Ls and pressed measures that would allow them to be more freewheeling. In 1987, in committee caucuses, he urged a lower recapitalization of the Federal Savings and Loan Insurance Corporation. This is what Speaker Jim Wright pushed in the House. Thrifts were not eager to see a large refinancing of the FSLIC for several reasons: They would have to pay the tab; the money would be used to close down ailing S&Ls, an admission that the S&L industry faced a severe problem; and they realized that if only a small recapitalization at that stage was set up, it could lead to a taxpayer bailout down the road. Which it did.

"Alan Cranston is not playing a large role in the public interest on that committee," says Peggy Miller, a banking lobbyist for the Consumers Federation of America. As an example, she points to community reinvestment legislation, which she maintains should interest a liberal well known for his advocacy of housing programs. Miller complains that groups backing community reinvestment legislation, which would require banks to take into account local needs when they review their lending patterns, cannot get help from Cranston: "With the exception of housing, whenever we try to have an impact on the financial community we don't bother with him."

One of Cranston's more notorious actions occurred in April 1987. As reported in the *National Thrift News*, Cranston and four other Senators—Dennis DeConcini, John McCain, John Glenn, and Donald Riegle Jr.—held a meeting with four representatives of the San Francisco Federal Home Loan Bank and urged the regulators to reappraise the real estate investments of a California-based thrift, Lincoln Savings and Loan. This was "an unprecedented display of Senatorial effort on behalf of a thrift," the publication observed. Last year, the *Detroit News* noted that Cranston had received $41,900 in campaign contributions from executives connected to the American Continental Corporation, the owner of Lincoln Savings. (Cranston's office, like those of Johnston and Boschwitz, did not respond to requests for interviews.)

Recently, Cranston was given the chance to relive his 1987 small victory on the issue of junk bonds and thrifts. In April, when the Senate passed the S&L bailout, the bill emerged with a provision that allows S&Ls to count as capital their investment in subsidiaries that hold junk bonds. Because the Banking Committee prepared much of the bill in secret, the author of this provision was never publicly identified. But congressional sources told the *Washington Post* that Cranston was the culprit and that the bill's main beneficiary was a Beverly Hills S&L.

As long as members of Congress need to turn to well-heeled individuals, corporations, trade associations, labor unions, and other special interests to finance their runs for office, the favors will fly and the taxpayer will pick up the tab. As long as they accept from the same gang honorariums (which are direct personal income) and free travel, motives will always be questioned. And as long as key legislative work goes on in secrecy, suspicion will be well justified. Take the case of Cranston's opposition to Domenici's Amendment 59. Senator William Proxmire, then chair of the Banking, Housing and Urban Affairs Committee, also opposed the measure. But Proxmire, who retired last year, did not accept PAC money and declined honorariums from any group with an interest in Banking Committee legislation. In fact, he spent only $145.10 in his last reelection bid.

The big lie on Capitol Hill is that the flow of money doesn't pervert the legislative process. The system has become so poisoned (and the public and news media so cynical) that most episodes of special-interest legislating no longer outrage anyone. In a year marked by scandal and greed on Capitol Hill, the need for reform is obvious. The time is long past to close off the financial tap and open the committee room doors. If there is no noticeable change in the way Congress does business, then we can return to the old ways. The money will always be there.

In Defense of PACs

Phil Gramm

United States Senator, Texas, Republican

I would like to try to begin by taking a broader look at this question than normally is given to it. I start out by asking the question: Why do people give to politicians? Why do people contribute?

I would like then to address this whole issue about how, all of a sudden, because of the self-appointed "public interest" groups promoting their agendas, if 100 hardware and implement dealers in Texas get together and each of them gives $10 and they contribute it to me, that is special interest, and how, if some individual gives $1000, that is not special interest.

I would like to talk about how the political process works in terms of political power, about the fact that PACs did not create political power, and eliminating their influence will not eliminate it. Then I would like to suggest that if somebody really wants to address this problem, the solution really has nothing to do with eliminating the ability of people to contribute, it has to do with trying to affect the things that government does that encourage people to want to give for reasons that we deem not to be in the national interest.

When I ran for the Senate, I had about $10 million contributed to my campaign. I had about 80,000 individual contributors. So far as I am aware, that is more individual contributors than any incumbent candidate for the Senate in American history.

About 15 percent of my contributions came from PACs. I find that, in this last election, the average member of the Senate got 27.8 percent of his money from PACs. I guess what this means is, I need to get out and work a little harder.

Why did these people give to me? I am not going to speculate about why people gave to anybody else; why did they contribute to me? I think a lot of people gave to me because they agreed with me. They did not give to me because they liked my face; they gave to me because they agreed with what

I was saying. They looked at my record in the House and they liked the way I voted and they contributed. I like to think some gave because they love America and they thought my election might be good for America. But I would be naive not to think that a few people gave because they—mistakenly—thought, maybe later, they might influence me.

In fact, when you get right down to it, why do people give? They give because they like the individual candidate; they give because they think the individual candidate is promoting their philosophy in the interest of the country; they give because they want to influence government; they give because they hope their contribution will have some impact on public policy.

I submit to my colleagues that when somebody contributes to a campaign, that is democracy at work.

If you want to know who supports me, all you need do is walk down Main Street, America. You walk down the street and there is the independent baker, there is the independent banker. I could go on and on listing companies and groups that contributed to my campaign. That is not special interest any more than any contribution is special interest.

How do we bring together the concerns of all the special interest groups to make the national interest?

I submit, if we really wanted to do something about those people who contribute to try to influence government, the way to do that is to try to do something about the reason they contribute. If government controls the price of mustard seeds, we should not be shocked that people in the mustard-seed business are going to be active politically. Is that a problem with democracy? Because the government sets the price of a commodity, should we be trying to limit the ability of citizens who believe in the principles of Jefferson to further their interests? I think not. Maybe we ought to look at the fact that the government sets the price of mustard seeds.

I submit if we eliminated the ability of government to set the price of mustard seeds, then the people who are in the mustard-seed business would be contributing because they want to affect general policy, not because they want to affect the mustard-seed business. But I do not see those who support this reform effort urging us to stop government from doing all these things that create the special-interest demands. I do not hear that at all.

My point is that if people are in the political process through political action committees and other groups in trying to influence government policy, it is because the government sets the prices of things. It is because government exercises discretionary power, because government grants favors. If we are concerned about that, what we ought to do is change the law: Limit the amount of government intervention; limit the discretionary decisions that produce winners and losers, that give gifts, that fix things for special interests. That is the source of the problem. If one wants to argue that people are active politically because of special-interest concerns, deal with the concerns; do not limit the freedom of those who want to contribute.

How did political action committees suddenly become the main villain in the political process? If you read some of the editorials that are being written, if you read the "Dear Colleague" letter that was sent out, you might conclude that there is a problem and that it is getting worse.

Well, let me submit that PACs did not create political power. Political power is a zero sum game. If we voted to eliminate political action committees, we would not eliminate political power. Political power exists because government is powerful, because government spends money, because government sets policies that affect us and our children.

The truth is, those who scream the loudest about political action committees are the very special interest groups that lost power to political action committees. They are the groups that have powerful endorsements and big memberships that can be activated to go out and run political telephone banks. They are the groups that once exercised power, the political parties, the power brokers who operated from smoke-filled rooms, the media. Those are the people who complain the loudest about political action committees. Political action committees did not create a situation where government is a megaplayer in the economy. That existed before political action committees. The groups that complain the most about political action committees are the groups that feel they must now share power with another group, and they do not like it. They like having all the power themselves.

Well, if you believe in democracy, if you believe in the principles of Jefferson, you believe that you cannot do away with political power and the best that you can achieve is to disperse it in as many hands as possible. I submit that political action committees, as another competitor in the political arena, have helped to strengthen democracy, not weaken it. And many of those who self-righteously preach against PACs are the very groups that had the power before and now feel the heat of competition.

The truth is, there is nothing more special interest about a group of individuals who get together and give as a group than there is about one individual giving. It is basically a falsehood and myth that is perpetrated by those who hope to tilt the balance of political power in their own favor by constraining their competitors.

Let me talk about that problem very briefly, if I may. Running for office is expensive. I remember when I first successfully ran for office, I did not know many people. I was a college professor. I was running against the aide of the former congressman and against a fellow who had been on television as a weatherman. I was amazed, when I took my first poll, that the weatherman was better known in two-thirds of the district than the congressman who had served for 32 years. The aide I was running against was a good-looking fellow who responded to voters who asked him, "How do you feel about this issue?" he would always say, "Well, how do you feel? What do you say? I'm not going to Washington, like Phil Gramm, to represent a philosophy or a viewpoint, I'm going there to represent you." And let me tell you, it sold like hotcakes.

But there was a difference. The people who were concerned enough to contribute their money looked at everybody's record, and they decided I would be most effective. They contributed to me. I went out, told my story, put the issues before the people and I was elected.

If you start limiting the ability of people to contribute and be involved, who are you going to elect? You will end up electing media personalities to the exclusion of every other group of citizens. You are going to prevent people who have something to say, but do not happen to be well known and do not happen to be especially charming, from reaching the public with an idea that they want heard.

That is the problem with this amendment. First of all, this amendment does not lessen political power. All it does is give more power back to the power brokers, more power back to the smoke-filled room, more power back to the media, more power back to those special-interest groups that use different techniques to influence candidates and public opinion.

Is that good for the country? I say no, because it allows a smaller number of groups to exert political power.

Now, any time a member of this body is willing to say we need to do something about the desire of people to give because they want to affect policy for their own individual interest and therefore we should go out and look at everything government does that would induce individual groups to want to line their own pockets by getting contracts or by getting benefits or by government setting a higher price for their commodity, all you have to do is let me know and I would be interested in joining in that effort. But I am not interested in joining a self-righteous crusade to try to limit the ability of people who have just as much right to be involved as the myriad of "public interest" groups.

I submit that if you take the hardware and implement dealers, the bakers, the bankers, and their employees giving voluntarily, you have some special interests in there. But together they come a lot closer to producing the public interest than the self-righteous, self-appointed public interest groups that are trying to promote a single objective—more government.

Quite frankly, I think we ought to be running on the basis of a set of values. And let people decide if they support that set of values.

I am not worried about being bought by some special interest group, for a single reason—I am not for sale. When people contributed to my campaign, 80,000 of them in my last campaign, they knew what I stood for. As a result, I assume that when they contributed, they were supporting that philosophy—and if they were not, they probably have been disappointed. I believe the vast majority shared the values I hold.

The issue here is, will we allow democracy to work? Will we allow people to be involved? Will we allow power to be competed for, to lessen the power that any single group has?

QUESTIONS FOR DISCUSSION

7.1 As government plays a larger role in American life, more interest groups will have stake in public policy. Aren't PACs simply a manifestation of an activist government?

7.2 Should Congress limit PAC spending and overall congressional spending, who would benefit, incumbents or challengers?

7.3 Would it make more sense to limit campaign spending and grant candidates a certain amount of free television time, thus, reducing the skyrocketing costs of congressional campaigns?

Chapter
8

Do We Need to Overhaul the System of Political Campaigning and Strengthen Our Political Parties?

INTRODUCTION

Political parties were once the major source of funding for candidates. Today they have been replaced by the PAC. The ascension of the PACs and the decline of the parties raises serious questions about the future of the American political system. In contrast to the major political parties, which represent coalitions of interests, the PACs represent special interests. Many believe that diminution of party influence and the rise of PAC power has fragmented the political system and made it difficult for the Congress to reach a consensus on such difficult political issues as the federal deficit. As discussed in Chapter 7, PACs have put more campaign money into the hands of incumbents, have forced members of Congress to spend an inordinate amount of time at fund-raisers, and given big-time contributors greater access to a congressional office than the ordinary taxpayer.

In the following article, Senator David L. Boren (D-Okla.) argues that serious campaign reform, weakening the role of the PACs, would reduce the influence of special interests. His proposed legislation would place caps on senatorial campaign spending and require that PAC contributions be limited to only 20 percent of that ceiling. It would also outlaw "bundling"—a practice whereby PACs package individual contributions together and send them to the candidate without falling under the $5000 PAC limit.

Boren does not claim that his reforms would strengthen the political parties. In fact, he wishes to eliminate the provision in the campaign law that allows individuals to contribute up to $100,000 to political parties. Yet, can the role of special interests be reduced without increasing the influence of the political parties?

In his rebuttal, former Senator William L. Armstrong (R-Colo.) argues that by limiting PAC contributions and capping campaign spending, only incumbents would be strengthened. Few would have access to enough money to challenge a well-entrenched incumbent. In order to invigorate the political system, he would institute term limitations, reduce the numerous perks of congressional office, end the system of free congressional mailing, and limit the time that members can spend fund-raising.

It is interesting to note that throughout this debate over campaign reform neither side argues for making the parties themselves the major source of campaign funding and restoring them to their former place of influence. What does this say about the future of our parties?

Congress on the Auction Block

David L. Boren

United States Senator, Oklahoma, Democrat

Each spring, members of Congress participate in one of the most cherished aspects of their jobs as elected officials—giving commencement speeches at high school graduations in their states. I always ask how many of the idealistic, spirited graduates in my home state would be interested in holding elective office. A good number of hands always go up. I then ask how many might like to serve in the U.S. Senate one day. Again, quite a few hands respond.

Unfortunately, I then have to ask how many will be ready to raise the nearly $20 million they will need at a minimum to win that seat by the time they're old enough to run for the Senate. The disillusionment and disbelief in students' eyes because of this almost insurmountable hurdle renews my commitment every year to enact reform in the way congressional races are financed.

Congress celebrated its bicentennial during 1989, focusing on its history and the changes the institution has gone through since the first representatives and senators convened in 1789. However, we don't have to harken back that far in our history to look at the basic erosion in our grass-roots democracy due to the spiraling costs of congressional elections.

In 1976, the bicentennial of this country's independence, the average cost of winning a Senate seat was about $600,000. By 1986, the bicentennial year of our Constitution, that figure had grown five-fold to more than $3 million. During the last election in 1988, that figure increased to over $4 million—nearly a 33 percent jump in only two years! If current trends continue at the same rate, 12 years from now, when this spring's high school graduates will be eligible to run for the Senate, the average cost easily could be $20 million.

These figures paint a bleak picture. In essence, seats in Congress have been placed on the auction block and their price is going through the roof with no end in sight. Who or what is at fault? Certainly, inflation has forced an increase in the price of mailings, television and radio advertising, and other campaign costs. However, inflation increased by about 25 percent between 1982 and 1988. In that same period, the cost of winning a Senate race increased 570 percent.

At the heart of the rising costs of congressional races is special-interest money. Political action committees (PACs) contributed over $49 million in the 1988 election. More importantly, PACs gave four times as often to sitting senators as they gave to challengers, allowing incumbents to outspend challengers by more than $60 million.

In 1982, 98 sitting members of Congress were reelected, with over half their campaign funds coming from special-interest PACs. In 1986, that number went up to 195! Is it any wonder that 99 percent of the members of the House of Representatives are reelected year after year?

When additional money from special interests is pumped into the system, it ends up being spent and campaign costs soar. The rising tide of special-interest money from PACs exacerbates the fundamental problem that there is simply too much money in our electoral system.

An alarming problem with PACs is that these out-of-state money machines, coming from both business and labor groups, are discouraging new people with fresh ideas from getting involved in politics. With the overwhelming share of PAC contributions going to incumbents, rather than challengers, new candidates almost are forced out of running a serious campaign. Even though prospective candidates may be able to do well with voters in their home states or districts, they are squeezed out by Washington-based or out-of-state-funded special interests.

More importantly, the growth in the influence of PACs further fragments our nation and its elected legislative bodies. A PAC does not judge a senator or congressman on his or her over-all voting record or personal integrity the way voters and local supporters do. It does not balance his or her entire record to see if that performance serves the national interest.

Instead, PACs rate the member of Congress solely on how he or she voted on bills specifically affecting the particular financial interest groups they represent. Because congressmen and senators receive more and more of their funds from PACs, the narrow focus of special-interest groups makes it increasingly difficult to reach a national consensus on important issues. As Senate Minority Leader Bob Dole (R.-Kans.) once said, when PACs contribute to a candidate, "they expect something in return other than good government." Our decision-making process is being held hostage to the special interests that PACs represent.

With millions of dollars rolling into campaign coffers for members of Congress, the conduct of our elected officials has changed dramatically. Former Senator William Proxmire (D.-Wis.) described the influence of a PAC contribution as not necessarily "buying" a vote, but "it may come in a speech not delivered, in a colleague not influenced. It may come in a witness not invited to testify before a committee. It may come in hiring a key staff member for a committee who is sympathetic to the PAC. Or it may come in laying off or transferring a staff member who is unsympathetic to the PAC."

Even more disturbing is that, when votes are scheduled in the Congress—the essential component of our legislature—consideration often is given to the fund-raising schedule that night. Frequently, two- or three-hour "windows" are left open in the Senate's schedule to allow members to go to each other's fund-raisers that evening. Too often, members of Congress are spending time raising money to fund expensive campaigns, instead of using that precious time working to solve the pressing problems facing our country. As former Solicitor General Archibald Cox once said, "We must decide whether we want government of, by, and for the people or government of the PACs, by the PACS, and for the PACs."

THE NEED FOR REFORM

On average, senators must raise $15,000 each week in order to run a normal race every six years. With the virtually unlimited supply of PAC money in Washington, the present system has become one of "incumbency protection." Seats in Congress have become, in essence, lifetime appointments. Turnover in Congress today is almost due more to retirement than to lost elections. The system our Founding Fathers set up 200 years ago of elected officials being held accountable to the voters is now in disrepute and must be reformed.

What we desperately need is a more "level playing field" in the campaign spending system so potential challengers are not prevented from running solely because the cost of campaigning is too high. We need fairness and a return to grass-roots democracy so that congressmen listen more to local groups and voters than they do to special-interest groups in Washington.

The only way to reform the current system is to place a ceiling on campaign spending. This notion has bipartisan support. As former President Gerald Ford recently stated, "The cost of running for office today is outrageous. We ought to put a limit on how much can be spent on a congressional race."

During the 1970s, Congress attempted to reform campaign financing by placing mandatory spending caps on congressional races. Unfortunately, the Supreme Court struck down mandatory spending limits as an unconstitutional restriction on free speech in its 1976 decision, *Buckley* v. *Valeo*. Following this ruling, there is only one way to limit campaign spending—through a voluntary system of spending limits with strong inducements to convince candidates to abide by reasonable cost ceilings.

Under legislation I introduced in January, 1989, spending caps would be placed on Senate elections based on the number of voters in each state. If a senatorial candidate goes over the reasonable limit, his or her opponent would be eligible for benefits such as lower mailing and advertising rates, as well as direct public grants.

In addition, my legislation would place a cap on how much money candidates could receive from special-interest PACs. Currently, individual PACs can contribute up to $5000 to a candidate, but there is no limit on how much a candidate can receive in total from *all* PACs. There is also nothing to prevent one special-interest group from forming two, three, or more PACs to get around the $5000 maximum contribution limit. Compared to the current system, in which candidates are getting 50, 60, and sometimes 90 percent of their campaign financing from PACs, my proposal would allow only 20 percent of a candidate's funds to come from these special-interest groups.

Had this legislation been in effect during the last election, total spending would have been down by 32 percent and PAC expenditures would have been cut by two-thirds. In 1988, every single Senate incumbent running for reelection raised and spent more PAC money than would be allowed under my proposal.

One of the lessons from past attempts at reforming the campaign financing system is that today's piecemeal reforms are often tomorrow's problems. Smart lawyers will continue to find ways around the law until we enact overall reform. My proposal is a comprehensive approach that will not allow later abuse of the system.

Beyond placing spending caps on elections, the bill would close current loopholes in the law. Under one such loophole, special-interest groups are allowed to pour hundreds of thousands of dollars into elections "on behalf" of candidates through "independent expenditures"—for example, by paying for television advertisements.

In theory, these groups are acting independently, without the knowledge or planning of the candidate. Tiny disclaimers at the end of such TV ads show the real source of the advertisement, but they appear briefly and are difficult to read. A large part of the last election's negative campaign ads came from these sources.

My proposal would open this system up to the light of public disclosure. By forcing groups to reveal their role in elections, voters will know who is trying to influence the voting. In addition, the bill would provide compensation to candidates who are the victims of independent expenditures when their opponents are not complying with the spending caps.

"Bundling" is a second loophole that needs to be plugged. As the law stands now, PACs can serve as a conduit for individual contributions solicited from their members. It is possible for PACs to receive these individual contributions, "bundle" them together, and send them on to a candidate without falling under the $5000 individual PAC contribution limit. Hundreds of thousands of dollars can be contributed this way with all the implied special-interest strings attached.

Another loophole is known as the "soft money" problem. Currently, individual voters can contribute only $1000 to a specific candidate's campaign. However, they can pay up to $100,000 to political parties for general "party-building" efforts. Too often, the Democratic and Republican national and state parties funnel this money into large-scale contributions to candidates. Since there is no regulation of "soft money," we do not even know how many millions of dollars were spent through this loophole in the last election to influence Senate and House elections. We do know that $40 million–$70 million was used to affect the presidential election.

We need a total reform package in order to turn the tide against the flood of special-interest money corrupting our electoral process. Loopholes must be fixed and overall spending ceilings need to be placed on congressional elections.

PAST EFFORTS

In 1985, along with Senator Barry Goldwater (R.-Ariz.), I introduced the first major campaign finance reform legislation since the 1970s. Our bill would have limited PAC contributions and their influence on increasing the cost of campaigns. The now retired senator and former presidential candidate recently told me, "As I sit on the outside now, and look at my time campaigning, I almost get sick at the amount of money I had to spend."

In 1987, I joined with the Senate Majority Leader, Robert Byrd (D.-W.Va.), in introducing a total reform package. A clear majority of the Senate supported our proposal and we had over 50 co-sponsors of the bill. Unfortunately, a minority of senators successfully "filibustered" it and prevented even one vote from ever occurring on the measure.

At the start of the 101st Congress, I introduced a revamped version of the "Boren/Byrd" reform proposal. While there has been one committee hearing on the bill, a minority again is preventing the Senate from acting on the proposal.

Also during the 101st Congress, the House of Representatives and the Senate set up task forces on congressional ethics, including campaign finance reform. However, as one leader in the House indicated during recent deliberations, to change the financing of elections is to tamper with a "congressman's lifeline."

Over the last five years, there has been a ground swell of grass-roots support for reforming the system. Newspapers across the country have endorsed placing caps on congressional spending, and I have heard from thousands of Americans supporting campaign reform. Everyone interested in real reform needs to speak up now to build the momentum necessary to ensure that Congress acts. We cannot allow another election to go by without a change in the system.

The time has come for the American people to demand that elected officials face up to their responsibility and reform the corrupt campaign financing system. An overwhelming majority of the American people support placing a cap on congressional campaign spending. A recent survey by the National Federation of Independent Business found that 83 percent of their members said "yes" to the question: "Should limits be placed on campaign spending of congressional candidates?" Only 12 percent said "no."

If we are to achieve meaningful reform in our election process, a strong sense of statesmanship must prevail in the debate. We must not allow partisan bickering to prevent Congress from acting in the national interest to protect the integrity of our electoral system. Campaign finance reform is not a Republican or Democratic problem—it is an American problem that demands a bipartisan solution.

In the process, we can salvage the dream of today's high school students who aspire to serve their country as public servants in the next century and ensure that tomorrow's voters will judge them on their goals, values, and new ideas instead of how much money they can spend. That is the challenge to all of us in Congress, and we are accountable to them to guarantee that their dreams indeed can be realized.

Voters should write their congressmen stating their concerns. We cannot wait for a national scandal involving inappropriate campaign contributions to call Congress into action. That call must come now from all Americans.

Campaign Reform
An Exercise in Cynicism

William L. Armstrong

United States Senator, Colorado, Republican

As the Senate revs up to pass campaign reform legislation, enthusiasts should recall how the last batch turned out. As usual, the do-gooders seem to have done more good for themselves than for the general public.

The 1989 "reform" of congressional ethics turned out to be a backdoor pay raise for members of Congress. The "reform" of franked mail regulations was heralded as curtailing the number, size, and cost of the free mailings which have given members of Congress an almost insurmountable advantage over challengers. Instead of reducing such mailings, however, the cost in the House of Representatives practically has doubled—from the $41 million budgeted for 1990 to an estimated $79 million—to boost incumbent name identification with the voters back home. No wonder Congress loves reform, and no wonder the public is unenthusiastic about the campaign legislation gathering steam in the Senate.

The campaign reform measures now being negotiated behind closed doors toward a "bipartisan compromise" are another example of incumbent self-perpetuation disguised as statesmanship. The evils to be vanquished are "unlimited spending," according to the Democrats, and "special interests," say the Republicans. They are both wrong.

What the Democrats really want is full public financing of campaigns and even greater perks and security for incumbents. (Most of the incumbents *are* Democrats!) What the Republicans really want is to block the Democratic schemes without appearing to be against "reform." So what the entire enterprise boils down to is not Democrats vs. Republicans. It's Incumbents vs. Challengers; Imperial Congress vs. Voters.

Indeed, the three campaign reform proposals on the table (those of the Senate Democrats, the Senate Republicans, and the president) have one feature in common—they all appear to violate the Constitution's guarantees of free speech and association.

Campaigns cost too much, say the Democrats. In introducing their bill, they bemoaned "the money chase [which] has corrupted the political process of this country" and "the escalating arms race of fund-raising that is destroying the system." Their prescription is to implement public financing and set overall campaign spending limits—a notion that goes far beyond the current policy of curtailing the amount groups or individuals can contribute to a candidate. Democrats stress that the spending limits are *voluntary,* but apparently no one will volunteer for the advantages of spending limits without substantial government benefits: low-cost television time, subsidized campaign mail (there they go again), and public funding to match money expended by independent groups and "excessive" spending by an opponent.

To collect all these campaign goodies, the incumbent merely has to promise not to spend more than a certain limit. However, if the challenger, swimming upstream against the powerful current of incumbent advantage, spends more than the limit, the incumbent gets millions more in public money and the spending limit is removed.

Republicans oppose spending limits. The centerpiece of their "reform" proposal is the abolition of political action committees. The much-maligned PACs, it is argued, are "special interests" that dominate campaigns and give more to incumbents than challengers.

The Democrats recently jumped on the "Kill PACs" bandwagon with the GOP, and the "good government" game now is shifting into bipartisan high gear. In speeches on the Senate floor and in most press accounts, senators on both sides of the aisle are seen promoting "cleanup of the process"; responding to "public demand" for integrity in campaigns; and declaring that the system, put in place largely by campaign finance laws in the 1970s, isn't working. They roundly denounce "special interest money." They confess that they are so preoccupied with raising money for campaigns, they're neglecting the important public duties they were elected to perform. They all agree campaigns are too expensive, making it hard for challengers to take on incumbents.

Initial posturing is completed. Partisan positions are staked out. Bipartisan negotiations are under way. Now, observe the next step in this typical congressional reform dance. In the coming weeks, there will emerge a bipartisan compromise, and there will be great back-patting among the reformers—Democrats and Republicans alike. If the scientists measure the hot air coming from the Senate wing of the Capitol, they'll probably identify it as a critical source of global warming.

The truth is, there always have been special interests in American politics, and there should be. People get into politics because they are interested in something, are mad about something, or want to get something done. If teachers, oil workers, or accountants have a beef with Washington, aren't independently wealthy, and want to band together to support or oppose a candidate for Congress—what's wrong with that?

Nothing is. That's the way our system should work. It's one of the animating principles of our Constitution. Madison explained in *The Federalist Papers* that a multiplicity of "interests" are fundamental to republican government. Alexis DeTocqueville observed the unique propensity of Americans to form associations for the promotion of their "self-interest," as properly understood: "As soon as several inhabitants of the United States have taken up an opinion or feeling they wish to promote . . . and as soon as they have found one another out, they combine. From that moment they are no longer isolated men, but a power seen from afar, whose . . . language is listened to." Perhaps the moralists and would-be reformers of today should reflect upon DeTocqueville's conclusion that the banding together of citizens to promote these special interests enhanced both individual rights and the common good.

PACs make special interest money both public and accountable. The alternative, at least in the past, was that special interests exerted influence behind closed doors—unknown to the voters and unaccountable to anyone. For example, read Robert Caro's recent book on Lyndon Johnson. During the 1948 Senate campaign, his aides took $50,000 cash donations from oil tycoons in paper bags, Caro claims.

PAC money today comprises 23 percent of campaign money vs. 64 percent from individuals in the 1987–88 period for all Senate campaigns. Like PACs, individuals also give more to incumbents then they do to challengers. The solution of eliminating PACs makes no more sense than that of eliminating individuals.

PACS AND THE FIRST AMENDMENT

Most important of all, eliminating PACs probably would be unconstitutional. In *Buckley* v. *Valeo,* the Supreme Court left no doubt that campaign contributions and expenditures are protected as a form of expression by the First Amendment. PACs, as voluntary associations of free citizens seeking lawful political aims, are protected by the Constitution as well.

Also in dubious constitutional standing are the provisions in the Democratic bill which guarantee that public revenues will be used to match "excessive" spending by an opponent or by independent expenditures. What does it do to the protected political expression of a challenger who, as he spends more money—as he must necessarily do to take on a powerful incumbent—has his expression effectively nullified by an ever larger public subsidy flowing to the incumbent?

Granting of reduced TV broadcast rates and mail costs to candidates using public money, while denying them to those using private money, also is likely to run afoul of the First Amendment. The ACLU calls this "effort to micromanage the content of political speech . . . wholly inappropriate and unconstitutional," declaring: "Surely, there is no justification for allowing a publicly benefited candidate to pay only 25 percent of the price of a first-class stamp, while a privately financed candidate pays full rate."

Incumbents claim they're forced to spend too much time chasing campaign money, at the expense of their jobs in Congress. If that is true, why was 1989's House average for roll call vote attendance 94.4 percent and the Senate's 97.9 percent? If there really is not adequate time to address the pressing lawmaking needs of the nation, how do members of Congress find time to act on bills designating "National Tap Dance Day" or "National Juke Box Week"? Those measures, and hundreds of similar ones, have become public law recently, so the complaints about the heavy burden of fund-raising should not cause Americans to melt with sympathy.

Then, there is the claim that campaigns are too expensive. True, spending for congressional campaigns, like everything else, has gone up, but put it in perspective. A total of $459 million was spent in the last election on *all* House and Senate campaigns—including primaries and general elections, winners and losers. That's less than the amount spent on network television advertising for snacks and soft drinks—about $493 million! In 1988, each of 52 American companies spent more on advertising than the combined cost of all the campaigns for the U.S. Senate that year. Incidentally, that amount was $201.4 million—or less than one dollar per American citizen.

Like so many "reforms" Congress institutes, these proposed measures will not fix what's really wrong, which is not campaign finance—it's what goes on in Congress itself. If people are serious about promoting changes that truly would limit the power of incumbents, bring fresh blood and competition into congressional races, and correct some related abuses in Congress, they should insist on:

- **Ending free mail.** Congressional newsletters, sent under the franking privilege at no cost to members of Congress, give incumbents a huge advantage over challengers. Reforms, controls, and limits haven't worked.

  In fiscal year 1989, one senator sent out 10.3 million items of mail at a cost of $1.7 million. That senator, up for reelection in 1992, fired out 2 million pieces of mail in the first quarter of fiscal year 1990.

  In 1988, the last year for which figures have been disclosed, members of both houses mailed 805 million newsletters and other franked items—more than seven pieces for every household in America—at a postal cost of $113.4 million, according to the estimates of the House clerk. All "free" congressional mass mailings should be eliminated.

- **Term limitation.** A return to the concept of the citizen legislature is the most important step in restoring the health of Congress. The permanent, career Congress, with its 98 percent incumbent reelection rate, has become a breeding ground for cynicism, which has reached epidemic proportions.

We have strayed far from the Founders' idea of landholders, merchants, farmers, and those in the various professions coming to represent their fellow citizens for a time in the national legislature. We have forgotten that, in a civic sense, the returning home is as important as coming to Washington in the first place.

Limiting representatives to three terms and senators to two seems reasonable. An outstanding member of Congress still could stay in Washington representing his constituents for 18 years.

- **Cutting congressional spending.** The money Congress spends just on itself is outrageous. It took it 191 years to reach an annual budget of $1 billion in 1980. Just 10 years later, the Congressional budget climbed to $2 billion. A sharp cut would do wonders to focus attention on the important at the expense of the frivolous. With reduced budgets, fewer staff members, and less perks of all kinds, incumbents could perform the duties of their office and have less idle time and resources to waste.
- **Shortening the campaign season.** Establish, for example, a Senate rule that no fund-raising may take place until 12 months before any given election. That would be truly equitable and productive. Think how it would free members of Congress to devote their attention to important legislation!
- **Insisting on openness.** Full disclosure of all campaign contributions, from every source, is the best accountability imaginable. Then, citizens would have the freedom and the power to band together, contribute to candidates, and get involved in the process. Voters would know everything and could make their decisions accordingly.

Pundits and politicians profess to be concerned about the growing cynicism of American voters. We all ought to reflect upon their concern in light of the campaign reform proposals before the Senate. It is exactly this kind of legislation—masquerading as reform, but promoting incumbency, inhibiting citizen participation, and trampling the Constitution in the process—that fosters cynicism from Portland to Pueblo to Peoria.

QUESTIONS FOR DISCUSSION

8.1 In this era of high-tech campaigning, which often costs in the millions, can our political parties ever gain access to the campaign funds necessary to give them real influence of the candidates?

8.2 Is our allegiance to the parties a thing of the past and should we concentrate upon opening up the system and thereby reduce the power of incumbents?

8.3 Is there a single reform that would eliminate the dominant role of PACs and strengthen the role of the parties?

Chapter
9

Should the Private Lives of Public Figures Be Subject to Media Scrutiny?

INTRODUCTION

Thirty years ago there was an unwritten rule among reporters who covered politics that they would not divulge information about the private lives of public figures. The drinking habits, the sexual foibles, and other assorted vices that politicians harbored were hidden from public view. A senator could stagger drunk onto the Senate floor, mutter some incomprehensible speech, and no mention would be made of it in the papers the next day. Even a matter so potentially explosive as President John F. Kennedy's affair with a girlfriend of a major mafia don was kept from the public.

In the late 1980s and early 1990s, this convention no longer held. A leading presidential candidate, Gary Hart, was forced to withdraw from the race in 1988 when the press uncovered an extramarital affair; a nominee for the Supreme Court, Judge Douglas Ginsburg, was forced to withdraw the same year when it was disclosed that he had used marijuana as a young law professor; former Senator John Tower's nomination to be Secretary of Defense was defeated in the Senate as a result of his reputation as a heavy drinker; a story in a tabloid newspaper concerning the alleged extramarital affairs of Governor Bill Clinton (D-Ark.), the Democratic presidential candidate in 1992, became a major campaign issue.

When does the private life of a political figure become the public's concern? In the following editorial from the *New Republic,* the editors suggest several questions that reporters should ask themselves before disclosing such information: (1) Will such behavior affect performance on the job?; (2) Was the law broken?; (3) Was the public lied to?; (4) Does the office make special demands? (meaning, for example, that the Surgeon General shouldn't smoke). Garry Wills argues that the question of character is relevant to political office, but the standards by which the society judges character are constantly changing. Public attitudes on religion, divorce, and sexual preference are far different today from what they were 50 years ago. Thus, argues Wills, as we define what is acceptable private behavior for politicians, we are also defining our own evolving American character.

Privates on Parade

Editorial from New Republic

From the fuss over Ralph Abernathy's book, you might think he was saying something new about Martin Luther King, Jr. But apart from a few specific details about King's final night, there are no real surprises. We already knew that the great man was also, as the old joke goes, a man. King is important enough that this is worth knowing and trying to understand. The outcry against Abernathy, however understandable as an expression of hurt feelings, is misguided—particularly since the burden of that outcry is not that what Abernathy is saying is untrue, but that he shouldn't be saying it. Reporters who wouldn't hesitate in applying tough-minded standards of truthfulness to punier, living personages such as Jim Bakker—or to historical equals of King such as Jefferson or Franklin Roosevelt—have tongue-lashed Abernathy for his candor about King's philandering. William Raspberry, the normally unsentimental *Washington Post* columnist, pronounced Abernathy a Judas for telling tales out of school, and Bryant Gumbel lectured Abernathy on NBC's "Today Show" for defacing the King "legend" and abetting his enemies. If these journalists really prefer myth to fact, they are in the wrong business.

The King case is an easy one. The trouble the media is having with it reveals a deeper confusion about issues of personal morality, privacy, and the public's right to know. These questions seem to be arising almost continually in our public life. The House, at the moment, hums with scandals involving the sexual behavior of four representatives. In addition to Barney Frank of Massachusetts, whose troubles have been massively publicized, there are Democrats Gus Savage of Illinois and Jim Bates of California, up on sexual harassment charges, and Republican Buz Lukens of Ohio, convicted of having sex with a minor. The Gary Hart case had its immediate echoes in the exposure of the extramarital love affairs of Governor Richard Celeste of Ohio and Mayor Henry Cisneros of San Antonio. John Tower was voted down partly because of his fondness for drink, made vivid by a reputation for unsubtle barroom flirtatiousness. Douglas Ginsburg missed the Supreme Court on account of the odd joint of marijuana. Accompanying these media feeding-frenzies (four of those mentioned above made the cover of *Newsweek*) has been an increasing amount of soul-searching by journalists about where to draw the line between public and private and about how to make such decisions.

Hart was supposed to be a special case, but the many cases since have made it clear that once a scandal has surfaced, prurience carries the day. The issue gets resolved in favor of investigation, exposure, and publication. The revelation of salacious details is justified on the basis of news value or competitive pressures or insight into "character"—in short, on any remotely plausible basis except disapproval of adultery itself (which violates an elite social taboo against moralism). Once the details are out, the discussion ensues about what should have been disclosed. First the *Cleveland Plain Dealer* exposed Celeste for "womanizing" on the pretext that his presidential ambitions made it news. Afterward the paper aired objections to its decision—too late for the Celeste family. Once one paper prints a story, others have the excuse that the lid is off, or that the way in which the victim of the disclosure is "handling" the disclosure is news, even if the disclosure itself isn't. Before the next sex story strikes, it makes sense to articulate some principles by which the conflicting claims of public and private can be arbitrated.

This is one debate in which the extremes both have something to recommend them. On one side are those who contend that a holder or seeker of office is as entitled to a private life as is any other citizen, and that the public has no more right to inquire into his or her sex life than does any other employer or prospective employer. On the other side are those who contend that self-government means citizens must be free to cast their votes and petition their representatives on the basis of whatever information they deem relevant. There's merit in both views. The former derives from respect for personal privacy, the latter from the democratic instinct. And both yield a satisfying "bright line" that answers the question of whether to invade the boudoir in any given instance.

Yet neither is quite satisfactory, in theory or in practice. The purist position in favor of privacy doesn't acknowledge that private misbehavior sometimes does intrude on public conduct. To take only one example, John F. Kennedy's libidinous excesses opened him to mob blackmail. This is not to say that he should not have been president; but it was not the place of the White House press corps to shield the public from a truth all its members knew. (Had the press been less routinely compliant, by the way, the president almost certainly would have behaved more wisely.) And this position both overestimates the public's censoriousness and underestimates its ability to put such matters in perspective.

The purist right-to-know position, on the other hand, gives the public too much credit for disinterested concern. Gossip is always fascinating, and we will concoct justifications for listening to it even where it has no direct relevance (as is usually the case). This view also disregards the way sex scandals happen in practice. Seldom is factual information about the private lives of politicians "out there" for reporters to print or not as they see fit. Journalists are familiar with scores of rumors, some fraction of which might be true. There is no way to investigate them without prying into the intimate affairs of those who have done nothing at all or whose private behavior has no public implications.

Rejecting these alternatives opens the great, gray void between "never" and "always." But there is no alternative to judging individual cases on their merits. The way to reach a decision about whether a matter should be made public is to ask questions about its relevance.

Is it material to the job? Everyone's sex life—even the lack of one—explicates his or her "character" or personality. The public, however, has no intrinsic right to understand its leaders and their motivations at this level; and it is a coarse parody of Freudianism that imagines that a superficial study of a person's sexual behavior yields insights into character that a deep study of his or her public record leaves obscure. The test is whether private conduct impinges on public performance. In the case of Gus Savage, accused of sexually harassing a Peace Corps volunteer on an official trip to Zaire, this test is clearly met. A legislator in the habit of showing up drunk on the floor of the Senate would also meet this criterion. But if John Tower merely went on the odd after-hours bender, it shouldn't have disqualified him from running the Pentagon.

Was the law broken? Though Congress often operates on the opposite principle, it seems reasonable to demand that those who make laws also obey them. Law-breaking is a basic criterion for legitimate public interest. An attempt must be made to substantiate any allegation of violations of law that emerge. The press cannot ignore Stephen Gobie's charges against Barney Frank, though it is far from clear that Frank knowingly broke laws. But the fact that some legal transgression may have taken place in no way excuses efforts, such as those of the Moon-owned *Washington Times*, to engineer the story for maximum destructiveness to Frank's career. It should also be remembered that not all laws are of equal magnitude. Many states still have oral sodomy statutes on the books that are unenforced and unenforceable; unprosecuted victimless misdemeanors do not on their own justify "investigative" enthusiasms.

Is the public being lied to? A measure of hypocrisy is indispensable to any social order, and is implicit in any notion of privacy. And appearing with the wife and kids in a Christmas card photo while carrying out an extramarital affair is too banal, too common a contradiction, to justify exposure and vilification. At some point, however, the contrast between personal conduct and public facade becomes intolerable, as in the case of former Representative Robert Bauman, who advocated anti-gay laws while soliciting male prostitutes in a D.C. gay bar. But if a politician consistently maintains that his private life is no one's business but his own, and his record shows he respects other people's privacy as well, then there's no excuse for invading his bedroom.

Does the office make special demands? The Surgeon General should be a non-smoker. The Drug Czar shouldn't get stoned. It seems reasonable that Supreme Court Justices be held to the highest standard of adherence to the law. Many jobs do involve setting a specific moral example. In these cases, behavior that would otherwise be private becomes pertinent to one's qualification. In the case of presidents, questions of judgment as well as moral example come into play. The holder of the most important post in the world, with his finger on the proverbial button, must be sober and controlled at all times. If a presidential candidate is recklessly promiscuous (not just quietly adulterous), it legitimately raises the question of his good sense. If reporters have information to this effect—and during a national campaign they're apt to find out—they should share it.

The problem is that in the wind tunnel of national publicity, perspective gets blown away. Gossip explodes into news and wrecks lives and careers. The punishment doesn't fit the crime. Before Hart's sexual indiscretions could be thought over by the voters he was finished. Perhaps his presidential candidacy deserved summary execution, but his public career did not. He may lack the caution and stability we look for in presidents, but he remains eminently qualified to serve in the Senate or elsewhere. Yet today he is a political untouchable.

Hart and others have gotten caught in the gears of massive changes in public attitudes about private mores. Respect for the *public institution* of marriage is on the decline, while demand for the *private authenticity* of marriage is on the rise. That is why we are now more willing to tolerate divorce than adultery in our presidents, a complete reversal of the attitudes of a generation ago.

Indeed, however much it may seem otherwise, public tolerance in general grows as a result of these periodic media overreactions. We don't like to see our leaders disgraced for infractions that are familiar in our own lives. By the time the next Douglas Ginsburg comes up for confirmation, the public will be closer to understanding that for an American 40-year-old, not to have smoked pot qualifies as deviant behavior. There are bound to be martyrs in the meanwhile. That's a shame, but it doesn't justify journalists putting themselves in the godlike position of deciding what the public is sophisticated enough to handle. It's an argument instead for serious, unsensational reporting of low sex in high places when, and only when, it makes a difference.

How Pure Must Our Candidates Be?

Garry Wills

"Has the press gone too far?" is a question that has been asked more frequently in this presidential campaign than any other. At a time when politicians are being canvassed on their love lives, their acquaintance with marijuana, and the originality of all their sayings, the question seems to answer itself. The "character issue" has become, in many people's eyes, a hunting license. The prey are intimidated even when they are not eliminated, made to seem vulnerable, "on the run" instead of running for office. The character issue seems to reverse its intended effect and puts in question all of a candidate's merits if he or she cannot measure up.

According to political managers like Raymond Strother (once Gary Hart's media adviser) and Robert Beckel (who ran Walter Mondale's 1984 campaign), the search for character has blighted any chance for charisma, for the kind of respect that makes governing possible. After making candidates scurry in fear from intrusive, petty, trivializing questions, how could the American public turn around and accord the winner a decent esteem?

These are all good questions. Do we really want to know as much as we are being told about other people's (even public people's) private lives? Are we going to make it impossible for public figures to have any private lives at all? The scrutinizing process has become, in the eyes of many, an incredible shrinking machine that diminishes all its participants—the prying reporters, the candidates shying off from the hunt, and a public torn between embarrassment and titillation. There seems to be no escape from knowing about Pat

Robertson's premarital sex or Albert Gore's most recent experience of marijuana (which occurred, significantly, when he was a journalist).

Nor is this kind of inquiry limited to presidential candidates, as Judge Douglas Ginsburg learned when he tried to move from a lower court to the highest one. It was found that in his various screenings for Justice Department and judicial appointments, he had exaggerated some things and minimized others. One of the things he minimized was any mention of drugs, including the putatively harmless (or at least temporarily expected) use of marijuana in his past. Widely expressed was a fear that the media would now enforce a "generational vendetta," disqualifying for public office those of a certain age bracket—that group of people coming of age in the 1960s, when custom seemed temporarily to exempt the young from the law against marijuana possession or use.

Of course, there have always been generational tests and barriers in our politics. After World War II it was almost impossible for men of a certain age to run for public office if they had not been in the armed forces. In the courts, too, it was a disqualification, for some time after the Civil War, for any judge to have served with the Confederacy. More recently, generations of Southern senators were brought up with an instilled certitude that keeping the "nigra" in his place was not only wise but the best thing for the "boy" himself. Many of these senators woke up in the 1970s to discover that their generation was being attacked for racial views that were accepted in an earlier time.

The rules are always changing in our politics, though never perhaps so rapidly as over the last two decades. Some lament that this changing of the rules will exclude worthy candidates. We are constantly warned that if Tendency X is allowed to run its course, no one of any self-respect will submit to the indignities of running for office.

But the changes in the rules that have occurred in recent years have worked mainly not to exclude candidates but rather to include vast new parts of the electorate. President Reagan is himself a prime instance of this. A generation ago, as a divorced and remarried man, he would have had a slim chance or none of being elected. Changing attitudes toward sexual morality—greater tolerance—made possible the presidency of a man who calls for a return to the good old days of strict sexual abstinence and just saying no. Some people, at least, count that change a blessing.

More clearly a blessing in my eyes is the fact that we have in our time what no American preceding us could boast of: the prospect of serious candidacies by blacks and females. It was not until the 1960s that a Catholic could be elected president. Now we are at the point where a Jewish candidacy will soon be viable. My own nominee for the person to fill that slot is Barney Frank, the gay congressman from Massachusetts who lost 70 pounds so he would not stick in the door while coming out of the closet. Any process that will include Barney Frank in the roll of serious candidates is clearly widening the pool of talents available, not narrowing it.

Paradoxically, the same processes that have led to the election of a divorced man have led to the scrutiny of adulteries committed by Gary Hart. The same opening up of taboo subjects, the same willingness to reassess the relevance of sexual behavior to public respectability made people bring up questions earlier suppressed. The ban on divorced men, or on Catholics, or Jews, or blacks, was never explicit in our politics. Neither Congress nor the Constitution, nor any party rules or guidelines expressly forbade the nomination of minority candidates. It was an unspoken prohibition, a gentlemen's agreement cloaked in civil reticences. The whole structure of suppression rested on an imperviousness to scrutiny or public challenge. It was simply unthinkable that a woman, for instance, could be president.

Well, now it is thinkable. But for that to happen, vast changes in our social assumptions had to take place—the entire feminist movement, for instance. That, in turn, could not have occurred without the preceding civil rights movement, during which arguments, debates, and demonstrations broke the rules of contained discourse that had countenanced Jim Crow laws.

Within the past few decades there were struggles over the most disturbing, wrenching things that went to society's inmost ties, to the makeup of the family, to relations between husband and wife, parent and child. They called into question interlocked patterns of authority, the instilled respect for parents and teachers and officers of the law. They were resisted, advocated, articulated, household by household, and the struggle is far from over. Generations overlap. The losing side has enclaves where it is still in the majority. Many try to deny that changes have taken place at all or that they are permanent. President Reagan speaks for that denial when he claims that the social values of the past have not been eroded or discredited.

But the sexual revolution, for instance, has occurred, despite those who believe that sexual roles will resume their old configuration if we just stop talking about them. Don't mention condoms in schools, these people insist, don't discuss AIDS in front of the children, keep it out of the media, don't bring it up. There is an aching desire to return to some of the social taboos, the unspoken arrangements that once kept people in their place. This is reflected in the fad for Allan Bloom's book *The Closing of the American Mind*, arguing as it does that exposure to more than one culture system destroys the very idea of morality.

Our society in general is questioning past attitudes toward race, gender, and authority, and sex is one of the most touchy but inevitable arenas where this self-questioning goes forward. One clear sign of that was the advice of some people to Gary Hart. They thought he should have immediately said, "Of course, I slept with Donna Rice. So what?" That reflects the attitude of many in our society, and it shows that what some see as prying into one man's privacy is seen by others as a vindication of what they believe is acceptable. After all, we live in a time when many respected figures live openly together in what used to be called sin. Barney Frank and others openly say that they are gay, that there is nothing wrong with that, that they have nothing to be ashamed of. That is not a position that would be as acceptable in many places as it is in Frank's Boston area. But it puts homosexuals in a difficult position—should they be ashamed of being ashamed? If it is all right for a gay person to be a political candidate, shouldn't one fight to establish that right rather than hide from the struggle? Yet who has the right to compel another to enlist in such a way? The questions circle back and back on each other. And in an open society all such shifting evaluations are expressed through the media, our forum for encountering each other as members of the same large and disagreeing community. The rules are changing for everyone, whether one wants to admit that or not. Parents admit it when they accept the new sexual behavior of their children, if only by averting their eyes from it. Society's consensus is distributed, with large areas of change and equally large enclaves of resistance. That is how profound social alteration, going deep into moral attitudes, is always effected.

So candidates are rightly confused. They are caught in a social situation where conflicting signals are being sent, clashing attitudes expressed; where there is widespread disagreement on fundamental premises. The presidential race itself is one of the ways this country decides what kind of society it wants to be, what symbols it will honor, what authority figures it finds persuasive. It always mattered that the nominee for president was male, white, Protestant, presumably happily married (but only once), and presumably heterosexual. In fact, it was always decisive to be most or all of those things. If you were not, you were simply out of the running from the outset. There were race and gender assumptions so securely in place that they never had to be brought up. There was little discussion of a candidate's private life because the range of a candidate's options in his private life was so narrow.

Those who did not bring up religion in an election wanted the reigning religious exclusions to continue. So religion ruled the situation far more rigidly when it was not discussed than it does now, when the fact that Bruce Babbitt is a Catholic is somewhat relevant, but not the decisive factor, as it was with Al Smith, nor a disproportionately relevant factor, as with John Kennedy. The issue had to get more relevant, to be brought up and openly addressed, before it could become less relevant. Only in that way could society make up its mind publicly on the matter and signal a new set of presidential rules: more inclusive for Catholics (though not yet for Jews).

Bringing such matters up, even before the children, is the way we discover jointly that we have changed our communal attitude. We discover the change while making the change, in public interchanges with our fellow citizens. We could not know the shift had occurred until it was thrashed out in public forums of social acceptance—forums like the presidential race, our leading symbol of social choice and cohesion.

Does smoking pot in the sixties have any relevance to a political career in the eighties? That, too, is a question we could not know the answer to until it was brought up. For Bruce Babbitt and Senator Gore, the answer seems to be no. But this is a question on which society itself has been somewhat hypocritical. For one thing, there has been a lag in time, or a lack of fit, between behavior and the law—the sort of thing we experienced under Prohibition. Law enforcement figures still preach against marijuana; this First Lady takes her campaign against it into the schools; Justice Department prosecuters have to declare whether they themselves have broken this particular law, detailing times and circumstances. It was an institutional hypocrisy that caught Ginsburg in the anomalous position of being higher in the Justice Department than some who had been disqualified because of what he did or that put him on the way toward being a high court justice who might have to pronounce on a crime (if that is what it is) that he himself had committed. And if it is not a crime, then why have it on the books? As I say, the "youthful indiscretion" argument seems to work for a Gore or a Babbitt, who did not have the institutional procedure of the Justice Department and the specific legal mandate that Judge Ginsburg sought. The Ginsburg case posed in its most pointed way this question: How does one go from challenging authority figures—as Ginsburg did, not only by smoking marijuana and growing a beard and long hair but by demonstrating against a war being conducted by the political authorities of the United States—to becoming an authority figure oneself? Even with all these factors weighing against him, Ginsburg would not necessarily have been denied office if other matters—possible conflict of interest and misrepresentations of his experience—had not also come into play.

The question of who deserves authority is complicated and must be decided case by case, person by person, but smoking marijuana is relevant precisely because the sixties were a generation that challenged authority so effectively and had such readily identifiable symbols for doing that. We are still caught in the turmoil caused by such questioning, and the sixties generation will have to sort out its attitudes in the world it helped change, with all the doubts that follow on successful challenges to authority. How do you reestablish authority? On what grounds of agreed values? These are the large questions that underlie such apparently trivial points as whether one broke a law that is still on the books, whether one supports that law now or would favor abolishing it.

There is probably no better way to thrash out all this than in a political race. From the time of George Washington, the choice of president has been a symbolic endorsement of certain values. He, more than any other president, was chosen for character, apart from the issues. Admittedly he was chosen by an electoral college that still had real independence. Nonetheless, that college voted for a man who would be a convincing, persuasive, unifying leader of the people at large—which he proved to be. He was chosen for his war record and, even more, for his resignation of military authority, for his peacetime self-restraint during the troubled period of transition from the Articles of Confederation to the present Constitution. Washington was an embodiment of what America was striving to be as a nation when we did not yet have a cluster of symbols and institutions that made the national identity and authority.

If we have trouble finding a similar figure now, it is because we do not have as firm a consensus of our values or as easy a way of signaling our identity. It was not held against Washington that he was a slaveholder. That was no disqualification for the presidency down through Andrew Jackson's time; after him, it became a liability, if not a disqualification. Slaveholding had by then been brought up and made relevant. Today, of course, we exclude slaveholders from running for office. We have even eliminated the electoral college except as a counting device—going more directly to more voters than ever in the search for a rallying figure in this large, heterogeneous nation. This is a risky process, and some want to reverse it. In a recent symposium sponsored by *Harper's* magazine, Raymond Strother said: "We force a man or woman to run for president of the United States as though he were a city-council candidate in Dubuque. . . . The race for it [the presidency] should be nobler and larger."

The only way to maintain the charisma and distance of the office is to avoid the demeaning process of seeking votes in Iowa, exposing oneself to endless questions that reflect the confusions of the society at large. Charisma is protected (if not created) by not talking about certain things in front of the children. Robert Beckel agreed with his fellow symposiast: "These primaries don't enhance a candidate. They mold the public's opinion of a candidate and almost always mold it negatively. . . . This system has got to be overhauled, and we have to get this word 'democracy' out of the way. We have to get back to selecting delegates in a rational way that gets us our best nominee with the least amount of fighting."

Though he seems to be calling, on the face of his words, for a return to smoke-filled rooms crowded with "brokers," Beckel is actually expressing a deeper yearning for the original electoral college—for people who know what the voters *should* want, rather than what they *think* they want, and can do the choosing for them. The only trouble with this is that a modern electoral college would have to consider the same things the original one did: how to find a candidate who is convincing, persuasive, authentic in the role of speaking for America. And no candidate can be that anymore unless he or she goes directly to the people, with an open and inclusive campaign, rather than rely on an elite of the sort that ruled America in the 1780s. The "character issue" is simply the modern way of stating the abiding problem of the American presidency: How is one person to express the character of the American people, a character that is never entirely made up, yet one that emerges (so far as that is possible) precisely through transactions like the campaigns for the presidency?

We are always changing the rules in this process, simply by talking to each other every day. It is called self-government. And we talk to each other through the presses and the cameras, by what we read and see, or refuse to read or see, about Americans at some distance from us coping with the same questions we have. In an electronic age we must plug in to the process in order to become aware of all our fellow citizens. The community exists only so long as its parts are in electronic touch with each other. This leads us, if not toward consensus, then at least to a sense of the boundaries of our disagreement, the rules and limits within which we can keep on disagreeing, keep bringing up questions that matter to any of us, and still be conscious of ourselves as part of a larger community, one that, despite all the changes of recent years—or, rather, *because* of the changes that have brought in more women, more blacks, more gays, more of the deprived and handicapped—is a society achieving "a more perfect union."

QUESTIONS FOR DISCUSSION

9.1 Can one separate private morality from public morality? Are there character faults that could affect someone's conduct as a public official? One voter was quoted during the 1992 campaign as saying, "If a man can cheat on his wife, he can cheat on the country." Is that fair?

9.2 In the 1950s Adlai Stevenson's divorce was considered a political liability. Yet in the 1980s Ronald Reagan's divorce was barely mentioned and had no discernable impact on his campaigns. Will the same be a case for homosexuality in the future?

9.3 Is it fair to judge candidates based upon choices they made in their youth concerning such things as drug use and the draft?

Chapter
10

Does the First Amendment Protect a Reporter from Violating the Confidentiality of Sources?

INTRODUCTION

Journalists have long claimed that they must guarantee their sources' confidentiality in order to do effective investigative reporting. Without this assurance, important sources of information, vital to the public, could disappear. Such individuals may fear some form of retaliation—loss of a job, physical danger, legal prosecution—should their names be made public. Reporters insist that their relationship to their sources is privileged and confidential, similar to those of a doctor and patient, lawyer and client, and priest and penitent. Thus, they insist that they should not be forced to divulge the identity of a confidential source in any legal proceeding.

Common law usage has not granted journalists the same privileges and standing as professionals in medicine, law, and the clergy. Since freedom of press is enjoyed by all citizens, anyone, theoretically, can be a journalist. Unlike lawyers and doctors, for example, journalists require no minimum educational standards, no license to practice, and no formal certification.

Yet freedom of the press does involve the right to know. And the public's right to know is dependent on vigorous reporters digging out scandals and getting people to speak frankly and without fear of disclosure.

The first Supreme Court case that considered this issue was *Branzburg* v. *Hayes* (1972), in which the Court decided that the First Amendment did not protect a reporter's right not to divulge his sources to a grand jury. But the Court was closely divided (5–4), with Justice Byron White writing for the majority. Justice White argued that defining who among the press is qualified for such a privilege would "embark the judiciary on a long and difficult journey to . . . an uncertain destination." White felt that such distinctions would be impossible to make since "liberty of the press is the right of the lonely pamphleteer who uses carbon paper or a mimeograph just as much as of the large metropolitan publisher."

Justice Potter Stewart's dissenting opinion claimed that the First Amendment guaranteed the full flow of information, and that such rights "require special safeguards." He felt that courts should be required to demonstrate "a compelling and overriding interest in the information" before they could require a reporter to disclose his sources.

In the face of *Branzburg* several states passed shield laws, which protected journalists from divulging certain information to state grand juries and trial courts. Congress has considered a federal shield law but, due to a lack of a consensus about who and what should be protected, has failed to pass one. In 1992 the leaders of the Senate Rules Committee refused to subpoena testimony from two reporters who had been given confidential material concerning Anita Hill's charges of sexual harassment against Clarence Thomas. A special Senate counsel sought to compel the reporters to reveal the sources of their information. In refusing the request, Committee Chairman Senator Wendell Ford (D-Ky.) said "[the subpoena] could have a chilling effect on the media and could close a door where more doors need opening."

Majority Opinion

Branzburg v. *Hayes* (1972)

Justice Byron White

Petitioners Branzburg and Pappas and respondent Caldwell press First Amendment claims that may be simply put: that to gather news it is often necessary to agree either not to identify the source of information published or to publish only part of the facts revealed, or both; that if the reporter is nevertheless forced to reveal these confidences to a grand jury, the source so identified and other confidential sources of other reporters will be measurably deterred from furnishing publishable information, all to the detriment of the free flow of information protected by the First Amendment. Although the newsmen in these cases do not claim an absolute privilege against official interrogation in all circumstances, they assert that the reporter should not be forced either to appear or to testify before a grand jury or at trial until and unless sufficient grounds are shown for believing that the reporter possesses information relevant to a crime the grand jury is investigating, that the information the reporter has is unavailable from other sources, and that the need for the information is sufficiently compelling to override the claimed invasion of First Amendment interests occasioned by the disclosure. Principally relied upon are prior cases emphasizing the importance of the First Amendment guarantees to individual development and to our system of representative government, decisions requiring that official action with adverse impact on First Amendment rights be justified by a public interest that is "compelling" or "paramount," and those precedents establishing the principle that justifiable governmental goals may not be achieved by unduly broad means having an unnecessary impact on protected rights of speech, press, or association. The heart of the claim is that the burden on news gathering resulting from compelling reporters to disclose confidential information outweighs any public interest in obtaining the information.

. . .

A number of states have provided newsmen a statutory privilege of varying breadth, but the majority have not done so, and none has been provided by federal statute. Until now the only testimonial privilege for unofficial witnesses that is rooted in the Federal Constitution is the Fifth Amendment privilege against compelled self-incrimination. We are asked to create another by interpreting the First Amendment to grant newsmen a testimonial privilege that other citizens do not enjoy. This we decline to do. Fair and effective law enforcement aimed at providing security for the person and property of the individual is a fundamental function of government, and the grand jury plays an important, constitutionally mandated role in this process. On the records now before us, we perceive no basis for holding that the public interest in law enforcement and in ensuring effective grand jury proceedings is insufficient to override the consequential, but uncertain, burden on news gathering that is said to result from insisting that reporters, like other citizens, respond to relevant questions put to them in the course of a valid grand jury investigation or criminal trial.

This conclusion itself involves no restraint on what newspapers may publish or on the type or quality of information reporters may seek to acquire, nor does it threaten the vast bulk of confidential relationships between reporters and their sources. Grand juries address themselves to the issues of whether crimes have been committed and who committed them. Only where news sources themselves are implicated in crime or possess information relevant to the grand jury's task need they or the reporter be concerned about grand jury subpoenas. Nothing before us indicates that a large number or percentage of *all* confidential news sources falls into either category and would in any way be deterred by our holding that the Constitution does not, as it never has, exempt the newsman from performing the citizen's normal duty of appearing and furnishing information relevant to the grand jury's task.

. . .

The argument that the flow of news will be diminished by compelling reporters to aid the grand jury in a criminal investigation is not irrational, nor are the records before us silent on the matter. But we remain unclear how often and to what extent informers are actually deterred from furnishing information when newsmen are forced to testify before a grand jury. The available data indicate that some newsmen rely a great deal on confidential sources and that some informants are particularly sensitive to the threat of exposure and may be silenced if it is held by this Court that, ordinarily, newsmen must testify pursuant to subpoenas, but the evidence fails to demonstrate that there would be a significant constriction of the flow of news to the public if this Court reaffirms the prior common-law and constitutional rule regarding the testimonial obligations of newsmen. Estimates of the inhibiting effect of such subpoenas on the willingness of informants to make disclosures to newsmen are widely divergent and to a great extent speculative. It would be difficult to canvass the views of the informants themselves; surveys of reporters on this topic are chiefly opinions of predicted informant behavior and must be viewed in the light of the professional self-interest of the interviewees. Reliance by the press on confidential informants does not mean that all such sources will in fact dry up because of the later possible appearance of the newsman before a grand jury. The reporter may never be called and if he objects to testifying, the prosecution may not insist. Also, the relationship of many informants to the press is a symbiotic one which is unlikely to be greatly inhibited by the threat of subpoena: Quite often, such informants are members of a minority political or cultural group that relies heavily on the media to propagate its views, publicize its aims, and magnify its exposure to the public. Moreover, grand juries characteristically conduct secret proceedings, and law enforcement officers are themselves experienced in dealing with informers, and have their own methods for protecting them without interference with the effective administration of justice. There is little before us indicating that informants whose interest in avoiding exposure is that it may threaten job security, personal safety, or peace of mind, would in fact be in a worse position, or would think they would be, if they risked placing their trust in public officials as well as reporters. We doubt if the informer who prefers anonymity but is sincerely interested in furnishing evidence of crime will always or very often be deterred by the prospect of dealing with those public authorities characteristically charged with the duty to protect the public interest as well as his.

Accepting the fact, however, that an undetermined number of informants not themselves implicated in crime will nevertheless, for whatever reason, refuse to talk to newsmen if they fear identification by a reporter in an official investigation, we cannot accept the argument that the public interest in possible future news about crime from undisclosed, unverified sources must take precedence over the public interest in pursuing and prosecuting those crimes reported to the press by informants and in thus deterring the commission of such crimes in the future.

. . .

We are unwilling to embark the judiciary on a long and difficult journey to such an uncertain destination. The administration of a constitutional newsman's privilege would present practical and conceptual difficulties of a high order. Sooner or later, it would be necessary to define those categories of newsmen who qualified for the privilege, a questionable procedure in light of the traditional doctrine that liberty of the press is the right of the lonely pamphleteer who uses carbon paper or a mimeograph just as much as of the large metropolitan publisher who utilizes the latest photocomposition methods. . . . The informative function asserted by representatives of the organized press in the present cases is also performed by lecturers, political pollsters, novelists, academic researchers, and dramatists. Almost any author may quite accurately assert that he is contributing to the flow of information to the public, that he relies on confidential sources of information, and that these sources will be silenced if he is forced to make disclosures before a grand jury.

In each instance where a reporter is subpoenaed to testify, the courts would also be embroiled in preliminary factual and legal determinations with respect to whether the proper predicate had been laid for the reporter's appearance: Is there probable cause to believe a crime has been committed? Is it likely that the reporter has useful information gained in confidence? Could the grand jury obtain the information elsewhere? Is the official interest sufficient to outweigh the claimed privilege?

Thus, in the end, by considering whether enforcement of a particular law served a "compelling" governmental interest, the courts would be inextricably involved in distinguishing between the value of enforcing different criminal laws. By requiring testimony from a reporter in investigations involving some crimes but not in others, they would be making a value judgment that a legislature had declined to make, since in each case the criminal law involved would represent a considered legislative judgment, not constitutionally suspect, of what conduct is liable to criminal prosecution. The task of judges, like other officials outside the legislative branch, is not to make the law but to uphold it in accordance with their oaths.

. . .

In addition, there is much force in the pragmatic view that the press has at its disposal powerful mechanisms of communication and is far from helpless to protect itself from harassment or substantial harm. Furthermore, if what the newsmen urged in these cases is true—that law enforcement cannot hope to gain and may suffer from subpoenaing newsmen before grand juries—prosecutors will be loath to risk so much for so little. . . .

Finally, as we have earlier indicated, news gathering is not without its First Amendment protections, and grand jury investigations if instituted or conducted other than in good faith, would pose wholly different issues for resolution under the First Amendment. Official harassment of the press undertaken not for purposes of law enforcement but to disrupt a reporter's relationship with his news sources would have no justification. . . . [The Court reversed the decision in the *Caldwell* case and affirmed the decisions involving Branzburg and Pappas.]

Dissenting Opinion

Justice Potter Stewart

Mr. Justice Stewart, with whom Mr. Justice Brennan and Mr. Justice Marshall join, dissenting.

The Court's crabbed view of the First Amendment reflects a disturbing insensitivity to the critical role of an independent press in our society. The question whether a reporter has a constitutional right to a confidential relationship with his source is of first impression here, but the principles that should guide our decision are as basic as any to be found in the Constitution. While Mr. Justice Powell's enigmatic concurring opinion gives some hope of a more flexible view in the future, the Court in these cases holds that a newsman has no First Amendment right to protect his sources when called before a grand jury. The Court thus invites state and federal authorities to undermine the historic independence of the press by attempting to annex the journalistic profession as an investigative arm of government. Not only will this decision impair performance of the press' constitutionally protected functions, but it will, I am convinced, in the long run harm rather than help the administration of justice.

I respectfully dissent.

I

The reporter's constitutional right to a confidential relationship with his source stems from the broad societal interest in a full and free flow of information to the public. It is this basic concern that underlies the Constitution's protection of a free press.

. . .

The right to gather news implies, in turn, a right to a confidential relationship between a reporter and his source. This proposition follows as a matter of simple logic once three factual predicates are recognized: (1) newsmen require informants to gather news; (2) confidentiality—the promise or understanding that names or certain aspects of communications will be kept off the record—is essential to the creation and maintenance of a news-gathering relationship with informants; and (3) an unbridled subpoena power—the absence of a constitutional right protecting, in *any* way, a confidential relationship from compulsory process—will either deter sources from divulging information or deter reporters from gathering and publishing information.

It is obvious that informants are necessary to the news-gathering process as we know it today. If it is to perform its constitutional mission, the press must do far more than merely print public statements or publish prepared handouts. Familiarity with the people and circumstances involved in the myriad background activities that result in the final product called "news" is vital to complete and responsible journalism, unless the press is to be a captive mouthpiece of "newsmakers."

It is equally obvious that the promise of confidentiality may be a necessary prerequisite to a productive relationship between a newsman and his informants. An officeholder may fear his superior; a member of the bureaucracy, his associates; a dissident, the scorn of majority opinion. All may have information valuable to the public discourse, yet each may be willing to relate that information only in confidence to a reporter whom he trusts, either because of excessive caution or because of a reasonable fear of reprisals or censure for unorthodox views. . . .

. . .

Finally, and most important, when governmental officials possess an unchecked power to compel newsmen to disclose information received in confidence, sources will clearly be deterred from giving information, and reporters will clearly be deterred from publishing it, because uncertainty about exercise of the power will lead to "self-censorship." . . .

After today's decision, the potential informant can never be sure that his identity or off-the-record communications will not subsequently be revealed through the compelled testimony of a newsman. A public-spirited person inside government, who is not implicated in any crime, will now be fearful of revealing corruption or other governmental wrongdoing, because he will now know he can subsequently be identified by use of compulsory process. The potential source must, therefore, choose between risking exposure by giving information or avoiding the risk by remaining silent.

The reporter must speculate about whether contact with a controversial source or publication of controversial material will lead to a subpoena. In the event of a subpoena, under today's decision, the newsman will know that he must choose between being punished for contempt if he refuses to testify, or violating his profession's ethics and impairing his resourcefulness as a reporter if he discloses confidential information.

. . .

The impairment of the flow of news cannot, of course, be proved with scientific precision, as the Court seems to demand. Obviously, not every news-gathering relationship requires confidentiality. And it is difficult to pinpoint precisely how many relationships do require a promise or understanding of nondisclosure. But we have never before demanded that First Amendment rights rest on elaborate empirical studies demonstrating beyond any conceivable doubt that deterrent effects exist; we have never before required proof of the exact number of people potentially affected by governmental action, who would actually be dissuaded from engaging in First Amendment activity.

. . .

II

Posed against the First Amendment's protection of the newsman's confidential relationships in these cases is society's interest in the use of the grand jury to administer justice fairly and effectively. . . .

Yet the longstanding rule making every person's evidence available to the grand jury is not absolute. The rule has been limited by the Fifth Amendment, the Fourth Amendment, and the evidentiary privileges of the common law. [Attorney-client, doctor-patient, and husband-wife privileges not to testify are common.] . . . [A]ny exemption from the duty to testify before the grand jury "presupposes a very real interest to be protected."

Such an interest must surely be the First Amendment protection of a confidential relationship that I have discussed above in Part I. As noted there, this protection does not exist for the purely private interests of the newsman or his informant, nor even, at bottom, for the First Amendment interests of either partner in the news-gathering relationship. Rather, it functions to insure nothing less than democratic decisionmaking through the free flow of information to the public, . . .

In striking the proper balance between the public interest in the efficient administration of justice and the First Amendment guarantee of the fullest flow of information, we must begin with the basic proposition that because of their "delicate and vulnerable" nature, . . . and their transcendent importance for the just functioning of our society, First Amendment rights require special safeguards.

This Court has erected such safeguards when government, by legislative investigation or other investigative means, has attempted to pierce the shield of privacy inherent in freedom of association.

I believe the safeguards developed in our decisions involving governmental investigations must apply to the grand jury inquiries in these cases. Surely the function of the grand jury to aid in the enforcement of the law is no more important than the function of the legislature, and its committees, to make the law. . . .

Accordingly, when a reporter is asked to appear before a grand jury and reveal confidences, I would hold that the government must (1) show that there is probable cause to believe that the newsman has information that is clearly relevant to a specific probable violation of law; (2) demonstrate that the information sought cannot be obtained by alternative means less destructive of First Amendment rights; and (3) demonstrate a compelling and overriding interest in the information.

This is not to say that a grand jury could not issue a subpoena until such a showing were made, and it is not to say that a newsman would be in any way privileged to ignore any subpoena that was issued. Obviously, before the government's burden to make such a showing were triggered, the reporter would have to move to quash the subpoena, asserting the basis on which he considered the particular relationship a confidential one.

The error in the Court's absolute rejection of First Amendment interests in these cases seems to me to be most profound. For in the name of advancing the administration of justice, the Court's decision, I think, will only impair the achievement of that goal. People entrusted with law enforcement responsibility, no less than private citizens, need general information relating to controversial social problems. Obviously, press reports have great value to government, even when the newsman cannot be compelled to testify before a grand jury. The sad paradox of the Court's position is that when a grand jury may exercise an unbridled subpoena power, and sources involved in sensitive matters become fearful of disclosing information, the newsman will not only cease to be a useful grand jury witness; he will cease to investigate and punish information about issues of public import. I cannot subscribe to such an anomalous result, for, in my view, the interests protected by the First

Amendment are not antagonistic to the administration of justice. Rather, they can, in the long run, only be complementary, and for that reason must be given great "breathing space."

QUESTIONS FOR DISCUSSION

10.1 What if a journalist's source is the only source concerning a committed crime? Should a shield law apply in such a case?

10.2 Is it possible to distinguish between professional journalists and all other people who may publish their views? Is Justice White correct in that making such a distinction would lead the courts "to an uncertain destination"?

10.3 Should the public's right to know be considered more important than the guarantees for a fair trial? How would you balance the two fundamental rights?

Chapter
11

When Do Campaign Contributions Buy Undue Influence?

The Case of Senator Alan Cranston and Charles Keating

INTRODUCTION

On November 20, 1991, the Senate Select Committee on Ethics presented a report to the full Senate "strongly and severely" reprimanding Senator Alan Cranston (D-Calif.) in connection with conduct relating to Charles H. Keating and his company, the Lincoln Savings and Loan, a failed California S&L. Specifically, the Senate charged that Senator Cranston intervened on behalf of Lincoln with the Federal Home Loan Bank Board (FHLBB) while soliciting and accepting substantial political contributions from Mr. Keating. Due to Senator Cranston's failing health and his decision not to seek reelection in 1992, the committee chose not to ask the Senate to take a formal vote censuring him.

Cranston was accused of an impermissible pattern of conduct that linked fund-raising and official activities. But the Senate rules governing favors for constituents and contributors were vague. Cranston could not be accused of violating any law or any specific Senate rule. The Committee rather reprimanded him for "improper conduct that reflects upon the Senate."

In the following excerpt from the Senate debate, Senator Howell Heflin (D-Ala.), chairman of the select committee, justifies the reprimand, despite the absence of clear rules. Senator Heflin argued that, "A senator may be disciplined for improper conduct which violates unwritten but well-established norms of Senate behavior, even though the senator's actions violated no specific law or Senate rule." The linkage between Keating's contributions and Cranston's intervention with the FHLBB seemed too close for the Senate Committee to ignore.

Cranston, in his own defense, insisted that his motives were "well-intentioned and honest" and that it was not unethical to intervene with the bureaucracy on behalf of a constituent simply because he was a contributor. But had Mr. Keating been an ordinary constituent who had given little or nothing to the campaign, would Senator Cranston gone to such lengths on his behalf? When is the linkage between contributions and political service improper? Senator Heflin cited the late Justice Potter Stewart, who claimed that he could not define obscenity but that, "I know it when I see it."

Michael Waldman tries to sort out what is and what is not improper behavior. He understands that there is a fine line between treating a constituent as an ordinary citizen in need of legitimate assistance and treating a big donor as a high-priced lawyer/lobbyist would deal with a client.

Quid Pro Whoa

Michael Waldman

It was late 1988, and the worm-probe industry was up in arms. Worm probes, which resemble straightened-out wire coat hangers, are thrust into the ground by earthworm breeders; a jolt of electricity sends the creatures wriggling to the surface for harvest. Unfortunately, according to the Consumer Product Safety Commission, worm probes led to the electrocution of at least 28 people; the agency was trying to remove the product from the shelves. But that might put the manufacturer of Worm Gett'rs, located in Caldwell, Idaho, out of business. So Republican Senators Steve Symms and James Mc-Clure of Idaho quietly blocked reauthorization of the CPSC, which had lacked a full legal mandate for nearly a decade. Consumer groups struggled to break the worm-probe filibuster, but to no avail. The legislation died, the agency remained crippled, and Worm Gett'rs stayed on the market.

As the saga of these hayseed Charles Keatings indicates, dubious constituent service is a problem not confined to the S&L and HUD scandals.

Nonetheless, the senators now in the dock for their activities in these de-bacles have innocently protested that they are merely giving the voters what they want. Al D'Amato, for example, explains his involvement in the HUD morass by declaring, "I'm not going to stop fighting for the people of this state." Senator John McCain of Arizona compares his efforts on behalf of Lincoln S&L to his routine assistance for an elderly constituent who needs help in prying loose a Social Security check from the bureaucracy.

Senator Don Riegle of Michigan is blunter still. His intervention for Keating, Riegle asserts, was no different from his routine help for other powerful corporations. In a bitter eight-page letter to the *Detroit Free Press*, Riegle compared the Lincoln case to "a particularly celebrated local case with some very interesting similarities." In sarcastic detail, he recounted Michigan lawmakers' efforts to secure antitrust clearance for a joint operating agreement between the *Free Press* and the rival *Detroit News*. (Riegle added that he met with regulators from the Federal Home Loan Bank Board not to help "constituent" Keating, but merely to "provid[e] Banking Committee perspective and insight.")

Of the thousands of favors done each year by members of Congress, the vast majority are legitimate. Like metal filings to a magnet, congressional offices inevitably attract pleas for help. We want our representative to pummel the bureaucracy on our behalf for a veterans check, disability benefit, small business loan. But some requests clearly cross the line, elevating the interests of constituents—or worse, contributors—over the public weal. With more than 100,000 people working directly or indirectly for business lobbies in Washington, D.C., pressures can grow intense.

What's a senator of average intelligence, ethics, and backbone to do? "The system is wrong, it's bad, it's corrupting," says William Proxmire, former chairman of the Senate Banking Committee. "But there's nothing developed to help. I feel sympathetic for [John] Glenn and those fellows—there is so little in the way of guidance."

Most attention has rightly focused on campaign finance laws. But Congress also desperately needs some new, explicit rules to help distinguish appropriate intervention from sleazy shilling. Here are a few:

Don't handcuff the cops. Members of Congress should not interfere with ongoing individual criminal investigations or prosecutions. Sounds obvious, but recall that at least two of Keating's supporters continued their advocacy after being informed by regulators in 1987 that a criminal referral would be made to the Justice Department. As late as two years later Arizona's Dennis DeConcini and California's Alan Cranston urgently phoned regulators in an effort to block the seizure of the S&L. . . . And D'Amato phoned Rudolph Giuliani to ask the U.S. Attorney to review sentences for two mobsters, according to the *Village Voice* and *New York Daily News*.

Is that a regulator in your pocket, or are you just glad to see me? "What the Keating Five did different was the scale," argues Harvard political sci-

entist Morris Fiorina. "Other than that, they did what other members of
Congress do all the time, and have been doing for 200 years."

Well, yes and no. Every day lawmakers carry water for big contributors,
through tax loopholes, trade provisions, and liability limitations. But when
Keating's allies summoned regulators to the two now notorious meetings on
Capitol Hill in April 1987, the goal was to get an independent agency to back
off from an ongoing enforcement proceeding. That's not only wrong; more
unusual for Washington, it's rare. At the first meeting, Edwin Gray has testified under oath, DeConcini offered him a deal on behalf of Keating. A week
later they met again, this time with regulators from San Francisco who were
conducting the Lincoln examination. Many of the senators' assertions were
couched as questions, but the message was unmistakable. Gray and other
former regulators who served in the Carter and Reagan administrations say
they can't remember anything like it.

"Once a regulatory body is established as an independent body, it is as
wrong to lean on them as it is a judge," argues Proxmire. "Even if there are
no campaign contributions whatsoever, if a legislator has influence because
he's a chairman of a committee or because he's an influential member of a
committee, he shouldn't be putting pressure on an independent or semi-
independent agency on behalf of a constituent." Former Arizona Governor
Bruce Babbitt, who turned down a Keating request to lobby for Lincoln,
agrees. "Where an administrative proceeding is in the nature of a law enforcement proceeding, as most of these bank procedures are, then I believe
it is improper to intervene," he said. Even most politicians doing favors for
their donors understand this unwritten rule.

This standard too involves nuances. On-the-record comments by members of Congress in an agency rule-making—as opposed to enforcement—
proceeding can enhance policy-making. And any standard should encourage
legitimate congressional oversight—such as when a senator, in the course of
a public hearing, urges vigorous enforcement of the law. But the opportunity
for inappropriate congressional special pleading increases the more an agency
action focuses on a specific company or person.

"Nice little agency you have there. Pity if something should happen to
it." "You can't control the problem by saying, 'Congressman, you can't call an
agency about a grant for your district,' " notes Babbitt. "The question is at
what point does it become extortionate." Wherever that point is, there you
will find Al D'Amato. New York's junior senator stands out not because his
was the only congressional name on the HUD phone logs, but because of the
relentlessness of his quids and quos. In case after case, D'Amato demanded
HUD funds for projects built by developers who had contributed to his campaigns, or who had retained as counsel the senator's brother, Armand. HUD
officials, mostly handpicked patronage employees, readily complied; if not,
D'Amato hounded the agency until it did. (One top regional official had a
speed-dial button on his phone that enabled him to contact his mentor

quickly.) In essence, D'Amato operated the New York region of HUD as a classic protection racket: First, monopolize the supply (through control of the agency); then extract your monopolist's fee.

The granny exemption. Broadest latitude should be given to routine help for average citizens. Former FTC chair Michael Pertschuck suggests a sort of means test: "The rule really should be the less money you have, the more help you get." There is less argument for discretion when it comes to an entitlement such as Medicare than when deciding whether to seize a bank or ban a pesticide.

Indeed, if ever there was a case of the people getting what they wanted, this would seem to be it. Given a choice between James Madison and Jacoby & Meyers, most voters would probably choose the caseworker. The problem is not any ethical taint associated with such help, but rather too much of a good thing. Senator William Cohen, who in 1982 co-authored *Getting the Most Out of Washington: Using Congress to Move the Federal Bureaucracy,* estimated that "as much as forty percent of staff time is spent in casework." Congress could rescue itself from the drudgery of endless paper shuffling if it heeded former Representative Henry Reuss, who proposed that an ombudsman's office be set up to discern trends of abuse by executive agencies, which would in theory eliminate the worst problems.

When bringing home the pork, keep it kosher. Standards are inevitably murkier when it comes to everyday contract hustling and grantsmanship. Still, some rules, if followed, could purify the process. Consider a congressman who is asked by a developer to help win a HUD grant for a hometown project. At a bare minimum, the lawmaker should conduct an independent investigation, even a cursory one, to see if the constituent's claims are valid or self-serving. "You can usually find out with just one phone call what's going on," said one Democratic administrative assistant. "And that will often be to the agency itself, so it accomplishes the mission of letting them know you're watching." And most intervention should be limited to inquiring about the status of a proceeding, rather than thumping for a result.

More important would be a requirement that lawmakers do all their advocacy for private citizens in public. Members of Congress, like other citizens, are not supposed to make secret contacts with regulators during a formal proceeding. Executive branch officials in many agencies are required to log any contacts they have with the public; Congress should be subject to the same standard. Quietly sleazy help for financial contributors, not workaday assistance for veterans, would potentially embarrass members of Congress under a full disclosure system.

When in doubt, do the right thing. Finally, solons should refrain from pushing for the district's interests if they differ from those of the country. Today, too many lawmakers see their job as being similar to that of a lawyer—represent the client, no matter what the cost. Civics-text earnestness of this sort might be no match for hard political reality, but DeConcini's defense of his actions in the Keating case illustrates why it is needed. "Did we do anything wrong by interceding? That's what I do for you, ladies and gentlemen," he told an Arizona audience recently. "That's my job." He pointed proudly to another recent intervention: When the Department of Defense wanted to buy 60 Apache helicopters, manufactured in Arizona, DeConcini and other legislators met with Secretary Dick Cheney and forced the agency to buy more. Maybe this was good for some residents of Arizona (though that state's citizens pay taxes, too), but it's a lousy way to construct coherent budget policy—and the main reason that dovish Democrats are as great an obstacle to arms reductions as the administration.

Some guidance may come from the ongoing Ethics Committee investigations of fully 6 percent of the Senate this spring. In themselves, these probes are extraordinary, coming from a committee so drenched in old-boy bonhomie that it didn't act against ABSCAMmer Harrison Williams until after his felony conviction.

But Senate ethics rules governing favors for constituents and contributors are maddeningly vague. The rules' closest brush with specificity is an admonition that senators not receive compensation or benefit from any source "by virtue of influence improperly exerted from his position as a Member." House rules are more precise, although the Ethics Committee read them very broadly in ruling on Jim Wright.

Quirky specificity may snare some senators; for example, the rules most explicitly restrict actions that personally benefit the lawmaker or his family. Thus, D'Amato's actions benefiting his brother might receive special scrutiny, or McCain's family's investments with Keating (even though he appears less culpable than others involved). These fortuities aside, committee members may lack the political resolve to find that contributor service violates the norms of the Senate. One consequence of the Ethics Committee probe could be a legislative desire for more explicit standards.

Ultimately, even these rule changes will fail if not preceded by campaign finance reform. Without a comprehensive campaign overhaul, lawmakers will continue to be hard-pressed even to distinguish between contributors and constituents. After all, right now a majority of House members received more than half of their campaign funds from political action committees, which are almost by definition the tools of Washington lobbyists. Some members—such as Al Swift, chairman of the very subcommittee that has jurisdiction over campaign reform—garner as much as 75 percent of their funds from these PACs. So routine is the intermingling of favor-dispensing and fund-raising that Senator Rudy Boschwitz provided contributors with special stamps to affix to letters sent to his office.

In contrast, examples of congressional self-restraint are rare—and are more rarely rewarded. Babbitt was chided by the *Arizona Republic* for being "fastidious" when his views were publicized there. Representative Mike Synar, a fifth-term Democrat from Oklahoma who declines all PAC money, also refuses to seek grants for his district, in particular refusing to sign on to letters signed by his colleagues in the state delegation. In light of his colleagues' conduct, Synar's reticence has raised eyebrows at home. "There are a lot of members in my Oklahoma delegation who wonder why I don't do this. There's been lots of conversations," he said. "It has hurt me. But I'll tell you what—it's given me an independence that I enjoy. We help a lot of people here, but only to make sure they're treated fairly. That's a lot different from going in there and trying to guarantee a result."

Only scandals produce seismic changes in congressional rules, if not mores. We may be at that point now. Let's hope so. Otherwise, the dominant ethos will continue to be that of the senator's aide who referred to a favored firm as her boss's "client." Client? "Client, constituent," she told startled consumer lobbyists. "It's the same thing in this context, right?"

Does the Senate Have Unwritten Ethical Standards?

Senator Howell Heflin versus Senator Alan Cranston

If, in all of his actions, Senator Cranston violated no law and violated no specific Senate rule, why is he, nevertheless, being reprimanded by the Ethics Committee? As amended, Senate Resolution 338 of the 88th Congress authorizes the Ethics Committee to receive complaints and investigate allegations of violations of law, violations of the Senate Code of Official Conduct, violations of rules and regulations of the Senate, and "improper conduct that reflects upon the Senate," and to make appropriate findings of fact and conclusions with respect thereto.

As written codes of conduct have been adopted by the Senate, there has been a recognition that the new rules did not, in the words of Senator John Stennis, "replace that great body of unwritten but generally accepted standards that will, of course, continue in effect."

The path to judgment is easy when a specific law or rule has been violated. But, for those who believe in the rule of law, violations of unwritten ethical standards are far more difficult to resolve. Although a finding of "improper conduct that reflects upon the Senate" is subjective in nature, it must ultimately rest upon a violation of an existing and well-understood norm of behavior. Before making such a finding, Senate practices and customs and their interrelationships must be carefully evaluated.

In reprimanding Senator Cranston, unwritten but commonly understood standards of Senate behavior were relied upon by the committee—in the same way that those standards have historically been relied upon by the full Senate in disciplinary cases occurring before as well as after the adoption of written codes of conduct in the Senate. Thus, Senate precedent is clear. A senator may be disciplined for improper conduct which violates unwritten but well-established norms of Senate behavior, even though the senator's actions violate no specific law or Senate rule. This has always been and must continue to be the case, if we are to protect the public's trust in the integrity of the Senate.

This brings me to a second aspect of the committee's resolution which I want to discuss. When is the well-established Senate norm applicable to the facts of this case, and how did the committee determine that Senator Cranston violated that norm?

In determining that a well-understood but unwritten standard of Senate behavior applies to a specific case, the committee looks to and is guided by relevant statutes, rules, rulings, and resolutions, the common and individual experiences of senators, and the history of Senate disciplinary cases.

In this case, having evaluated these sources in light of our own experience as senators, members of the committee unanimously concluded that commonly understood and well-established norms of behavior in the Senate do not permit linkage between official actions and fund-raising. The committee also determined that Senator Cranston's conduct substantially linked his official actions and his fund-raising, in violation of this established Senate norm. How did the committee arrive at the conclusion that such linkage existed?

The fact that two events occur at or near the same point in time may be an important fact in deciding whether the events are impermissibly connected. In and of itself, however, this coincidence of timing does not mean that the events are linked. On the other hand, to find linkage, it is not necessary that one of the events directly or indirectly caused the other. And certainly fund-raising and official actions may be impermissibly linked although the member did not intend them to be.

Also, such linkage is improper, even though the official actions involved may not, in and of themselves, be detrimental to the public interest. For example, in the case of Lincoln Savings and Loan, the committee found that the evidence clearly showed that the contacts by the five senators with federal regulators regarding Lincoln did not cause the eventual failure of Lincoln or the thrift industry in general, and that the evidence did not establish that their contacts affected the regulators' treatment of Lincoln. Nevertheless, the linkage between Senator Cranston's official actions and his fund-raising was improper.

Senator Paul Douglas, whose writings on government ethics may not have been familiar to senators prior to the public hearings in this case, offered advice in this area. Although his writings are not binding upon senators, they provide some guidance. Of the connection between contributions and official actions on behalf of contributors, he said:

> [T]he possibility of . . . a contribution should never be suggested by the legislator or his staff at the time the favor is done. Furthermore, a decent interval of time should be allowed to lapse so that neither party will feel that there is a close connection between the two acts. Finally, not the slightest pressure should be put upon the recipients of the favors in regard to the campaign.

I am reminded of the well-known words of Supreme Court Justice Potter Stewart when he wrote about the meaning of obscenity. The Justice noted that although he was not able to define obscenity with specificity, he knew it when he saw it. In my view, Justice Stewart's statement is a frank recognition that not all standards offer the opportunity to arrive at easy judgments through the mechanical application of a fixed formula. Recognition that a standard may not be easy to apply, however, does not mean that it does not exist or that it is not sound, nor does it imply that the standard cannot be reasonably applied.

As in all cases of this nature, the committee's decision in Senator Cranston's case was based upon the totality of the circumstances, and it was from this totality that the committee determined that Senator Cranston engaged in an impermissible pattern of conduct in which fund-raising and official activities were substantially linked. The pattern which the committee found so disturbing was unequivocally manifest through a series of activities and occurrences involving Senator Cranston over a period of at least two years. Some of the actions which created the linkage were taken by Senator Cranston personally, some by his staff, who often acted with his knowledge or permission and often under his direction or supervision.

Some of the occurrences which led the committee to conclude that substantial linkage existed between Senator Cranston's fund-raising and his official activities were included in the committee's resolution, and I will not repeat them all. On their face, some acts or occurrences were obviously more troubling than others. One notable example is the incident in November 1987, where delivery of $250,000 in contributions from Charles Keating for voter registration groups took place at the same meeting in the Capitol where the senator agreed to contact a regulator on Keating's behalf. The committee has not found that the events were causally connected, but the incident does indicate linkage.

But the committee's decision was not based upon any single action or event standing alone. Woven together over time, however, Senator Cranston's actions and the actions of others who acted with his knowledge or permission, or at his direction, created an unmistakable pattern in which the senator's official actions were intertwined with his fund-raising activities. None of the acts violated any law or specific Senate rule. However, in combination these actions violated accepted Senate standards which do not permit official actions to be linked with fund-raising.

Also, most of the money raised by Senator Cranston in this case was contributed to 501(C)(3) organizations, which are listed as charitable organizations. Although this case has made painfully obvious the urgent need for comprehensive campaign finance reform, we must remember that the Senate prohibition against linking fund-raising and official duties applies to charitable as well as campaign contributions.

While this committee has said that a senator must be mindful of the appearance that may be created by his or her conduct and take special care to try to avoid harm to the public trust, the committee's strong and severe reprimand of Senator Cranston, like discipline administered by the Senate in prior cases, is based upon the senator's improper conduct. Senator Cranston's improper conduct also appeared to be improper, but it was his improper conduct, and not the appearance of impropriety, that caused the committee's reprimand.

Senator Howell Heflin

I ask that each and all who are interested, and particularly each of you, my colleagues, take a look at that documentation.

It deals with the four incidents that were referred to by Senator Rudman. I believe it casts a different light upon them. And there are other details that have been dealt with by Senator Heflin, Senator Rudman, and the resolution which I think are not exactly accurate, but I do not propose to go into that sort of detail in my remarks now.

Mr. President, up to the very last moment of the committee's long, long deliberations—and they were very long—I considered waging an all-out battle against its verdict. If the committee had called for any action by the full Senate against me, I would have fought it tooth and nail, with the help of the man who sits beside me, Professor Alan Dershowitz, one of our nation's leading defenders of human rights. Let me tell you why I would have done so.

First, I ask each of you, I ask everyone to note that the committee found and acknowledged the following: that nothing I did violated any law or specific Senate rule; that I acted without corrupt intent; that no evidence was presented to the committee, no evidence that I ever agreed to help Charles Keating in return for a contribution; that none of the contributions constituted a personal gift to me; and that I did not receive or intend to receive any personal benefit from any of the funds I raised.

The committee found and acknowledged that all my actions regarding Lincoln Savings and Loan were legal and proper, and violated no law or Senate rule; that the money I raised was legal, proper, and properly reported.

The committee found and acknowledged that I had substantial reasons relating to the jobs and financial security of thousands of my constituents for intervening with federal officials on behalf of Lincoln; that I had information which raised legitimate questions about the regulation of Lincoln.

Senator Rudman, I had that information before I attended those meetings. Lincoln was vouched for by two of the big eight accounting firms, Arthur Young and Arthur Anderson, and by Alan Greenspan, now chairman of the Federal Reserve Board, a man with tremendous impact upon the economy of our entire nation. Alan Greenspan told me that Lincoln was well managed and viable for the foreseeable future.

The committee found and acknowledged in its earlier February 27 resolution that my contacts and the contacts of the other so-called Keating Five senators with regulators regarding Lincoln did not cause the eventual failure of Lincoln and did not cause the eventual failure of the thrift industry in general.

The committee found and acknowledged in its February 27 resolution that my attendance and the attendance of other Keating Five senators at two meetings with the regulators violated no law or Senate rule. It was those two meetings, my colleagues, that started this prolonged and painful saga. Yet, the committee found and acknowledged that I attended one of those meetings for approximately 1 minute. The record shows that all I said at that meeting was that I shared the concerns of the other senators.

The record shows that all I did at the other meeting was to ask why an audit of Lincoln was taking so long. It was the longest audit ever. The end apparently was never in sight. And the only other thing I did at that meeting was agree with Senator Glenn that if Mr. Keating had broken any law he should be prosecuted, but if he had not broken any law, the regulators should get off his back.

Thus, it is clear, Mr. President, my colleagues, whoever else is observing this, it is clear that I have not been reprimanded for doing anything improper for Mr. Keating.

I have been reprimanded because there was, or appeared to be, a proximity in time between legitimate charitable donations that I accepted—for bona fide charities—and legitimate official actions that I took. There has been no charge, no charge, that there was any other connection between the donations and the actions, and it has been acknowledged today on the floor that I did not take any action, there is no evidence that I did, because of any contribution.

The record is replete with evidence that there was no other connection of any sort. The record shows, too, that my official actions were not only proper but were *de minimus* in nature. They were all routine status inquiries or requests that somebody see somebody or requests of various proposed sales of Lincoln be carefully considered. It is not unusual for me and for many of you to work with great diligence for constituents.

Let me give you an example of another time I did so. Back in the seventies, another large corporation, Lockheed, was facing bankruptcy. The livelihoods of many thousands of my constituents and their families were at risk, as was the case with Lincoln. I devoted far more time and effort and made many more phone calls about Lockheed than I ever did about Lincoln as I successfully fought to obtain a government-guaranteed loan for Lockheed. Lockheed was not a supporter of my campaign or causes. Lockheed had supported and raised money for my opponent in the previous election.

I sought the charitable donations in question because of my zeal in a cause that relates to the very foundation of our democracy: voter participation. The deplorable decline in the number of citizens who vote puts the essence and vitality of our democracy at risk. My long and deep dedication to this cause stems from what I witnessed and lived under in Hitler's Germany, Mussolini's Italy, and in Communist countries where citizen participation was forbidden.

Since my motives and my actions were well-intentioned and honest, I recognize now that I failed to anticipate that raising these funds could be looked upon as improper. And that is what we are now talking about—appearances.

I failed in that respect for a couple of reasons. First, most of the donations went for nationwide nonpartisan registration drives conducted by organizations which were approved by the IRS for tax deductibility and in which I had held no position and whose use of the money was not under any control.

Second, these donations were made after my 1986 reelection for registration drives conducted all across the country in 1987 and 1988. Obviously, they could not benefit my 1986 campaign.

In retrospect, nonetheless, I now realize that what I did looked improper. But I differ, and I differ very, very deeply, with the committee's statement in the resolution that my conduct "violated established norms of behavior in the Senate." If I had chosen to fight, I would have challenged that statement even more forcefully than I now will.

There are no such established norms of behavior in the Senate. There is no precedent and there is no rule establishing that it is unethical for a senator to engage in legitimate constituent service on behalf of a constituent, because it was close in time to a lawful contribution to the senator's campaign or to a charity that the senator supports.

In its consideration in this case, the committee acknowledges that it has referred to sources for ethical guidance which may be largely unknown. It also acknowledged that there were no "written guidelines of the Senate" in several relevant areas.

Justice Black once referred to a tyrant king who wrote his laws in a hand so fine and placed them so high and so far from view that his subjects could not read them. That is the essence of tyranny. The essence of due process is to have laws written in advance so all can know them.

I have stated repeatedly that my actions were not fundamentally different from the actions of many other senators. My statements fell on deaf ears, perhaps because I was undergoing treatment for cancer and unable to present my case strongly at a crucial stage of the committee's proceedings.

Whatever the reason, I was left with no alternative except to see if I could prove that I am far from being the only senator to do what I have done. I found abundant evidence that I could do so. The evidence is available in various studies, reports, and documents—all in the public domain. I was prepared on the advice of Professor Dershowitz to demonstrate to the Senate and to the nation, through example after example of comparable conduct, that my behavior did not violate established norms.

But instead of using examples, I will now simply summarize what I found. At least two-thirds of my colleagues in the Senate are involved with charities or foundations. Some are institutions set up by a senator or by his or her friends, admirers, and contributors which bear the senator's name or advance causes related to the senator's legislative efforts.

In many cases, the senator raises funds for the institutions or permits others to raise the funds in his or her name. The contributors include a great many individuals and corporations that have a direct interest in matters before the Senate and government agencies. More than a few of these contributors have benefited from actions taken by the senator involved, sometimes close in time to a contribution.

Many of the contributions are immense—$750,000, one contribution; $500,000; $250,000; $200,000—there are many $100,000 contributions. The totals run into many millions.

In many instances, there are overlapping campaign contributions, PAC contributions, and honoraria payments to senators from the individuals, special interests, corporations and their officers and directors who contribute to the senator's causes.

I tell you all this, my colleagues, for several reasons.

First, and most importantly to me, to demonstrate that I did not violate any established norm for Senate behavior.

Second, to warn every one of you who plays any part, direct or indirect, in fund-raising for a charity or a foundation or whatever, that you are in jeopardy if you ever do anything at any time to help a contributor to that charity—no matter how worthy the cause, no matter how proper the need for help, no matter how proper the help you render. I stand before you as an illustration of that jeopardy.

Third, to suggest that reform is needed to protect you and to protect the Senate. I doubt that anything less will do than a ban on charitable fund-raising by senators or in their names. If you engage in such fund-raising, sooner or later some of those who help you will want your help. If they have a legitimate need, you will be hard put to refuse their request simply because they responded to your request. And then you are headed for trouble. On the other hand, how can you not help them?

Let me turn to the matter of political contributions.

The committee stated on February 27:

> It is a fact of life that candidates for the Senate must solicit and receive assistance in their campaigns, including the raising of campaign funds.

Of course, we all know that. Raising these funds can often lead, as we also know, to charges of wrongdoing. It is now more likely than ever to lead to charges of wrongdoing because the Ethics Committee has enunciated formally a new principle: that it is improper for a senator to engage in a legitimate constituent service on behalf of a contributor close in time to a lawful contribution to a senator's campaign or PAC.

It seems to me, and it seems to my attorney, Alan Dershowitz, that the committee has applied this new principle to me in an *ex post facto* fashion. But this point really has less to do with me than it does with most of you. My fund-raising for my campaigns is over since I decided not to run again. And my political fund-raising was not a major issue with the Ethics Committee. I received less in such political contributions than the other Keating Five senators; in one case 80 percent less.

Congress, the House and our Senate, is the branch of government closest to the people. We represent the people. We must serve the proper interests of the people who support us and elect us. If we do not, our constituents won't get the help they need and deserve, and we won't be reelected.

I ask you this—about this question—How can you rationally refuse to give legal and proper help at any time to someone who seems to have a reasonable grievance because he or she has contributed to your campaign? Can you only help people who have not contributed? Or can you only help people who have not contributed lately? How lately? And must you refrain from helping people who might contribute in the future? How far in the future?

A majority of senators feel it necessary to raise money all the time. Campaigns now go on for six years. Constituents, whether contributors or non-contributors, seek help all the time. Inevitably, contributions and actions sometimes overlap, time-wise.

How many of you, after really thinking about it, could rise and declare you have never, ever helped—or agreed to help—a contributor close in time to the solicitation or receipts of a contribution?

I do not believe any of you could say never. I am sure you do not really know at any time exactly who has contributed and who has not, and how much, and when. But all a political opponent, a reporter or anyone else has to do to find out is to look at your contribution report with the Federal Election Commission and match it with what appears in the *Congressional Record* and committee records about your official acts—speeches, motions, amendments, votes—and then, to make you look bad, charge improper conduct.

I assure you that the examples they could use are plentiful. The present system makes it virtually impossible—virtually impossible—for a senator to avoid what some will assert is a conflict of interest. There is no Senate rule stating when you can and when you cannot help a contributor. I do not see how one can be formulated.

The Supreme Court, in the wise ruling in 1964 that I wish applied to Senate rules as well as to statutes, observed that, "A statute which either forbids or requires the doing of an act in terms so vague that men of common intelligence must necessarily guess at its meaning and differ as to its application violates the first essential of due process of law."

I believe the only remedy is to get money out of politics. Therein lies salvation for you, for the Senate and, most of all, for the American people who are the ultimate losers until we end the role money plays, or seems to play, in our decisionmaking, and end the business of senators and would-be senators having to spend more and more of their time chasing the money needed to fund a successful campaign.

That means public financing. Nothing less will suffice. Let us end the practice, a practice we engage in here unfortunately, of considering campaign reform on the basis of what will help or hurt Republicans, Democrats, incumbents, and challengers. That way, everybody loses. Let us enact a campaign reform measure that will benefit the Senate, our country, and all the people. If we do not, what happened to me and the other Keating Five senators can happen to any one of you.

I am particularly troubled by one other aspect of the resolution, and you should be, too. I differ with the suggestion that the way I handled so-called access differs from the established norm in the Senate. How many of you could stand up and declare you never, ever decided to see or take a call from someone whose name you recognized, be it a friend, a prominent leader in your state or the nation, a volunteer in your campaigns, or a contributor, while asking your staff to tend to someone you do not recognize. I doubt that any of you could honestly do so.

Furthermore, you know and I know that the Democratic Senatorial Campaign Committee, the Republican Senatorial Campaign Committee, and the White House stage events where lobbyists and other individuals who pay $10,000, $15,000, $20,000 or even $100,000 a year can mingle with the president, the vice president, cabinet members, and senators.

The more people contribute, the more exclusive and intimate the event they may attend. That is access. And events are not the only time and place these generous contributors get access. So let me ask, since I have been singled out for a reprimand on access today, who among you can be sure you will not be singled out for a reprimand on access tomorrow? Here, but for the grace of God, stand you. There is only one way out: Get money out of politics; enact public financing and enact it now.

There is another reform I urge upon you. Before any of you who have not yet endured this experience land before the Ethics Committee, it should be restructured. I recognize that the committee labored under particularly difficult circumstances in my case, but its role is difficult in all cases, and difficult most of all for the senators who are brought before it. Today, there is no real due process in the Senate for senators. We are not afforded constitutional rights that are available to all other citizens. So long as ethics charges are dealt with by senators, our fellow senators, we are about as far away as we could possibly be from a jury that comes from anonymity and returns to anonymity when its work is done.

Unlike a sequestered jury, the senators on the Ethics Committee read the press. They are public figures whose decisions will be weighed by their constituents. They have been buffeted in my case by vicious and inaccurate leaks that violated the rules, by press pressures, by perceived public pressures, and by mood swings in the public and within the Senate, especially in the wake of the Thomas-Hill affair and the matter of bounced checks over on the House side. And apparently the committee was deadlocked along partisan lines for months.

It has been suggested that the committee should be revamped so that its members would consist not of sitting senators but, instead, of former senators, former judges, and outstanding laymen. I endorse that concept until and unless something wiser is proposed.

Senator Alan Cranston

QUESTIONS FOR DISCUSSION

11.1 Was Senator Cranston correct in claiming that he was denied due process by being reprimanded for violating something as vague as "the established norms of the Senate?" Or does the Senate have the discretion to examine improper behavior even if there are no written laws or rules?

11.2 Is it possible to establish guidelines defining an improper linkage between campaign contributions and constituent service?

11.3 Would public financing of all congressional campaigns eliminate the problem presented by the Cranston case? Could there be other improper linkages, such as between constituent service and business associates, close friends, future employers?

Chapter
12

Should There Be Term Limits for Members of Congress as There Are for Presidents and Governors?

INTRODUCTION

In the early 1990s, when the economy drifted into recession and the federal deficit continued to grow, there was a public reaction against politics and politicians. Some of this discontent was manifest in a movement to limit the terms allowed to members of Congress (the Twenty-second Amendment already limits presidents to two terms of four years each, and many states have limits on the number of terms governors may serve). But there was also a partisan dimension to this discontent. The 1988 Republican platform endorsed a 12-year limit for Congressional terms. Republicans had not controlled the House of Representatives since 1955 and were especially concerned that incumbency was becoming close to a guarantee of reelection. In fact, more incumbents (most of whom were Democrats) were running and more were being reelected. The reelection rate in the House had been running at over 90 percent for twenty years, and, in 1990, over 96 percent of the House incumbents were reelected, with an average of 63.5 percent of the vote.

The issue of term limits goes beyond popular discontent or partisan politics and touches upon essential issues of political accountability and responsible government. In the following selection, Mark Petracca argues that

Congressional careerism creates a distance between representatives and constituents. "America's revolutionary thinkers," Petracca argues, "generally agreed that, in a republic, government should be kept as near to the people as possible, chiefly through frequent elections and rotations in office." Representative Lee Hamilton (D-Ind.) disputes such argumentation and claims that term limitations would enhance the power of entrenched bureaucrats whose expertise would overwhelm new members. As a consequence, Hamilton claims, "Representative democracy would be the loser, and bureaucracy the winner."

Nonetheless, term limitations will remain an issue on the political agenda as long as public dissatisfaction with government remains high.

The Poison of Professional Politics

Mark P. Petracca

Fearing disintegration of the Confederation, Alexander Hamilton called upon the delegates meeting at Annapolis, Maryland, in September, 1786, to reconvene the following May to "devise such further provisions as shall appear to them necessary to render the constitution of the federal government adequate to the exigencies of the Union." Out of despair and frustration arose the Constitutional Convention of 1787 and, with it, America's second birth as a democratic republic.

The American republic again is at risk. This time, the threat lies not in internal disorder or foreign predators, but in the contemporary exigencies of professionalism and careerism that dominate U.S. politics. These poison the prospects for political representation in America and threaten the promise of democratic government.

The professionalization of politics is incompatible with the essence of representation. Although it may be useful for a society to encourage the development of professional lawyers, nurses, social scientists, or physicians, the qualities and characteristics associated with being a "professional" politician run counter to the supposed goals of a representative democracy. In a great many arenas, especially in Congress, evidence of the professionalization of American politics is mounting. In response, a national movement to limit the terms of congressmen and state legislators is gaining momentum.

In the last decade of the twentieth century, mounting evidence of the professionalization of American politics is beginning to pique the attention of pundits and citizens alike. What is a professional politician? Conventionally, we use the phrase to refer to someone who makes his or her living from politics.

Professional politicians proliferate both in and out of government. The total size and policymaking discretion of the huge federal bureaucracy continue to expand despite the anti-bureaucratic rhetoric of the past two decades. Although some devolution and privatization occurred during the Reagan years, expenditures as a percentage of gross national product remain high and the deficit continues to set records every year. In addition, the size of the government continued to grow during the Reagan Administration. In 1981, there were about 2.8 million federal civilian employees; by 1990, the number had risen to approximately 3.1 million.

The expansion of legislative staffs has accompanied the growth of the executive bureaucracy, dominating much of the decisionmaking politicking constantly taking place in Washington. A fourfold increase in the number of staff members assigned to the House and Senate occurred between 1960 and 1980 alone.

Out of government, there have been two notable developments in the professionalization of politics in the last decade and a half. First, there has been a spectacular increase in the number and potential influence of organized interest groups and political action committees (PACs). That army of lobbyists has been joined by an explosion of lawyers, corporations, trade and professional associations, and public interest organizations. What do all those interest groups and lobbyists want? According to the Cato Institute's David Boaz, their first priority is money, closely followed by the many other valuable services available from the modern state.

Second, professional political consultants have all but taken over the running of American elections for national office and are well on their way to controlling the process of public policymaking as well. The number of consulting firms doubled during the 1980s. In elections at all levels of government, it has become the rule, rather than the exception, to hire a consulting firm to run a candidate's campaign. These organizations are assuming an increasing role in shaping the substance and direction of the electoral process.

Bureaucrats, staff lobbyists, PACs, and consultants are not alone in making a career out of politics. America's elected representatives do so as well, serving seemingly never-ending terms in the national and state legislatures. Incumbents are all but guaranteed reelection if they seek it, thus creating a permanent government made up of career politicians. In turn, the existence of a permanent government justifies the need for professionals with the skill and expertise to navigate the shoals of the new political hierarchy. Such permanence and symbiosis are clearly evident in Congress.

No longer citizen-legislators, congressmen have converted the privilege of representing American people into lifelong careers. During the second half of the twentieth century, elected officials have spent more time in public office than during any other period in U.S. history. Throughout the nineteenth century, congressmen served an average of one or two terms before voluntarily returning to their communities to resume careers or pursue other endeavors. During the last 40 years, the average length of service in the House has ranged from four to five terms. An average of 15 percent have held office for 20 or more years.

As more congressmen have spent more time in office than ever before, turnover has declined precipitously. Throughout the nineteenth century, the average was slightly higher than 50 percent at each election. Today, turnover due to death, retirement, or electoral defeat hovers around 10 percent.

During the last 40 years, the institution of Congress has been redesigned to facilitate and accommodate the career aspirations of its members at the expense of its representational and legislative responsibilities. Congressmen have achieved reelection by creating new federal programs that grant wide decision-making discretion to the Federal bureaucracy, potentially causing a variety of political and policy-specific problems. As a result, constituents with grievances or demands on the Washington establishment approach their congressmen for relief or assistance. Instead of acting as dutiful representatives dedicated to solving local and national problems, they achieve career security by serving constituents as ombudsmen vis-à-vis Washington's burgeoning bureaucratic establishment.

TRUSTEE OR DELEGATE?

The professionalization of politics is incompatible with the essence of representative government. At its most basic, the exercise of a profession entails a set of role relationships between experts and clients in which the professional is an expert who offers knowledge and judgment to clients. The culture of professionalism disconnects and distances the professional—whether journalist, doctor, attorney, social scientist, or politician—from those whom he or she intends to serve.

Conversely, representative government is characterized by the close connection that necessarily must exist between the representatives and represented. It aspires to minimize the distance or space between the two sets of citizens.

There are differing theories of representation. However, the classic distinction between the representative as a trustee and the representative as a delegate (or agent) remains a useful key to the conceptual boundaries of representation. Trustees depend on their own conscience, what they think is right, or their considered judgment of the facts relevant to a particular decision. The representative as delegate must express the will, and speak the opinions, of the constituents that depute him.

In practice, representation usually lies somewhere in between these models. As the business of government has grown in complexity and become less locally centered, it is probable that the representative has become less of a delegate and more of a trustee. On the other hand, a representative cannot easily ignore constituent interests or the popular will (when there is one).

Theory is one thing; representation in practice is something else. America's founders were sensitive to the complexity of the concept, but they also had a commonsense understanding of its essence—that representation requires the representative to strike a balance between representing the interests of the constituents and occasionally acting on their behalf. That approach was put simply by Abraham Lincoln during his reelection campaign to the General Assembly of Illinois: "I shall be governed by their will on all such subjects upon which I have the means of knowing what their will is, and upon all others I shall do what my own judgment teaches me will best advance their interests."

The delicate balance of the two views was captured by Walter Lippmann in *The Public Philosophy:* "[The representative] is in duty bound to keep close to the interests and sentiments of his constituents, and, within reasonable limits, to do what he can to support them." The professionalization of representatives makes it impossible to maintain that delicate balance. Whereas representative government aspires to maintain a proximity of sympathy and interests between representative and represented, professionalism creates authority, autonomy, and hierarchy, distancing the expert from the client. Professionalization encourages an independence of ambition, judgment, and behavior that is at odds with the inherently dependent nature of representative government. For representation to resolve that paradox, representatives cannot become experts and constituents cannot be treated as clients. Yet, those are precisely the new roles in which they are cast by the professionalization of politics in America. As a result, the term professional representation as applied to politics is an oxymoron. The oft-touted expertise of professional politicians as representatives is in contradiction with the essential function of political representation in a democratic republic—namely, to connect the people to the government through representatives who share their values and stay in touch with the reality of their day-to-day lives.

Suspicion of professional representatives is well-advised. They not only pose a threat to the quality of representation in government, but, through the power of incumbency, restrict the entry of amateurs—citizen-legislators—into the governing process. As historian Daniel Boorstin explains: "The representative of the people . . . must be wary of becoming a professional politician. The more complex and gigantic our government, the more essential that the layman's point of view have eloquent voices." Today, the layman's voice in the halls of Congress has been silenced by a chorus of career legislators and other professional politicians. Since "democracy is government by amateurs," Boorstin warns that "the survival of our society depends on the vitality of the amateur spirit in the United States today and tomorrow." However, there scarcely is any room left for amateurs in the modern American legislature. "We must find ways to help our representatives preserve their amateur spirit," he proposes. Appreciating America's experience with the republican principle of rotation in office and its contemporary counterpart, term limitation, may be one way to restore the amateur spirit to legislatures and to begin the process of recovering American politics from the professionals.

ROTATION IN OFFICE

America's revolutionary thinkers generally agreed that, in a republic, government should be kept as near to the people as possible, chiefly through frequent elections and rotation in office. The principle of rotation in office dates back to the practice of democracy in the ancient city-state of Athens. During the fifth and fourth centuries B.C., the Athenians selected their council of 500 annually by lot, with the further provision that no one could serve on it more than two years in his lifetime. The principle of rotation also reflects Aristotle's understanding of the proper relationship among equal citizens—there is a reciprocity of "ruling and being ruled in turn." Thus, democratic citizenship is produced by experience in two different political roles; that of the ruled and that of the ruler.

Three distinct advantages that are evident in Western intellectual heritage often appear in the thinking of America's revolutionaries and their constitutional designs. First, rotation provides an opportunity for a greater number of individuals to serve in government. Second, it acts as a check on tyranny and the unbridled usurpation of political power. Third, the American revolutionaries believed that rotation both facilitates and affirms the experiential connection that must necessarily exist between representatives and the represented. The bill of rights contained in the new constitution of Virginia (1776) expressed the expectation that the threat of oppression would be diminished and the qualities of representation enhanced if public officials were frequently "reduced to a private station."

Presumably, the connection between the representatives and the constituents is strengthened and the exuberance of government is tamed when representatives know that they must soon return to live in the community they have helped shape through their actions in government. That view was stated by Thomas Paine in *Common Sense* (1776), one of the most influential tracts of the revolution: "That the interest of every part of the colony may be attended to . . . the elected might never form to themselves an interest separate from the electors, prudence will point out the prosperity of having elections often, because as the elected might by that means return and mix again with the general body of the electors in a few months, their fidelity to the public will be secured by the prudent reflections of not making a rod for themselves. And as this frequent interchange will establish a common interest with every part of the community, they will mutually and naturally support each other, and on this . . . depends the strength of government and the happiness of the governed."

The Articles of Confederation (1781) called for the annual appointment of delegates, provided for their recall at any time, and set limits on the length of time a delegate could hold office. Section V of the Articles stated, "No state shall be represented in Congress by less than two, nor by more than seven members; and no person shall be capable of being a delegate for more than three years in any term of six years."

This revolutionary zeal for rotation in office started to diminish during the mid-1780s, in large measure as a result of the disintegration of the Confederation and the forced retirement of six popular and effective executives in states with mandatory rotation for executive officeholders. At a meeting of the Pennsylvania Council of Censors in 1784, the Republican Society criticized the principle of rotation, claiming that it deprived men of an incentive to serve and the state of able servants. In addition, it charged that rotation was anti-democratic since "the privilege of the people in election is so far infringed as they are thereby deprived of the right of choosing those persons whom they would prefer."

Despite such criticism from the state with the most stringent rotation requirements, the principle still was considered important enough to merit inclusion in the Virginia Plan presented to the Constitutional Convention in 1787 by Edmund Randolph. Section 4 stated that "members of the first branch of the National Legislature" would be "incapable of reelection" for a period of time to be determined by the convention "after the expiration of their term of service." However, after rather brief debate on different occasions throughout that summer, neither mandatory rotation nor ineligibility for office was included for either the House or the Senate in subsequent drafts of the Constitution.

While the Federalists shied away from the principle of rotation in office in the Constitution, its absence widely was denounced by the anti-Federalists. They focused most of their concern and scorn on the absence of rotation for senators and presidents, which would make the Senate "a fixed and unchangeable body of men" and the president "a king for life, like the king of Poland." In general, the anti-Federalists feared that the elimination of annual elections, rotation in office, and recall, together with the extensive powers given to Congress, would make the "federal rulers . . . masters, and not servants."

Despite constitutional silence on the matter, rotation in office, much of it voluntary, remained a popular principle of republican rule throughout the nineteenth century. Washington's voluntary retirement after two terms as president was followed a few years later by Jefferson's statement that rotation in office would prevent the formation of a permanent bureaucracy. Jefferson, too, served only two terms as president.

Responding to the commonly made arguments that rotation in office meant lost experience and talent, John Taylor asserted in 1814 that "more talent is lost by long continuance in office than by the system of rotation." Taylor held that rotation did not squander talent and that "ability was stimulated by the prospect of future employment and smothered by the monopoly of experiences."

JACKSONIAN DEMOCRACY

The most extensive and principled nineteenth-century defense of rotation in office took place during the presidency of Andrew Jackson. Dedicating a healthy portion of his 1829 inaugural address to a discussion of its merits, he gave a new democratic twist to many of the arguments that had been used to defend rotation by the revolutionaries and anti-Federalists. Instead of merely advocating this principle on the grounds that it opened up opportunities for citizen involvement in the process of governing, Jackson argued for the capability of all men to hold public office: "The duties of all public officers are, or at least admit of being made, so plain and simple that men of intelligence may readily qualify themselves for their performance."

Not only should citizens have the opportunity to govern, but the quality of governance would be better for it. Jackson observed that "there are, perhaps, few men who can for any great length of time enjoy office and power without being more or less under the influence of feelings unfavorable to the faithful discharge of their public duties." Although integrity might suffice to protect officeholders from corruption, the longer they remained in office, the more likely they would be to yield to temptation.

Rotation would reduce the chances of corruption born of familiarity with government and reinstate service on behalf of the public interest as the norm for elected officials. No one should "treat public office as a species of property," nor view government "as a means of promoting individual interests," proclaimed Jackson. Government is "an instrument created solely for the service of the people"; rotation in office would keep it that way.

Throughout most of the nineteenth century, voluntary rotation in office was the prevailing norm of behavior for national legislators. By century's end, many commentators echoed James Bryce's observation that "rotation in office was, and indeed by most men still is, held to be conformable to the genius of a democracy." Expressing a sentiment rekindled in recent years, A. Lawrence Lowell of Harvard University explained in 1913 that "The American citizen is far less attracted by the idea of experienced public servants who retain their positions so long as they are faithful and efficient than he is repelled by the dread of bureaucracy."

American disdain for permanent government has deep roots indeed. An assessment of Congressional tenure in 1903 by historian James Albert Woodburn reveals the profound differences in representational expectations then and now:

> A congressman is elected for two years. Occasionally a man of distinction is continued in service for several consecutive terms, and the most distinguished congressional leaders are those who have sat for long terms by successive re-elections. But the local influences in the States, the ambitions and schemes of the political wire-pullers and workers, and the practice of rotation in office that has been considerably cultivated have tended to limit the average length of service to four to six years.

Such an observation is unthinkable in the 1990s.

America's lengthy experience with rotation in office grew out of a belief in creating opportunities for citizen-legislators, a desire for checks on tyranny and abuse of government power, and prerequisites for authentic political representation. Jackson added a strong democratic flavor to the revolutionary and anti-Federalist advantages of rotation. A belief in its utility and efficacy in office also reflects a political culture hostile to the concentration of political power, permanence in government, professional politicians, and bureaucratic power. This experience largely has been ignored or forgotten during the recent debates about constitutional and political reform.

What antidotes are available to cure America of professional politics? Are we as a nation even in a position to administer the remedy or remedies if revealed to us, or is the patient beyond recovery? Political reform always has been a daunting task in the United States. However, it is especially difficult when the intended object of reform—such as professionalism or careerism—widely is accepted by average Americans in the ordinary practices of daily life.

Term limitation increasingly is proposed, and is gaining popularity, as a response to permanent government and legislative careerism. For advocates, term limitation is an idea whose time has come and the intervention that will put Congress on the road to recovery. For opponents, term limitation is "a solution in search of a problem" and "an illusory fix for a symptom rather than a cure." In one form or another, Presidents Truman, Eisenhower, Kennedy, and Bush supported term limits for Congress. Three states—Oklahoma, Colorado, and California—have passed initiatives limiting the terms of state officeholders. Similar movements are under way in at least a dozen others, and public opinion polls show overwhelming popular support for state and congressional term limits by the American public, even though the state of Washington voted down such a proposal in November 1991.

Is term limitation the antidote for professional politics in the United States, as many are suggesting? Of course, it isn't. The proposal merely is a first response to the problem. Periodically throwing the "rascals" out of office will do little to remedy the other pressing issues of professional politics. Term limitation alone is not enough, but it is a start, especially if accompanied by serious state and national debate about the causes and consequences of professionalized politics.

America needs to get serious about the burgeoning, immortal bureaucracy; explosive costs of political campaigns; irrelevance of political parties; skewed proliferation of organized interest groups; dependence of candidates and officeholders on political consultants; and supremacy of legislative staff in addition to grappling with the rise of legislative careerism. A comprehensive approach to the poison of professional politics would be ideal, but nothing in American history would lead any sensible observer to conclude that such a course is probable, or even possible.

Thus, as usual, we must settle for incremental improvement. Greater appreciation of the reasons for the American tradition of rotation in office can smooth the way for term limitation as the first step on the arduous road to the restoration of political institutions capable of nurturing representative democracy, democratic citizenship, and self-government.

The Case Against Term Limitations

Representative Lee H. Hamilton

The public frustration about government in general and the Congress in particular continues to grow. The savings-and-loan crisis is the principal focus of discontent, and Hoosiers are frustrated over the budget deadlock and issues like the congressional pay raise. They often charge that the Congress and, more broadly, the federal government lack common sense and simply are not accountable to the American people. In general, there is a sour mood toward Washington. I understand their dissatisfaction, and, to a degree that often surprises them, I share it. The Congress and the president simply are not meeting many of the problems facing our nation as effectively as they should. Neither branch of government is performing to our expectations.

One manifestation of the frustration with the performance of the Congress is the proposal for a constitutional amendment to limit the number of terms a member of Congress may serve. After six terms in the House or two terms in the Senate, for example, members would be unable to run for re-election. Supporters of this proposal argue that the high rate of reelection for members of Congress has made the Congress unresponsive to the people. Members certain of returning to Congress are less concerned about performance while in office and more likely to put off hard decisions such as reducing the budget deficit. Proponents further argue that the two-term limit on presidential service has worked reasonably well and similar limits should be applied to legislators.

My view is that dissatisfaction with a Congress that has not always performed satisfactorily does not justify removing all members of Congress, the good members as well as the bad, after a certain number of years.

First, arbitrary limits on how long a person may serve in the Congress would usurp the power of voters. We ought to have more faith in democracy. The limitation of terms proposal reflects a distrust of the voter. It denies the people a choice of representatives and unnecessarily limits democracy.

Second, limiting the terms a member may serve would deprive the country of the services of many outstanding public servants whose experience and wisdom have accumulated over long years of sensitive and sensible service. Almost all congressional leaders in the House and Senate would be affected by such a proposal. Today's America is an extremely complicated country. To assume that a member of Congress can learn all about government in a few years is simplistic. The premise behind the proposal to limit terms seems to be that anyone new is better and that experience is an obstacle to good performance. Few private sector companies would endorse the view that performance would improve by requiring all employees to leave after 12 years.

Third, members should be judged on their own record, not on the record of Congress as a whole. Congressional decisions are usually reached by majority votes in the House and Senate, with 535 members each making choices as he or she sees fit. Discriminating persons should always separate, and judge separately, the performance of an individual from the performance of the institution to which that individual belongs. We do not, for example, judge a doctor on the basis of what the American Medical Association does.

Fourth, limiting the terms of members would create a power vacuum, and bureaucrats would seek to fill it. New members would find themselves confronting bureaucrats made more powerful by the legislators' inexperience. The power of unelected and entrenched bureaucrats would far exceed that of members whose tenure was sharply limited. Their expertise, formed over many years, would overwhelm members. Representative democracy would be the loser, and bureaucracy the winner.

Fifth, the proposal would increase the power of special interests. Members of Congress who knew that after 12 years they had to seek other work may well seek that work with the very interests that lobby them. In such a situation, members would be tempted to favor special interest groups that could offer them employment after their legislative careers are over.

Sixth, the proposal would make members of Congress less responsive to the views of the public during their final term. Knowing that they would not have to face voters again, members would not be bound to respect the views of their constituents. This could result in a loss of the effectiveness of representative democracy. With a large number of members serving their last term, the Congress's obligation to reflect the wishes of its constituents could be undermined.

Seventh, limiting the terms of members is an example of politics by distraction. This measure emphasizes a simple solution without directly addressing the many substantive problems facing our country. The process of amending the Constitution to adopt this proposal could take years to complete, while the important problems facing Americans are not addressed.

Eighth, such a limit on time of service for the Congress would be a new political experiment. No states and no other industrialized countries have limits on how long legislators may serve.

Finally, the notion of a permanent Congress is exaggerated. Three-fourths of the current members have been in office for less than 12 years, and the average member today serves about 10 years.

Nonetheless, supporters of the proposal have a valid point: The Congress is not working well and should do better. Members of Congress need to get at the underlying cause of dissatisfaction with the Congress, by doing a better job of addressing the major issues of the day. The Congress also should focus on election reforms. Steps could include campaign finance reform and enforcement mechanisms against abuse of the franking privilege or other congressional perks. Making elections more competitive by implementing such reforms would assist voters in making decisions about who should represent them in the Congress.

QUESTIONS FOR DISCUSSION

12.1 Are term limits, by restricting the ability of the public to select candidates of its choice, inherently anti-democratic?

12.2 Is Petracca correct in claiming that the longer representatives stay in Washington, the more interest they have in expanding governmental programs?

12.3 Are there more effective and less drastic methods for making elections more competitive, such as restrictions on PAC contributions and public financing?

12.4 Would the president's influence vis-à-vis Congress increase with the enactment of 12-year term limits?

12.5 Is the task of representation so complex that it requires years of experience before a member can match the expertise of those in the federal bureaucracy?

Chapter
13

What Are the Responsibilities of Government in Meeting the Health Care Needs of Its Citizens?

INTRODUCTION

In 1992 the issue of health rose to the top of America's political agenda. Making his support of national health care a central issue, Senator Harris Wofford (D-Pa.) upset former Republican governor and Attorney General Dick Thornburgh in a special 1991 Pennsylvania Senate race. The rising costs of health care programs such as Medicare and Medicaid were major contributors to the burgeoning deficit and the spiraling of entitlement spending. Americans who lost their jobs in the recession of the early 1990s were also faced by the loss of their health benefits. Even those who had jobs feared that the costs of health insurance would force employers to reduce existing benefits.

Americans in 1990 were paying approximately 12 percent of the gross national product on health care, a staggering $650–$670 billion. At the current rate of increase health care costs could climb to $1.6 trillion by the year 2000. Liberals and conservatives alike agree that substantial reform is required, but they disagree sharply on the nature of that reform.

Former Representative Marty Russo (D-Ill.) proposes a Universal Health Care Act, whereby government would pay for all health care with revenues from payroll, income, and corporate taxes replacing insurance premiums and current public programs. The government would set fee schedules for doctors and budgets for hospitals. This concept would guarantee coverage for all and could eliminate the costs of administering and marketing many different plans. Critics contend that the costs under the plan could skyrocket because Congress would not muster the courage to contain expenditures. If costs were contained, the bureaucrats then would be faced with the task of rationing expensive care.

In March, 1992, President Bush introduced proposals for a tax credit or a voucher payment to all citizens to purchase health insurance on the open market. Supporters, such as Senator Alan Simpson (R-Wyo.) in the speech that follows, argued that it would help cover the presently uninsured and would cost considerably less than the proposals for universal health care. Opponents of the Bush proposal maintained that it would not reduce administrative costs and that the voucher payments to the poor would soon trail behind the costs of insurance. Proponents of the Bush plan are vague about how it would be financed. Some have suggested a reduction in the Medicare subsidies to the upper-income elderly and a cap of the federal contribution to Medicaid plans for welfare recipients. None of the plans are simple and none of the solutions are painless.

How to End the Health Care Crisis

Representative Marty Russo

The U.S. health care system is in a state of crisis. In 1990, we spent 12.2 percent of our Gross National Product on health care—$671 billion—up from 11.6 percent in 1989. This is three times greater than the average annual increase in the past 30 years. Without major reforms, we will expend 20 percent of our GNP—more than $2 trillion—on health care by the year 2000. This means $4500 a year for every man, woman, and child by the end of the decade.

The United States spends far more on health than any other industrialized country. In 1989, these expenditures were 40 percent more per person than Canada, the next highest-ranking nation, almost twice as much as in

France and Germany, and well over twice as much as Japan and Britain spend. What's more, this gap between the United States and the rest of the world continues to widen.

Despite such an outlay, the United States ranks thirteenth in life expectancy and an appalling twenty-fourth in preventing infant mortality. It also is the only major industrialized country without a national health care plan.

The proposed Universal Health Care Act would help to strengthen Americans' ability to select the doctor of their choice by establishing a national, single-payer health insurance program. Such a plan would cut the nation's health costs, while guaranteeing comprehensive, high-quality care.

The proposed legislation, H.R. 1300, incorporates many of the strengths of the health care system that has been so successful in Canada, yet remains distinctly American. It's about the things Americans hold dear and have come to expect—freedom of choice, quality care, and the efficient and fair use of their hard-earned dollars. Above all, it's about providing the peace of mind they deserve so that, if their children are sick, they can take them to the doctor without having to worry about paying a high deductible; or that, when they change jobs, they will not lose their health insurance; or that, if their mother or father needs long-term care, they won't have to mortgage their home or postpone their kids' college education.

The act would cover all Americans for a wide range of health benefits, including hospital and physician care, prescription drugs, and mental health services, as well as dental, long-term, and preventive care. The ability of working and middle-income families to afford good health no longer would be limited by co-payments and deductibles. Parents would not have to worry about taking their child to the doctor immediately or waiting until the fever gets high enough to justify the expense. Consumers still would be free to choose their own physician, hospital, or health care provider.

The plan would put a lid on skyrocketing costs for 95 percent of Americans. Instead of the rapidly escalating insurance premiums, co-payments, and deductibles that impact on workers and their employers, the bill is financed through payroll, personal, and corporate income taxes plus state and federal contributions. The net effect of this shift from insurance company premiums to public financing will mean more money in the pockets of almost all families.

The elderly would save $33 billion a year because they no longer would have insurance premiums or deductibles. Businesses already providing health insurance would save as well. In 1989, companies spent an average of 11.6 percent of payroll for health care. Under this plan, they would contribute just 7.5 percent of payroll, allowing them to increase salaries. Since businesses that don't provide health insurance complain that it is too expensive, it provides an affordable way for them to contribute.

The bill achieves these savings by making the U.S. health care system more efficient. In 1990, $160 billion was required just to administer America's fragmented health care system. This means 24 cents of every dollar spent for health care were wasted on administrative and billing expenses.

A single-payer system dramatically can reduce these outlays because all Americans would be covered under a single comprehensive program. This means money no longer would be wasted on weeding out unprofitable groups and individuals; advertising, marketing, and commissions; or billing 1500 insurance agencies and millions of consumers. Doctors, nurses, and hospitals no longer would have to keep track of the eligibility requirements or the complicated definitions of covered services in hundreds of insurance plans. Currently, 18 percent of hospital spending is for administration and billing, and nearly 45 percent of gross physician income goes toward billing.

Canada spends 11 cents of every dollar on administration under their single-payer system. If the United States could reduce administrative costs to that level, it would save $100 billion a year. There already is one insurer in this country that has kept such items under 3 percent—Medicare.

In addition to cutting administrative waste, the bill contains costs by reimbursing providers more efficiently and establishing expenditure targets. Hospitals and nursing homes no longer would have to absorb millions in uncompensated care because they would be paid monthly based on annual global budgets. Physicians and other health care professionals would be reimbursed according to fee schedules. Other health care facilities, as well as home- and community-based services and group practices, also could elect to be paid based on global budgets, fee schedules, or another approved prospective payment system.

The program would be administered at both the federal and state levels. Annually, the Secretary of Health and Human Services would establish national and state budgets specifying health spending for the year and how that amount would be divided among the provided services. These would act as expenditure targets, so that, if the budget for a service were exceeded, the secretary could lower payments for it the following year.

SPIRALING ESCALATION

Though the federal government and large businesses have tried to control costs over the past decade, health care inflation has continued to spiral. This happens because, when one payer tries to contain expenditures, providers simply shift these costs to others. A single-payer system effectively can control medical inflation by preventing them from doing so.

To improve quality of care, the legislation incorporates Medicare's practice guidelines and outcomes research provisions and expands them to cover the entire health system. This would provide for much needed research into the quality, effectiveness, and appropriateness of medical care.

Groundbreaking studies have produced evidence of resources squandered in practices ranging from unnecessary hysterectomies to superfluous lab tests. Examining a sample of heart-bypass operations, researchers at the Rand Corporation concluded that 14 percent were inappropriate and 30 percent were "questionable." The Joint Economic Committee estimates that unnecessary tests and procedures run approximately $125 billion a year. The practice guidelines would help eliminate this waste, thus improving the quality of care as well as saving billions of dollars.

As costly new medical technologies have come into use over the past 50 years, relatively little has been done to measure their true effectiveness. Most agree that the United States overinvested in and overused many technologies. Hospitals competing for market share have installed equipment that stands idle much of the time or, even worse, is being used without good medical justification to generate reimbursement from insured patients.

This has triggered what has been described as a medical "arms race." For example, in a small Pennsylvania town, a hospital and a group of radiologists both bought Magnetic Resonance Imaging machines even though there is another MRI just outside the town. As a result, this area has three sophisticated diagnostic machines, each costing approximately $1.5 million. With them, the physicians performed more MRI scans per resident than were done in the entire city of Philadelphia and many other hospitals in that state.

The proposed bill would get rid of this waste and improve the quality of care because capital expenditure would be paid from a separate budget. This would allow the state to distribute funds for capital improvements in a rational manner and eliminate incentives for wasteful and duplicative spending. Quality would increase because complicated surgery and high-tech equipment would be concentrated in fewer hospitals by providers who perform procedures more frequently.

The United States can't afford to accept anything less than single-payer coverage. Partial solutions such as insurance reform or mandated benefits won't work because they would allow insurance companies to continue administering health care. According to the General Accounting Office, the only way the United States ever will slow health care inflation is through comprehensive reform. As the Congressional Budget Office has testified before the Ways and Means Committee, single-payer is the only system that can provide high-quality health care to all Americans without increasing the amount spent on health. Let those who call for "moderate" reforms explain where ordinary people can find the money to continue subsidizing insurance company red-tape and waste.

Americans trust and respect their doctors and nurses, but they are fed up with the wasteful way insurance companies manage the health system. Opinion polls indicate that 89 percent believe it needs fundamental change. A majority say they would prefer the Canadian system of health insurance where the government pays most of the cost of care for everyone out of taxes and sets all fees charged by physicians and hospitals, rather than the current U.S. system.

For the amount of money the United States now spends, Americans should be living two years longer than Canadians, not the other way around. The Universal Health Care Act does not attempt to answer every detail. Instead, it offers the framework for how health reform should be structured to guarantee that the United States has the *best* health care system in the world, not just the most expensive.

13-1   **The President's Health Care Plan**

On February 6, President Bush unveiled his plan to make health care more affordable for most Americans. His proposals are estimated to have a price tag of more than $100 billion over a five-year span. The plan has little chance of getting through the Democrat-controlled Congress, but should spur further debate toward solving this pressing national dilemma. The following are the highlights of the Bush proposals:

- A voucher worth up to $3,750 would be issued to poor families that could be used only to buy medical insurance.
- A tax deduction of up to $3,750 would be authorized for families with incomes up to $70,000, with a lower deduction for those earning between $70,000 and $80,000. There would be no deduction for families with incomes exceeding $80,000.
- The self-employed would be allowed to deduct medical insurance premiums fully.
- Insurance companies would be required to provide coverage to anyone willing to pay for it, regardless of pre-existing medical conditions.
- Small businesses would receive inducements to band together to purchase medical insurance for their employees, thus lowering their costs by spreading the risk.
- Medical malpractice and anti-trust laws would be changed to hold down medical costs.
- Use of health maintenance organizations by private plans, Medicare, and Medicaid would be encouraged.

The Case for Health Care Vouchers

Alan Simpson

United States Senator, Wyoming, Republican

Mr. President, for the past several years now we have been listening to and studying various proposals for health care reform.

We have heard shrill and emotional appeals for a nationalized Canadian style health care system—a system which would subject all of United States health care to the budget-driven political system.

We have heard calls for pay-or-play mandates, which, whatever its aesthetic merits and however expedient, is still at root definition a tax on labor, a tax on jobs—a danger we can all perceive with crystalline clarity right now.

We have heard unflinching ideological insistence on privatization of all health care in this country—a proposal too much at odds with our heritage and self-conception as a nation of compassion, with our communitarian ethic.

We have heard from virtually every major health care advocacy and trade association, the insurance industry and employers, organized labor, consumers, and a potpourri of foundations and economic institutes. My staff has a drawer full of bright glossy folders supplied by the stakeholders in this system.

All of these proposals have at heart an earnest desire to fix what is wrong with U.S. health care—to bring the disenfranchised into full and equal participation, to stem the costs, to improve quality. I know that. But each seeks first and above all to protect the interests, the stake of its sponsor. And that has been the problem thus far.

Mr. President, the public is growing very frustrated at our apparent inability to do what they elected us here to do: to find and execute a common ground that is in the best interests of the nation as a whole; to legislate solutions to pressing national concerns. In this instance, to make some meaningful progress on health care reform.

Today will mark a turning point in that process.

Mr. President, President Bush, and his very able Secretary Louis Sullivan, have consulted with all of the major stakeholders in our massive, $740 billion health care system. With help from the Steeleman Commission and the Horner Task Force and countless others, they have consulted with the providers and the insurers, the ideological purists and the advocates, the academics, the intellectuals, the economists, the taxpayers, and the beneficiaries. And in doing so they posed the question as it should have been posed from the beginning: "The depth and breadth of American health care is unparalleled; for 85 percent of the American people it offers ready access to the best medical care in the world. But it is too expensive, and for some it is inaccessible. How can we address what is wrong with this marvelous system without disrupting what is right?"

I commend the president, Dr. Sullivan, and the hundreds of contributors to this behind-the-scenes dialog, and congratulate them on the proposal released today.

The president's team found, as they spoke with the stakeholders in this world class health care system of ours, that its shortcomings and deficiencies could be readily addressed without dismantling or distorting the whole, without compromising its strengths.

The president's health care reform proposal offers real relief against the high cost of health care, even as it takes steps to ratchet down those costs. It is a comprehensive plan to assure all Americans full and equal access to the best medical care in the world.

As some of my colleagues have already described, President Bush's plan will provide access to all poor families through a fully portable health insurance voucher that will cover the cost of a health insurance policy.

The plan will expand access to workers in small businesses who currently don't have and cannot find affordable health insurance coverage, and do that through significant changes in the small-group insurance market.

The plan will give new help to the middle class by effectively reducing their out-of-pocket cost for health care coverage.

The plan will address the shortcomings in our health care infrastructure by vastly expanding the supply of health professionals and clinics in rural and inner city areas.

And the plan will clamp down on the health care cost spiral at all levels—patient, provider, and payor—that would otherwise undermine any reform effort.

With this proposal, the president has sounded the clear bell which should bring everyone in the room directly to the table. The president's plan contains elements common to virtually all of health care reform proposals that have as yet been seriously offered: help for employees and employers in small businesses; medical liability reform; cost containment through appropriately managed care; relief for medically underserved areas; critically needed assistance for the middle class with the cost of health insurance, and mainstream access for the poor and near poor.

Mr. President, these are the areas which not only the president but the American people have identified being the chief culprits in the health care crisis. In letters, phone calls, town meetings and committee hearings, the

American people have described the flaws in our current health care system with great clarity and precision. The president has responded with a precisely measured proposal for change.

QUESTIONS FOR DISCUSSION

13.1 Does the federal government have the moral obligation to provide decent medical care for all American citizens? Can this be done without adding substantially to the growing federal deficit?

13.2 Would a free-market approach, as proposed by President Bush, weed out the most wasteful and inefficient medical plans and make consumers more cost-conscious in spending their health care dollars?

13.3 The choice between the Bush plan and the Russo plan is a question of regulation versus competition. Is there a point of compromise between the two that would broaden health care coverage without adding to the costs and the power of the bureaucracy?

Chapter
14

Should Political Ideology Influence the President and the Senate in Selecting Supreme Court Nominees?

INTRODUCTION

Recent nominations to the Supreme Court have become occasions for intense ideological debates over such issues as abortion, affirmative action, and the right to privacy. Supreme Court nominees, once asked perfunctory questions about their background and approach to the law, have been grilled by the Senate Judiciary Committee about an entire range of legal and social issues. The unsuccessful nomination of Judge Robert H. Bork to the Court in 1987 by President Reagan set the stage for one of the most rancorous debates in recent history.

Judge Bork, who had served as a Yale law professor, solicitor general of the United States, and as an appellate court judge, had written numerous briefs, law review articles, magazine pieces, and legal opinions. His views on virtually every aspect of constitutional law were well documented. He had created a 25-year paper trail. During his confirmation hearings Bork was forthcoming about his particular legal and constitutional philosophy. He questioned the Supreme Court's decisions declaring the right to privacy (*Griswold* v. *Connecticut*), the principle of one man, one vote (*Reynolds* v. *Sims*), and the right of a woman to obtain an abortion (*Roe* v. *Wade*).

Consequently, numerous liberal interest groups—Leadership Committee on Civil Rights, the American Civil Liberties Union, National Organization for Women—organized to defeat his nomination. They were, indeed, successful, for on October 23, 1987 the Senate turned down his nomination by a vote of 58–42. The nominees that followed—Anthony Kennedy, David Souter, and Clarence Thomas—were far more circumspect and ventured few opinions about past Supreme Court decisions.

In the following essay Max Lerner, a noted scholar of American civilization, decries the focus on a Supreme Court nominee's judicial philosophy. By answering such questions, Lerner feels that a Court nominee compromises his "own right of privacy and independence, and his future freedom of choice." The Senate, Lerner contends, should look at a nominee's life, character, and judicial temperament. Francis Flaherty, who opposed Bork's nomination, feels that the Senate has every right to examine the nominee's philosophy and to exert its own independent judgement about it. Flaherty asserts, "the bestowal of a Supreme Court justiceship is a signal event, deserving of as much democratic input as possible."

But will these contentious and ideological debates over Supreme Court nominees only assure that future justices will be bland lawyers who come to the Court having said or written little that is controversial or even interesting?

Courting Rituals

Max Lerner

Even in the context of the Supreme Court tussles that have provided political entertainment since at least the 1930s, the 1987 saga of Robert Bork, Douglas Ginsburg, and Anthony Kennedy broke new ground. What made the play rougher this time was the heightened consciousness of the power stakes, a more aggressive deployment of the interest groups, and a greater sophistication in media use. If the overworked term "watershed" still conveys some meaning, it applies here to the future direction of confirmation politics. It is now evident that the crisis in the confirmation of judges will turn on the question of how much they will reveal under questioning about their future positions and thus how much of their judicial independence they will surrender.

In considering nominees for the swing seat of Justice Lewis Powell, Attorney General Ed Meese—guided by Assistant Attorney General William

Bradford Reynolds—made the prime blunder of imagining that a symbolic strict constructionist and "original intent" champion such as Robert Bork could survive the confirmation process. (The seat taken by Antonin Scalia had not been a swing seat; it was previously occupied by Chief Justice Warren Burger.) It was a rash decision by a man who thought he could nail down an "original intent" Court majority until the century's end and beyond. Meese was especially blind to the intensity of feeling in the liberal law school culture about making a growing number of "rights" (including privacy) the center-piece of constitutional concern, as against the Madisonian "balance" of free-doms and limits. And he was unprepared for the almost metaphysical passion that gave unity of purpose to a loose gaggle of interest groups concerned about the balance of power on the Court.

One can now see ironies in the whole performance. There was the irony of a liberal Senate and law school elite, committed to change and growth in con-stitutional interpretation but rigidly hostile to any similar change and growth in the constitutional journey of a legal thinker, denying evidence of it in his five years of decision-making on a high federal court. There was also the irony of Bork, eager to win the suffrage of marginal senators, earnestly an-swering their intrusive queries about his thinking—past and future—on case after case, doctrine after doctrine, thus giving legitimacy to a line of ques-tioning that concentrated on his intellectual rather than his legal record. Tra-ditionally, the Senate's role has dealt with the nominee's character, possible conflict of interest, and flagrant bias. Clearly the questions to Bork went be-yond this to his intellectual journey and future decision-making.

In retrospect, one need not mourn Bork overmuch. He lived by the constitutional sword in his grandly polemical articles, and in a sense he died by it—even running into the sword pointed at him by his enemies. He an-swered questions no nominee has any business answering if he means to be an independent judge.

But if the Bork story had saving ironies, the Ginsburg story had only absurdities. The Meese strategists, misreading the Bork disaster as due to his "paper trail" alone, too cleverly proposed Douglas Ginsburg, a young judge with no constitutional journey to speak of. This left the Democratic commit-tee majority opposing him with only the traditional "fitness to serve" strat-egy—the "character issue."

Enter the investigative reporters. Ginsburg's life yielded some trifles (a conflict-of-interest cloud, a second wife who had worked clinically in a hos-pital that performed legal abortions), and then—as the final blow that shat-tered the confirmation—an obscure episode of marijuana smoking while on the law school faculty at Harvard. The scandalized single-issue protest groups were no longer the devotees of rights on the left but the champions of rig-orous traditional values on the right. Coming of age in the exploratory early

1970s, Ginsburg had violated the just-say-no command of codal purity. Exit Ginsburg, an innocent too rashly chosen to start with.

Anthony Kennedy came at just the right point in the drama—where both camps, exhausted by their wars in the first two acts, wanted a third with a happy ending. He has proved to be a "safe" candidate for both sides to support—the very model of a modern judicial nominee. There were no behavioral lapses in his youth or early manhood, no ethical cloud over his lobbyist years in Sacramento, no turbulent adventures in constitutional interpretation in some 400 judicial opinions. The Republicans are willing to settle for a "true conservative." The Democrats—including their Harvard Law School prime adviser, Professor Laurence Tribe—are fearful of their victor image of excessive nominee-bashing, and welcome the chance to show themselves as "moderates."

At what cost to the judicial culture and the nation? Where Robert Bork was eager to answer questions the committee had no right to put to a nominee, Anthony Kennedy was deftly evasive in most answers but crossed the line on some. Bork often gave involved and unsatisfying answers; Kennedy—more adroit in avoiding confrontation—managed to give soothing ones. Asked about his restricted membership club, he assured the senators he was "sensitive to the subtle barriers" of racism—a commitment that is bound to crop up in responses to his future decisions on "affirmative action" cases.

Harried by Senator Dennis DeConcini on the "right of privacy," Kennedy tried to skirt it by positing a line beyond which "the government may not go." But DeConcini would not be put off on his right-of-privacy query: "But it's there? No question about it?" Kennedy's defenses collapsed. "Yes sir," he said. He thus gave away the treasure of a judge's own right of privacy and independence, and his future freedom of deliberative choice, all of which are central to the maintenance of a sturdy, knowledgeable, and independent judiciary. Questioned about his views on the meaning of the Fourteenth Amendment, Kennedy simultaneously embraced the historical intent (what the legislators "thought they were doing and intended and said when they ratified the Amendment") and added sweepingly that "*Plessy* v. *Ferguson* was wrong on the day it was decided" and that "a people can rise above its own injustice." His candy box has bonbons for every doctrinal taste.

What is going on in these questions and responses? It is, as I read it, nothing less than a movement toward plebiscitary control of the "advise and consent" process of judicial confirmation. The fact that it is enacted in a public hearing room and transmitted on a TV screen instantaneously around the world doesn't make it any less a form of political hostage-taking, under threat of an adverse senatorial vote.

This was not the way the historic judicial greats were chosen or confirmed. Whether they adhered to judicial restraint or activism, they would have met such questions and questioners with magisterial rebuffs. In their independence—from Holmes to Frankfurter and Jackson, from Black and Douglas to Brennan—they were models for many of the young in legal and judicial vocations. Under far lesser provocation than Bork or Kennedy, Felix Frankfurter, when pushed by a hostile senator about his associations and beliefs, responded more sharply than either of them. Bork slipped dangerously away from Frankfurter's example when he let Senator Arlen Specter pin him down on how he would interpret Justice Oliver Wendell Holmes's "clear and present danger" doctrine in future freedom-of-speech First Amendment cases.

The confirmation hearings of 1987 are bound to serve as precedents for future hearings on future nominees, perhaps irreversibly. This may haunt the Democrats when they come to power in this century. It will mean mischief unless the constitutional culture refuses to accept the prospect that no Supreme Court nominee will escape this kind of scrutiny. It is one thing to examine the life, character, and "fitness" of a nominee, provided it isn't pushed to absurdity. It is quite another for senators to extort commitments on a nominee's doctrinal positions and legal philosophy, which are either on public record for them to read or are in a zone of integrity and independence that no nominee should be asked to barter away in order to save his skin.

A Record That Speaks for Itself
Principle, Precedent, and Predictability

Francis Flaherty

Thumbs down on Robert H. Bork. But first a story to clear the air:

The lame-duck president announces his Supreme Court nominee, a lawyer and jurist of sterling credentials. The chairman of the Senate Judiciary Committee, a member of the opposition party, wholly dislikes the political tint of the nominee. He and his party consequently deploy every parliamentary tactic available to thwart the nomination: delaying and drawing out the hearings, stretching the Thanksgiving and Christmas recesses, filibustering the matter once it hits the Senate floor. The ruse works. The nomination is eventually withdrawn.

A scenario for 1987? No. This was 1968, when Lyndon Johnson nominated his liberal soulmate, Abe Fortas, to succeed Earl Warren as chief justice. Strom Thurmond (R-S.C.) was the chairman of the Judiciary Committee, and the result of his and his party's deft use of parliamentary procedures was the ascendancy of *their* ideological soulmate, Warren Burger, to the top judicial spot in the land.

The debate over Supreme Court nominee Robert Bork is an embarrassment of political posturing on both sides of the aisle. But the claim by Bork supporters that the Senate must lightly scrutinize the nominee, merely ascertaining his professional competence and ensuring that his views are not wholly off the judicial map, has made the matter particularly murky. And the claim is wrong. As the Fortas story suggests, full Senate scrutiny of Court nominees, including their philosophy and politics, and rejection or confirmation based thereon, is both historically common and constitutionally valid.

How typical is the Fortas affair? From George Washington to Richard Nixon, "almost one out of every five nominees to the Court has failed to gain the Senate's consent," wrote Harvard law professor Laurence Tribe in *God Save This Honorable Court* (1985). "No other nomination that a president makes receives more rigorous scrutiny." The Senate rejection of John Rutledge in 1795, Tribe continued, "began a tradition of inquiry into the political views and public positions of candidates for the Court."

Is this common practice constitutionally correct? Yes. Article II of the Constitution provides that the president "shall nominate, and by and with the Advice and Consent of the Senate, shall appoint, . . . Judges of the Supreme Court." One needn't be schooled in legal exegesis to perceive that this is a joint process, with neither branch assigned a greater role. If anything, constitutional history suggests the Senate may have the weightier voice. The debate in the Constitutional Convention over Court appointments focused on two alternatives: congressional or Senate election of justices, or Senate confirmation of presidential nominees. That the president would have the sole, or predominant, part in Supreme Court selections was never a serious proposal.

An equal Senate role in these appointments makes constitutional sense in other ways. It is consistent with the constitutional scheme of checks and balances, which requires the concurrence of two and sometimes three branches before government action can be taken. If, for instance, a president must sign each of the thousands of bills that Congress passes before the bills become law, how much more important to the constitutional vision is the concurrence of the branches when the issue is the appointment of a life-tenured member of the third and coordinate branch? This theory also explains the light Senate scrutiny accorded nominees for executive branch positions. In such intra-branch matters, a president deserves to have his own choice within broad parameters of acceptability.

Put another way, in our democracy the bestowal of a Supreme Court justiceship is a signal event, deserving of as much democratic input as possible. As the people's choice, President Reagan deserves to and will have his influence on the process; the Senate cannot move until he nominates someone. But the same citizens who chose Reagan also elected a Senate that is Democratic by a count of 54 to 46 Republicans. The only democratically authorized replacement for Lewis Powell—he or she will be our nation's one hundred seventh Court justice—is one acceptable to both the Republican administration and the Democratic Senate.

There are some things to like about Robert Bork, who has served for the past five years on one of the nation's most prestigious appellate courts, the U.S. Circuit Court of Appeals for the District of Columbia. For one, he boasts a mighty resumé: Chancellor Kent Professor of Law and Alexander M. Bickel Professor of Law at Yale School; solicitor general and acting attorney general in the Nixon administration; anti-trust scholar. His service in the Justice Department was of course marked by his firing of special prosecutor Archibald Cox, at the behest of Richard Nixon, in the midst of Watergate.

No dummy, then. Nor is he an invariable right-wing ideologue. In recent years, he has opposed such pet conservative initiatives as the balanced-budget amendment and the "court-stripping" bills that would have circumvented *Roe* v. *Wade* by removing abortion cases from federal court jurisdiction. He has paid for these positions: For a time, he was on a conservative blacklist for appointment to the Supreme Court seat now occupied by Antonin Scalia because of his congressional testimony against the court-stripping bills.

But Judge Bork still sits on the far right. And, understanding that they are authorized by history and the Constitution to do so, every senator who sits on the left of the far right should reject his nomination because of his politicojudicial preferences.

Those preferences are not hard to prove. For instance, Judge Bork strongly disapproves of the constitutional right to privacy established by the Supreme Court 22 years ago in *Griswold* v. *Connecticut*. In that case, the Court held that a Connecticut couple could not be jailed for using birth control in their own home. In an opinion by William O. Douglas, the Court held that, while there is no explicit right of privacy in the Constitution, the First, Third, Fourth, Fifth, and Ninth Amendments have "penumbras" and "emanations" that comprise a constitutional zone of privacy within which the government cannot intrude. That zone is a complex of intimacies, implicating the family, the home, contraception, and reproduction.

Since *Griswold*, the Court has expanded the privacy right. It has extended the right to use contraceptives to unmarried persons; established the right of women to have abortions in *Roe* v. *Wade* and subsequent cases; and found a right of families to live together in *Moore* v. *City of East Cleveland* and other rulings. Indeed, many hope that in time the Court will enlarge the zone of privacy still further, to include such areas as sexual orientation.

But Judge Bork will have none of that because he detects no penumbras, no emanations, and no right of privacy in the Constitution. Under his banner of "judicial restraint," Judge Bork believes that judges should not extract from the Constitution any rights that cannot be fairly derived from the document's text, history, and the intent of the Framers. *Griswold* is an "utterly specious" and "unprincipled" ruling, he declared six years after the decision was handed down.

At this juncture, Bork supporters quickly stress that their man's judicial conservatism means that he respects precedent. By this they mean that his placement on the Court will not automatically mean the reversal of *Griswold* and *Roe* v. *Wade* and the roping off of the zone of privacy. Perhaps true, but no one can fault women, single people, families, and others if they'd rather not take the chance. This is particularly so in light of Judge Bork's recent conversation with Senator Bob Packwood (R-Oreg.), an outspoken advocate of abortion rights and a member of the Senate Judiciary Committee. Judge Bork told the senator that he would have dissented in *Roe* v. *Wade* had he been on the Court. Packwood then asked him about his treatment of precedent. "He said certain precedents were so fixed, some issues so settled, that regardless of how you felt about them you shouldn't vote to overrule them," Senator Packwood told the *New York Times*. "He did not include *Roe* v. *Wade* in that category."

Even absent the abortion question, the right of privacy is a pivotal constitutional doctrine that provides a sanctuary of individual freedom in an age of growing governmental regulation and power. For anyone concerned about that right, Judge Bork's remarks to Senator Packwood should clearly offer sufficient reason for his rejection.

But on nearly every other judicial issue as well, Judge Bork sits on the conservative side. A sampler: He opposes affirmative action. He doubts the constitutionality of the Fairness Doctrine, the recently overturned 38-year-old Federal Communications Commission policy that required broadcasters to air both sides of important public issues. For a long time, he believed that the Free Speech Clause of the First Amendment protected only political speech; artistic and scientific speech and writing constitutionally could be censored or prohibited by the government.

His theory of the proper ambit of government also takes suspiciously convenient turns. In 1963, he opposed the public-accommodations title of the then-pending Civil Rights Act arguing that motel and restaurant owners had a liberty interest in banning blacks from their premises if they so desired. To enforce such a law merely out of the conviction that racism is morally wrong is an idea of "unsurpassed ugliness," he wrote in the *New Republic*. He disavowed that view in 1973, but it became clear in 1984 that his recantation may have been a mixed blessing. In a speech before the

American Enterprise Institute that year, he saw nothing wrong in curbing the liberty interests of homosexuals through morals legislation.

Unsettling as these sometimes troglodytic views are, the recent surveys of Judge Bork's judicial record are even more cause for pause. In a study of his votes in several hundred cases, the Public Citizen Litigation Group found Judge Bork almost perfectly conservative. In 50 non-unanimous decisions by the D.C. appeals court, for instance, the Nader-affiliated group found that the nominee voted against the underdog a daunting 96 percent of the time. Twenty-eight of the studied split cases pitted the government against an individual or a public-interest group; in 26 of these, Judge Bork voted for the government. But in the eight suits pitting the government against a business, the judge sided invariably with the latter. "One can predict his vote with almost complete accuracy simply by identifying the parties in the case," the report concludes.

Even in the conservative world of Republican-appointed jurists, Judge Bork sits on the right. A forthcoming *Columbia Law Review* survey of 1200 decisions by Eisenhower, Ford, Nixon, and Reagan appointees found the judges voted conservatively an average of 69 percent of the time. But Judge Bork, along with only three other Reagan appointees, ruled on the conservative side in 90 percent of their decisions. (The authors defined conservative votes as those for business interests and against criminal defendants, civil-rights plaintiffs, and public-interest groups.)

In a certain sense, it is disingenuous to voice outrage at the clear political content of Judge Bork's judicial record. Though the legitimizing function of the courts makes it a taboo topic, political values clearly play major roles in the rulings of judges of all jurisprudential stripes. No savvy Supreme Court observer, for instance, will have much difficulty predicting the positions of Chief Justice William Rehnquist or Justice William Brennan in any given case.

But there is a question of degree. First of all, the Columbia survey belies any claim by Judge Bork that he is a mainstream conservative. He is a good measure more conservative than Abe Fortas was liberal, and moderately conservative senators should take note of that.

Second and more generally, slavish adherence to a party line is bad judging and cynically endangers the legitimizing function of the courts. In 1978, Harvard law professor David Shapiro studied then Associate Justice Rehnquist's votes on the high court since his 1972 appointment. The justice's votes fell into three basic conservative patterns, and while the other justices had their preferred patterns too, Rehnquist was outstanding in his allegiance to his political druthers. This "unyielding insistence on a particular result," Professor Shapiro concluded, "appears to have contributed to a wide discrepancy between theory and practice in matters of constitutional interpretation, . . . to tacit abandonment of evolving protections of liberty and property, to sacrifice of craftsmanship, and to distortion of precedent." Judge Bork clearly courts the same danger.

There are different styles of conservative judging, of course. One of the three patterns Professor Shapiro detected in Chief Justice Rehnquist's jurisprudence, for instance, was a strong bias toward states' rights. Judge Bork seems to have his particular conservative patterns too, and liberals, moderates, and mainstream conservatives should be very worried about two of them.

The first is blindness toward bias. However maltreated, blacks, women, gays, and others will likely get no solicitousness at Judge Bork's bench. A former Yale Law School colleague, Dean Guido Calabresi, said a month after the nomination that Judge Bork "ignores the significance of discrimination." Judge Bork's opposition to affirmative action and his apparent belief that the Constitution requires no special scrutiny of claims of sexual discrimination are just two examples of this tendency, a tendency which ignores one vital function of the courts in this democracy: to protect minority rights from the inevitable depredations of majority rule. The United States is not a pure democracy; the majority can have its way only within the metes and bounds of the Constitution. In Judge Bork's United States, those boundaries seem perilously broad. Witness, for instance, his flirtation with the idea that the First Amendment protects only political speech.

The second theme is equally troubling, but oddly inconsistent with the first. Judge Bork seems to have little regard for the role of the courts as the referee of democracy, the institution that makes sure the game is played fairly. He has, for example, opposed the Supreme Court's ban on poll taxes in *Harper* v. *Virginia Board of Elections*, a 1966 ruling. He has also criticized the "one man, one vote" line of decisions, begun a quarter century ago, in which the Court redressed legislative voting malapportionments that made some citizens' votes worth only a fraction of others'. Typically in these cases, state or local legislatures used clever gerrymandering to dilute the voting power of blacks, rural folks, or members of disfavored political parties. Judge Bork also has a stingy view of the standing doctrine, which sets out the legal requirements for a person or entity to sue. In one of his circuit court decisions, for instance, the nominee ruled that bipartisan congressional leadership lacked standing to challenge, on constitutional grounds, an action by the executive branch.

All these positions bespeak unconcern with keeping the pathways of democracy clear, with ensuring that the constitutional checks and balances balance, with verifying that majority rule is truly majority rule. After all, if only people rich enough to pay the poll tax can vote, we have something less than majority rule. Judge Bork's lackadaisical approach to the court *qua* democratic referee contradicts his record of indifference to minorities. Why? Because this justification for the latter is deference to majority rule—a tenet he is judicially unwilling to protect.

What about Judge Bork's vaunted theory of judicial restraint? The one good thing about the theory is its proper quest for principles to prevent judges from reading into the Constitution anything they want. But otherwise, the doctrine, which requires courts to find in the Constitution only those rights fairly discoverable from its text, history, and authors' intentions, is hogwash. First, the phrases of the Constitution—"due process," "equal protection"—are too open-ended to determine what is fairly derivable from them. Second, sticklers for what Stanford Law Dean John Hart Ely calls "clause-bound interpretivism" inevitably confront anomalies that demand abandonment of their theory. For example, the First Amendment prohibits only Congress from abridging freedom of speech. Does this mean the president is free to do so? Finally, the many elusive, and often contradictory intentions of the 55 Framers are impossible to determine. As Professor Tribe has written, "No collective body can really be said to have a single, ascertainable purpose or intent." As the surveys of Judge Bork's record prove, judicial restraint is just a cloak of neutrality for conservatism.

Why is it important to keep this former Chicago antitrust lawyer off the Court? Clearly, he signifies a conservative vote, and one vote on a nine-member court means a great deal. *Miranda* v. *Arizona, Mapp* v. *Ohio, Furman* v. *Georgia*, and *University of California* v. *Bakke* are just a few of the Court's more famous 5-4 cases, and in them one vote made the difference in such crucial legal areas as the breadth of suspects' rights, the constitutionality of capital punishment, and affirmative action. And Judge Bork's vote is not just a conservative vote; it is a radically conservative one.

Judge Bork poses a particular risk to the political balance of the Court, given its current makeup of three conservatives, two liberals, and three centrists. Associate Justice Bork would mean that the Court's conservative faction need only persuade one of the three "swing" justices to assemble a majority of five in any case. Moreover, Judge Bork represents the critical fourth conservative justice needed to accept cases for review under the certiorari procedure known as the "Rule of Four." The Court has full discretion to select which 150 or so cases it will hear of the thousands of petitions presented to it yearly, and Court watchers know that the justices' political battles are just as furious in case selection as in case decision. For instance, suppose that the New York federal appeals court held under a novel First Amendment theory, that the right of free speech included the right to *hear* and that citizens' rights were therefore violated when a left-wing Latin American journalist was deported by the Reagan administration before she could deliver a speech. Conservative justices would of course be itching to grant "cert" and reverse the ruling. With Judge Bork on the Court, they undoubtedly would have that chance.

Judge Bork's benighted views and his threat to Court balance are sufficient for anyone with an ADA approval rating of 25 percent or more to hope ardently for his Senate rejection. But he deserves rejection for another reason: With all his theories of judicial restraint, he has no theory of personhood, and such a vision is vital for constitutional interpretation. In 1971, Judge Bork concluded that the First Amendment "does not cover scientific, educational, commercial, or literary expressions as such" and, therefore, the elected branches of government can prohibit or censor such speech without judicial interference. Though he later abandoned this stated conclusion, what vision of humanity permits the denial of whole universes of self-expression? For Judge Bork, people seem to be what's left over after the sectors of government have divvied up their constitutional power. Judge Bork has it backwards.

QUESTIONS FOR DISCUSSION

14.1 Will the defeat of Robert Bork's nomination reduce the possibility that legal scholars whose ideas on numerous questions of the law are on record will become Supreme Court justices?

14.2 Does a democracy have the right to question justices who may serve for life about any and all issues that may come before the Supreme Court?

14.3 Does it compromise a potential Supreme Court justice to have him or her expound on broad issues of constitutional philosophy and interpretation?

14.4 Have the debates over Robert Bork and Clarence Thomas politicized the Court and diminished its magisterial role in the American political system?

Chapter
15

Should We Legalize Drugs?

INTRODUCTION

The strategy of the American government in combatting drug use has had two prongs: reducing the supply of illicit drugs from abroad and reducing the demand at home through educational programs, rehabilitation centers, and drug testing in the workplace. While drug use has declined among certain population groups, it persists as a major problem in inner cities such as Washington, D.C., where the murder rate and other drug-related crimes have reached epidemic proportions.

Thus, some have argued that the most effective way of taking drug money away from the criminal element and reducing the hideous murder rate in the inner cities is to legalize the sale of drugs. This approach has never gained broad public support largely because many feel that the legalization of drugs would only encourage more usage.

In the following selection, Eric Sterling criticizes President Bush's War on Drugs. He feels that the profits from drug trafficking are too great and that too many people are tempted to enter the business for it ever to be stopped by force. Sterling criticizes the use of the National Guard in policing borders, the construction of prisons to hold more convicted drug sellers, and the purchase of more hardware for law enforcement officials. He feels that such a prohibition strategy imposes excessive burdens on the criminal justice system and is doomed to failure. Instead, he suggests that the sale of drugs be managed and regulated by law.

Richard Hawley argues that, "Legalizing drugs is the shallowest and weakest of responses to the nation's drug problem." Hawley emphasizes the impact of drug use on the health and behavior of individuals. Legalization would socially validate them and accelerate their use. Tough laws and tough law enforcement are the only effective means, he contends, of reducing drug use. He cites the experiences of China, Japan, and Western Europe in curtailing illegal drugs through prohibition and enforcement.

The Eighteenth Amendment (1919), which brought the Prohibition era and outlawed "the manufacturing, sale, or transportation of intoxicating liquors" is associated with the growth of organized crime and bootleg whiskey and was repealed in 1933. Hawley, going against the conventional view, argues that repeal may have been a mistake. He cites the subsequent increase in alcoholism, alcohol-related accidents, and violent crimes committed under the influence of alcohol. Hawley's position on drug legalization reflects the overwhelming public consensus. Few political leaders have endorsed such legalization and it is unlikely that the laws will be changed in the foreseeable future. The debate, nonetheless, raises important questions of individual liberty and social order.

Legalizing the Intolerable Is a Bad Idea

Richard A. Hawley

Laws that restrict the use and supply of psychoactive drugs have been devised for the same reason that laws have been made to prevent the discharge of toxic chemicals into public waterways or to keep known poisons out of food. There would be little public debate about keeping substances like marijuana, heroin, crack, and powder cocaine out of the public pantry if these substances, in addition to their several toxic effects, did not also deliver sensual pleasure.

Because various chemical preparations—whether stimulants, depressants, or hallucinogens—have the capacity to elicit powerfully reinforcing (for many, irresistible) pleasures, users are driven to repeat the drug-taking experience. Among adults, mental acuity, human relationships, commitments, job performance, and general health decline as drug use becomes chronic; among children, drug use retards or eclipses critical maturation and learning altogether.

The biological and medical impact of drugs on healthy functioning has never been more clearly understood. If substances that do *not* pack a pleasurable payoff were known to wreak the kinds of health and social havoc that psychoactive drugs have done over the past 30 years, we would arise as one to banish the culprits. At massive public expense, we have removed asbestos from school ceilings, boiler rooms, and plumbing closets, because we believe it to be toxic. Asbestos has not impaired even 1 percent as many people as have lost their learning, their health, and even their lives due to the availability of illicit psychoactive drugs.

Again, the confusing issue is pleasure. Because pleasure-inducing drugs create a deep and powerful desire in users to have more, drug use appears, at first, to be a choice. Choices and preferences are the birthright of a free person, of an educated citizen. And so, one specious line of argument goes, drug use should be protected as an expression of individual liberty.

But as drug abuse professionals, drug-dependent people, and their families know, drug use ultimately effaces the capacity to choose; freedom of choice, along with health and performance, may be lost altogether. There is no constitutional right protecting drug use or any other form of self-destruction.

HISTORICAL PERSPECTIVE

Physicians, drug-abuse counselors, school teachers, guidance staff, and the families of drug users—people who work closely with drug-impaired individuals—tend to oppose the legalization of drugs. Those favoring legalization are more likely to view the problem abstractly and statistically. Moreover, they are likely to come from university campuses—typically from academic departments, rather than from campus health facilities that work with drug users face to face.

Politically, legalization appeals to those who see it as a "nonjudgmental" and "nonconfrontational" solution to a massive and staggeringly complex social problem. It is comforting to maintain that drugs, drug use, and drug commerce are not the real problem; that, instead, an antiquated, perhaps puritanical "system" (designed by a benighted opposition party) is the problem. Make drugs legally available, allow the government to control and inspect them, and the nation will save and make billions of dollars, jails will be cleared of socially harmless persons, the mob will be outflanked, and the mayors of the nation's great cities can get back to business without crippling harassment from the press.

Why is this view so comforting? If the "system" is at fault, then no wrenching interventions need be undertaken, no political enemies made, no costly and dangerous law enforcement measures risked. If the system has been the culprit, then there has been no real crisis of values or commitment or courage in schools or workplaces or legislatures over the latter decades of this century. The error has been merely strategic.

But this kind of thinking will not stand up to the evidence. The performance of American schools has sunk to crisis levels in the very years in which illicit drug use became epidemic. It is important to remember that harsh drug laws did not cause the youthful drug epidemic of the 1960s and 1970s.

As the distinguished epidemiologist Nils Bejerot has made clear, the American and European drug epidemic of the 1960s was generated in the same way every other drug epidemic has been generated: Social norms were challenged and altered by a sufficiently large norm-breaking population. In the case of the United States, that population was the World War II baby boom as it reached college age, with the attendant freedom and mobility provided by campus life. When antidrug norms were successfully challenged—first by college students, then by adolescents generally—and when the norm-breaking was supported by popular culture, particularly its films and music (I'll "get high with a little help from my friends"), conditions were met for an exponential increase in formerly marginalized behavior: an epidemic.

The peak years of illicit drug use on the part of students were *preceded* by a softening of drug laws in some states and municipalities. Typically, that change might have been the "decriminalization" of possession of small amounts of marijuana.

But by the mid-1970s—as the epidemic was approaching its 1979 peak—forces concerned about the effects of drug abuse began to find their voice. A national parents' movement was started at the grassroots level and was loosely coordinated by the now international Parents Resource Institute of Drug Education (PRIDE) in Atlanta. Drug-abuse professionals, public and private educators, and pediatricians also began to close ranks in opposition to drug experimentation and use. As a result, many states rescinded their "decriminalization" measures and stiffened drug penalties. A drug-free schools movement was initiated and still persists, and drug-abuse prevention efforts have been stepped up in the armed services. There has also been continuing efforts in the private sector to promote drug-free workplaces, and such media gestures as Partnerships for a Drug-Free America have sought to rebuild a consensus that drug use is harmful and wrong.

In sum, the past 30 years have seen a weakening of the norms prohibiting drug use, then an epidemic of illicit drug use, followed by a growing attempt to restore antidrug norms. At present, there is reason for guarded optimism that the antidrug measures are producing an effect. The use of marijuana and powder cocaine is down significantly from a decade ago (although levels of use are still unacceptably high).

From an epidemiologic standpoint, the news is even better: Students are more than twice as likely as they were 10 years ago to believe that smoking marijuana poses a serious threat to their well-being.

WHAT LAWS MEAN TO CHILDREN

As Jean Piaget, Lawrence Kohlberg, and their contemporary disciples have taught us, nearly all preadolescent children—and many people throughout their lives—hold the law as their highest moral standard. Even for those "higher stage" intellects who think about the principles of justice that laws are designed to promote, the law stands as a lofty, politically critical standard for personal decision making.

For children whose conceptual capacity does not yet enable them to entertain abstract principles of justice, the law is the ultimate guide to what is right and true and fair. The universal values we share—truth telling, keeping commitments, not injuring others without cause—are supported by laws. When liars, perjurers, cheats, vandals, and killers are legally punished for violating those values, children learn a concrete, yet profound, lesson concerning right and wrong.

It was Aristotle's view—and it is a durable one—that we should habituate children to right action, so that when they are mentally able to understand why, say, honesty is the best policy, they will be in effect confirming a socially necessary, already accepted fact; they will realize in a new way what they already know. Laws help us and our children to become habituated to right action.

When laws are openly ignored, when lawmakers themselves break laws, or when laws permit repellent and harmful behavior, children are confused. They lose confidence not merely in the value of law, but in the value of any social standards.

Chemicals that retard, distort, or destroy healthy maturation and learning are harmful to children. Laws against using and trading such chemicals are consonant with the values we encourage children to embrace. Laws allowing even regulated use of these harmful substances undermine those values.

The legally available substances most comparable to illicit drugs are alcohol and tobacco. Each of them annually claims more lives and generates more pathology than all the currently illicit drugs combined. Moreover, unlike the illicit drugs of choice, tobacco has negligible psychoactive effects, and alcohol is typically consumed in such a way that users can monitor its intoxicating effects. Moreover, alcohol and tobacco, the drugs first and most frequently used by children, are legally available to adults. Adding more toxic and more dramatically psychoactive drugs to the legal marketplace will inevitably increase the use of those substances by children.

Legalizing and thus socially validating the use of psychoactive drugs would in effect "renorm" them in a more comprehensive way than the youthful counterculture managed to do in the 1960s and 1970s. History reveals that legalization of drugs accelerates new use and contributes to a larger population of chronic users—never the reverse. In Great Britain, where laws were changed to enable heroin addicts to receive the narcotics they required on a prescription basis, the number of users doubled every 16 months between 1959 and 1968.

By contrast, when states energetically enforce antidrug laws and policies, illegal drug use is reduced and eliminated. Internationally, tough laws and tough enforcement have been the *only* effective measures against drug abuse. Through such measures the Chinese government eradicated its centuries-old opium traffic in just two years, from 1951 to 1953. Cocaine use was similarly curtailed in Western Europe in the early thirties, and the Japanese successfully reversed an epidemic dependence on amphetamines between 1954 and 1958.

Advocates of legalization like to compare antidrug laws to the 13-year period of Prohibition. Yet looked at closely, the analogy with Prohibition actually undermines legalization arguments. Frequently portrayed as a triumph of Puritanism and conservatism, Prohibition was actually a progressive, strongly feminist movement. Women, politically disenfranchised and unable to establish credit or to gain access to many lines of employment, suffered most from fathers' and husbands' alcohol-related brutality and domestic irresponsibility. Sentiment in favor of Prohibition grew steadily from 1846, when Maine voted itself dry, to 1919, when the Eighteenth Amendment and the Volstead Act were passed.

Without question, Prohibition failed. Enforcement provisions were hopelessly meager, and alcohol continued to be marketed and consumed illegally—especially by middle-income and wealthy people. However, overall alcohol consumption did dip considerably between 1920 and 1933, and the incidence of alcohol-related illnesses, such as cirrhosis of the liver, declined dramatically.

If one accepts that Prohibition was not the answer to the nation's alcohol problems, one must also accept that repealing Prohibition has proved to be an even worse answer. Today, an estimated 7 adults in 10 use alcohol. Of approximately 110 million American drinkers, about 10 million are estimated to be problem drinkers. Alcohol-related accidents are the number-one cause of violent death in the United States. Drunk drivers are responsible for half of all highway deaths; every year 25,000 Americans die as a result of drunk driving, more than half as many as were killed in the entire Vietnam War. High percentages of sex offenses and other violent crimes are committed under the influence of alcohol, as well.

Once again, alcohol is a legally vended, proof-controlled, tightly regulated "minor depressant." Yet there are those who wish to make the likes of high potency cannabis, LSD, and powder and crack cocaine as accessible as alcohol.

OBLIGATIONS TO CHILDREN

If you tell my physician friends in Cleveland who volunteer to treat the growing legions of crack-impaired babies that drug abuse is a victimless crime, you are likely to get punched in the eye.

Legalize drugs, and certain busts and scandals may disappear from the newspapers. But the drug problem will not go away; it will persist and grow. Drugs impair the healthy functioning of users. *That* is the real drug problem. That is why there is no historical instance of an enduring society in which any of the substances currently controlled has been legally available for long.

We have never known more clearly what drugs do to those who use them. Caring people tend to act, to intervene. Those who confront drug use and attempt to curtail it are met with anger, fear, and cynicism by those who are so deeply enmeshed in the drug culture that they cannot imagine an alternative. Working to rid one's family or school or community of drugs will invariably lead to vilification, frustrations, and periodic defeats. Confronting the consequences of drug abuse always produces bad news and bad feelings, at least in the short run.

Like antidrug activists, drug laws remind us of a standard that is not being met. Getting rid of the standard is like shooting the messenger who bears disturbing news.

It is past time for all of us—schoolpeople foremost—to declare our values with respect to drug use and its related social consequences. The fact of the matter is that the availability and use of drugs are incompatible with healthy child development and with learning.

Moreover, we have reached a moment in history when exercises such as this one—airing the pros and cons of legalization in a "debate" format—may actually contribute to the problem. Whatever the strength of the contestants' arguments, the message of the subtext is stronger: "Experts" disagree. But experts—at least advocates for children—don't disagree.

There is a point at which the editors of the *Kappan* must decide where they stand on the availability of drugs to children. When I pointed this out to the editor who commissioned this piece, I was told, "We have always trusted our readers to come to their own conclusions."

But is this magazine really as value-neutral as that? Will there be a debate on the pros and cons of using children for the sexual gratification of adults? Will pro-Semites soon square off against anti-Semites in the pages of the *Kappan*?

I doubt it. I believe that the editors have resolved these last two issues to their ethical satisfaction; yet drugs hurt children as surely and as intolerably as sexual abuse and ethnic and religious discrimination do.

Legalizing drugs is the shallowest and weakest of responses to the nation's drug problem. It is an attempt to redefine the problem, so as to feel less bad about the data. But the data of failed lives and failed learning should make us feel bad. Legal failures are still failures.

I don't think we need to debate this topic anymore.

What Should We Do About Drugs?
Manage the Problem Through Legalization

Eric E. Sterling

We are considering today how to address an extremely complex social problem. The issue is not, "Should we 'legalize' drugs?" for their own sake. The issue is how does a society best address a complex economic, health, social, family, and spiritual problem. Recently I was in Philadelphia, Pennsylvania, at a conference on building a drug abuse prevention movement. That is a worthwhile way to describe the goal, far preferable to saying that we are going to build a "drug-free community." We must be careful how we define our terms. How do we define "drug," how do we define "drug abuse," and how we define "prevention?" We know that illegal drugs are having a tremendous negative impact on our community, our families, and our nation, but to effectively address the problem of drugs in our environment, we must know a great deal more.

Almost any citizen can outline some of the horrors of drugs.

Deaths
- People being killed by drug users in the course of robberies.
- People being killed by drug traffickers in the competition in the drug business.
- People dying of drug overdoses.
- Children dying of neglect and abuse by drug-using parents.

Crimes
- Robberies, burglaries, shoplifting, embezzling, fraud, prostitution—all to raise money to buy drugs.
- Money laundering and corruption by drug traffickers working to protect their profits.

Intoxication
- Accidents caused by people working or driving under the influence of drugs.
- Children failing to learn because they are under the influence of drugs in school.
- Lives of thousands of drug addicts wasted because of their addiction to drugs.
- Children born addicted to cocaine or suffering from Fetal Alcohol Syndrome.
- Half our motor vehicle fatalities involving drunken driving.

This is the widely known, daily newspaper-view of the "drug problem."

Now for many people, these problems are simply explained by the word "drugs." Drugs do this. Drugs did that. That is as simple, *and as wrong*, as it would be to look at the high proportion of black men in America's prisons, and say, "Blacks do this. Blacks commit crime."

We must understand more completely the complex impact of the drug phenomenon, and why it is the way it is so that we can effectively manage the problem.

Today I want to get beyond the "tip of the iceberg" thinking that surrounds the drug problem. I am not going to give you a better understanding of the tip of the iceberg, the number of illegal drug crimes or the number of cocaine addicted babies, you hear all that, *ad nauseam*, from people who hold important offices who feel they must be cheerleaders in the "war on drugs."

Because of the fraudulence, viciousness and perversity of the "war on drugs," I tend to be sarcastic about the established wisdom about the drug problem, and cynical about the motives of those who posture as antidrug warriors. Let me state at the outset that I feel deeply for those who are hurt by drugs. There are alcoholics in my family and I have cousins whose lives have been detoured by drug abuse. I know personally how illegal drugs are a very serious problem for our society and a tragedy for many families. But I don't let my emotion blind me to the facts.

The principal reason why illegal drugs like cocaine and heroin are as harmful as they are is not simply because of their physiological or psychological properties, but because of the vicious, racist, anti-democratic, and just plain stupid way our society has dealt with drugs.

I believe that the drug problem is a problem that must be managed like other complex problems. If there is anyone in this room who believes that in the next 20 or 30 years we can *eliminate* solid waste, water pollution, air pollution, acid rain, alcoholism, cancer, or birth defects, please raise your hand.

None of them will be eliminated, but all of them will be reduced because we will manage the problem, and because we will not take absolutist, unrealistic or moralistic approaches. For example, none of you would propose that we take a "zero tolerance" approach to solid waste or air pollution. No one proposes making it a felony to drive a car that emits air pollutants, we set standards for automobile emissions and motor vehicle fuels. No one would make it a felony to flush a toilet, or put plastics in the trash, we set plumbing codes and establish regulations. We deal with these problems comprehensively, dispassionately, and incrementally.

When we talk about drugs, we have to use the term "drugs" truthfully, and not on some absurd legally technical basis, like controlled substances. When we use the term "drug," we must first look at legal drugs, principally alcohol and tobacco. Almost all of us know that legal drugs are a much more serious problem than illegal drugs both in terms of deaths, health, and crime.

The leading deadly drug in Colorado, as it is for the entire nation, is tobacco. In 1988 the Surgeon General's Report to Congress on Smoking and Health stressed over and over: Tobacco is as addictive as heroin and cocaine. The Centers for Disease Control estimate national tobacco deaths at 400,000 per year. That's over 1,000 per day. Yet nationally, illegal drug deaths, from all causes, are at a maximum, in the range of 10,000 to 15,000 per year.

Alcohol is reported in surveys of persons in prison to have been used more frequently at the time of the commission of a crime than were illegal drugs. Alcohol use results in about 100,000 deaths per year in the United States.

When we think about the impact of drugs on Colorado, let's look not only at the headline story in the *Rocky Mountain News* or the *Denver Post* but also in the obituaries. When the obit says, Mr. Jones died at age 56 of a heart attack or cancer, it doesn't tell us that Mr. Jones has been addicted to cigarettes for 40 years, and has tried, unsuccessfully, to quit eight times.

Even aspirin kills about as many Americans in a year as does cocaine.

Second, when we hear the term, "the drug culture," what do we think of? Is it the 1967 "summer of love" in San Francisco, The Doors, Jimi Hendrix, Lenny Bruce, Janis Joplin—people who have been dead for 20 years? That is an anachronism.

You don't think of the Camel "Smooth" Character, "Spuds McKenzie" for "Bud Light," the "Schlitz Malt Liquor Bull," cigarettes "alive with pleasure," "Virginia Slims—you've come a long way, baby," "Anacin" for "FAST, FAST, FAST Relief," "Midol," because you "don't have time for the pain," "Motrin" IV, I mean IB, and more doctors recommend "Preparation H" which shrinks painful hemorrhoidal tissues fast, in time for "Miller Time," and "the night belongs to Michelob." That's the drug culture.

The drug culture is instant chemical relief, it is chemical sexiness, chemical camaraderie, chemical sophistication, chemical success and chemical self-esteem. The messages of the drug culture, and the values of the drug culture are created on Madison Avenue and bombarded at us and our children 24 hours a day.

Legal drugs are dangerous, they are killers, yet they are being promoted to us. Their promotion is one of the biggest industries in our nation, and our attitudes about drugs are being shaped in the context of that promotion.

If we want to deal with the drug problem, we have to deal with legal drugs and the drug culture of instant relief and surrogate sophistication. If we want to deal with the drug problem, we must be comprehensive and deal with all drugs more forthrightly and more effectively.

At a minimum when we think about the impact of drugs, we have to break the impacts down into the impacts of legal drugs and the impacts of illegal drugs. A part of our examination, even more important than asking "what are the impacts of drugs," is to ask "*why* do drugs have the impacts on our community that they do?"

What is drug "abuse?" Abuse is more than simply doing something which is risky and harmful over the long term. Responsible alcohol consumption may be injurious to some people because of particular physical sensitivities of their bodies. Playing professional football results in many serious, permanent injuries. Even with the best protection, and the best training and conditioning, those injuries are the *inevitable* risks of the activity. Because people are injured doesn't mean that abuse is involved.

Abuse involves going over some line, and the line isn't always clear. Playing football without protection is abuse. Drinking three or four beers during a Denver Broncos game is not generally drug abuse. But hopping behind the wheel at the stadium after drinking those beers is abuse. Smoking marijuana at home lounging around is not abuse. But for a student, smoking pot in school is abuse. Children drinking wine at a Passover Seder is not abuse. Children drinking "Bud Light" under the porch can become abuse. Drug use which breaks the law is not *per se* drug abuse.

Legal drugs have many of the adverse impacts that they do because they are widely promoted, because they are inadequately regulated, and because their dangers are minimized—particularly in comparison with illegal drugs. We bombard the society with the message to stay away from illegal drugs because they are dangerous—and the implicit message is that the legal drugs are not dangerous. For the tobacco and alcohol industry, that's a terrific message.

The harms of illegal drugs that are most obvious and most troubling are due to the inadequate way in which we regulate illegal drugs. Illegal drugs are totally unregulated, even less regulated than savings and loans, and we know how well that deregulation scheme worked. By making certain drugs illegal, we have given responsibility for selling them to organized crime, and we know how much social responsibility organized crime has.

The illegal drug laws are based on a simple premise: The American people are too stupid to know what's dangerous, and too lacking in self-control to avoid dangerous habits. Therefore they must be prohibited from using the illegal drugs. But prohibition, as we recall from the 1920s, is not a particularly successful way to deal with complex problems, and it has lots of undesirable side effects. And this premise of American stupidity and irresponsibility is fundamentally antidemocratic. Can we as a society decide that we are going to sell dangerous poisons, addictive drugs, drugs that create psychosis and breed crime? We decided that question in 1933 in the affirmative.

My thesis is that the undesirable consequences we see in the impact of illegal drugs in our community *are increased by prohibition,* and that the more promising strategy to reduce those impacts is to manage the problem through intelligent and comprehensive regulation.

I am not making the argument that drugs ought to be legalized along the lines of the alcohol model. Drugs, including alcohol, should not be promoted. Indeed, to address the problems of crack and angel dust, I believe, *requires* that we deal with "Schlitz Malt Liquor," "Cisco" fortified wine, and cigarettes and smokeless tobacco with more restrictive regulations.

This leads me to the question of "prevention." Prevention is rarely simple. When addressing complex behavior involving the use of many types of drugs, by many people, for a variety of reasons, prevention of abuse is complex. Prevention involves regulation, social policy, advertising policy, family values, schools, economic policy, spiritual values and culture. Prevention is not "Just Say No!" T-shirts. It starts with sex education, it involves avoiding teenage pregnancy, it includes prenatal care, it involves building strong, functional families, it involves early, positive experiences, good housing, it requires good schools and dedicated teachers, adequate recreation, adequate nutrition, positive role models, positive affirmations, love, more love, self-love, hope, trust, respect, opportunity. Prevention truly requires breaking down our society's indifference to poverty and racism. Specialized drug abuse education is a small part of a true preventive program.

We must make prevention our principal strategy. Unfortunately, the National Drug Control Strategy presented to the nation by President Bush makes military involvement in South America, enlistment of the National Guard, the construction of prisons, and the purchase of law enforcement hardware the foundation of the strategy. His strategy is the same strategy which has failed since President Nixon declared war on drugs in 1972, it just comes with a much bigger price tag. Bush requests a total of $11.654 billion for FY 1992. But *only 13 percent* for drug abuse prevention ($1.1514 billion), and *only 14 percent* for drug abuse treatment ($1.654 billion).

The budget calls for $1.158 billion for anti-drug activities in the Department of Defense alone, up from $800 million in 1990, now more than 10 percent of the entire request. The 1992 corrections request is $1.680 billion (more than 14 percent of the request), up $380 million in one year, the administration's goal is to double federal prison capacity by 1996. Yet drug abuse treatment is offered in only two federal prisons. The request for interdiction (to stop drugs coming in over the border and coastline), the most costly and one of the least effective components of the supply control program, is $2.109 billion, more than 18 percent of the request. It was $948 million in 1988 and only $473 million in 1983.

Yet the latest National Strategy cuts back on treatment and prevention programs: in FY 1991 $38.5 million was projected for reducing waiting lists at drug treatment programs—the President asks to eliminate that program to nothing in FY 1992. In FY 1990 and FY 1991 the Community Youth Program of the Office of Substance Abuse Prevention spent $20 million. This program was also "zeroed out" for FY 1992.

Basically our national strategy, and it has been Colorado's strategy, is a prohibition strategy. At least three vital aspects of our community which are being hurt because the strategy is a prohibition strategy: public safety, health, and the economy.

First Let's Look at Public Safety

1. In larger cities police don't respond to "911" calls for service unless illegal drugs are reported to be involved. Excessive attention to illegal drugs means that other important problems get less attention.

2. In larger jurisdictions police investigative resources are so overwhelmed that they can rarely investigate burglaries, robberies, rapes, or other crimes where the offender has fled. That means that these crimes are less likely to be solved, and the offenders are likely to commit more crimes.

3. Intelligent and ambitious police officers seek drug enforcement jobs where there is more fame, faster promotions, and more resources, instead of applying their intelligence and ambition to solving predatory crimes.

4. The U.S. attorneys and district attorneys are overworked on drug cases. Robbery, car theft, burglary, and theft are lower priority than drug cases.

5. Police laboratory services are devoted to drug cases instead of other cases such as examining evidence in rape cases or burglary cases.

6. Public defenders are overworked. Drug cases carry mandatory sentences and thus have higher stakes to the client. Public defenders have less time to adequately represent their clients generally, including those who are innocent and mistakenly accused.

7. Judges are now case processors, managing overcrowded dockets, being evaluated on the speed with which they dispose of cases. They no longer are evaluated on the degree of fairness or the quality of justice they dispense. Individuals don't get individualized justice, they are simply products of a judicial assembly line.

8. Correctional resources are overwhelmed with drug possession and drug trafficking cases. Many jurisdictions are under orders to reduce overcrowding. Releasing authorities are forced to let offenders, even violent offenders, out of prison early to make room for new, often nonviolent offenders.

These are criminal justice system impacts from the prohibition of drugs. Consider the crime impacts from the prohibition of drugs.

How many of you have ever had a disagreement with a business about something you purchased? If you have a disagreement, the Uniform Commercial Code provides rules for the nonviolent resolution of the conflict. If your supplier sends defective goods, you know how to solve that conflict. At worst, you get caught in a lawsuit. How many of you are worried that a dispute with a supplier or a customer in your business is going to result in you being shot?

How are disputes in the drug marketplaces resolved? In the illegal drug business, which has conflicts between market participants just like all businesses, the *only* way for a conflict to be resolved is through violence. A drug dealer cannot sue a supplier for delivering a short weight, or less-than-the-represented purity. A drug dealer can't sue a distributor to obtain payment for product delivered on consignment. These conflicts are resolved through violence.

The illegal drug dealer doesn't take checks or credit cards, or send invoices. Payments are in cash. Legal businesses with large cash volumes, a liquor store or a supermarket, hire a professional security service to provide a licensed armed guard for protection. The illegal drug business needs the same protection, but it is supplied by criminals. Drug dealers can't call the police if someone steals the day's receipts. They have to use violence against the thieves. Thus drug dealers accumulate armories of powerful weapons in our neighborhoods which are placed in the hands of those likely and willing to use them, not those who have been trained, like the off-duty police officers at the supermarket. Those weapons are available for use in any kind of violence in the community.

The prohibition strategy increases property crime and violence and at the same time undermines the criminal justice resources available to address those crimes.

Let's Look at the Health Consequences of Our Prohibition Strategy

Because of prohibition there are no regulatory controls on the manufacture, packaging, or distribution of illegal drugs. As a result poisonings from contaminated illegal drugs are widespread. And overdoses from batches of illegal drugs of unknown strength are widespread.

Prohibition means that drug addicts get lower-quality drugs, and all of the protections we associate with the regulated drug industry are missing. Life for drug users and addicts is made worse, not better, by prohibition.

Important, legitimate pharmaceutical pain relievers like Percodan or Dilaudid, that can substitute for heroin, are extremely valuable and popular among addicts because their purity is known and their strength is known. Use of legal pharmaceutical narcotics poses lower health risks to users. But because their strength and purity are dependable they are more valuable on the street drug market. Thus they are very frequently stolen from pharmacies. Thus many pharmacies will not carry such drugs, to discourage robberies and burglaries, which means that patients who need these legal drugs find them harder to obtain.

The increased risk of carrying such drugs makes them more expensive to legal customers. The increased price, plus the increased security, plus the cost of stolen inventory all result in higher costs to insurance companies, which means higher health insurance premiums for all of us.

Okay, first, there are more overdoses. Second, there are more poisonings. Third, legitimate painkillers are harder to get. Fourth, there are more pharmacy robberies. Fifth, insurance premiums are higher to pay for legal drugs made more expensive. We are just beginning to get below the tip of the iceberg in the health area.

Sixth, one of the biggest consequences of the prohibition approach to drugs is the spread of HIV and other bloodborne diseases such as hepatitis. This is because IV syringes, i.e. needles, are classified as drug paraphernalia, and are hence illegal. That makes clean injection equipment scarcer and more expensive, and discourages addicts from carrying their own "works." Possession of works, because it is illegal, is probable cause for arrest.

The "war on drugs" says that it is more important to "send a message" that drug use is unacceptable by banning the sale of injection equipment, than it is to save lives by preventing the spread of HIV through the sharing of needles. In a growing number of cities around the world legal-needle laws and clean for dirty needle exchange programs are cutting down on the spread of HIV.

Seventh, the blood supply is put at risk for spreading HIV and hepatitis because addicts sell their blood to buy expensive illegal drugs.

Eighth, ordinary patients suffer needlessly because pain medication is withheld or underprescribed because doctors fear investigation if they prescribe strong narcotic pain relievers. This has been confirmed by the World Health Organization as an international problem, and it is a serious problem throughout the United States.

Ninth, ordinary patients needlessly suffer because a drug such as marijuana used to treat glaucoma (one of the leading causes of blindness in the

United States), to treat the nausea of anticancer chemotherapy, or to treat spasticity; or a drug like heroin, used in Britain and Canada as legal pain reliever, is withheld from patients who could benefit from the drug in order to maintain medically false legal distinctions.

Tenth, drug users avoid medical treatment because their illegal drug use may be detected in an examination and reported to law enforcement authorities. Their medical conditions become more severe and more expensive to treat. The very people who the drug laws are supposed to help are discouraged from obtaining medical treatment. All of us pay a greater price as a result.

Eleventh, more babies are put at risk because pregnant drug users stay away from prenatal clinics because they fear being reported and jailed. Laws rationalized as helping to protect babies, drive their mothers away from the care that could improve the babies' conditions.

Twelfth, hospital emergency rooms and trauma centers must triage patients such as you, or your family, because they are overwhelmed with prohibition-fueled gun-shot victims, with drug overdoses and poisonings, or with AIDS cases. When your children are injured on an athletic field, or you are injured in an automobile accident, or your spouse has a heart attack, or your mother's hip is broken in a fall, you or they, with those serious injuries, have to get in line behind the terrible cases that the prohibition anti-drug strategy has exacerbated.

Thirteenth, research into new psychiatric drugs has been delayed or eliminated because of prohibition. Doctors looking at the new research about brain chemistry are discouraged from engaging in research with drugs that affect the senses, moods, or feelings.

Fourteenth, drug prohibition leads to the spread of HIV, hepatitis, syphilis, gonorrhea, and other sexually transmitted diseases through prostitution engaged in to raise the money to pay for illegal drugs.

Is it [in] our interest to keep the price of drugs high and the people who are addicts in penury, or in the criminal underworld?

This Brings Us to the Economic Consequences to Our Community from Prohibition

Why are illegal drugs expensive? Is it good for us that illegal drugs are expensive? The U.S. Drug Enforcement Administration used to measure their success by the degree to which drugs became more expensive.

Illegal drugs are expensive because of risk. They are not expensive because of the raw materials, or the complexity of manufacture, or the cost of transportation of the product, or because of scarcity. None of the usual economic factors that makes goods expensive are present, but one. Very high risk is the principal factor in keeping the price of drugs high.

That risk is obvious—it is the risk of being arrested and imprisoned for long periods of time. Now it is obvious to everyone here that when one undertakes a legitimate investment of high risk, one does so in anticipation of making high gain. That is the case in illegal economics. By making drugs illegal and by zealously enforcing the drug laws we guarantee that those in the business will make enormous profits.

Who benefits from the high cost of drugs? The sellers benefit. They benefit handsomely. In our success-oriented, capitalistic society, drug selling is an extremely attractive means to make money quickly. But like every risky business, many people are discouraged from entering. But our culture teaches us to persevere, to run risks.

Prohibition increases the demand for medical care and makes medicines and medical services more expensive. Therefore health insurance costs go up, premiums go up, and fewer people have access to health care.

Prohibition increases the price of drugs. Therefore the amount of crime needed to be committed to pay for a given amount of drugs goes up. This increases costs, and increases the taxes to pay for more police, courts, and prisons.

Prohibition increases property crime: Therefore security costs go up, inventory losses increase, insurance losses and costs go up, therefore prices for all goods and services go up.

Prohibition strategists however point out one advantage to the society and the drug addict from increasing the retail or street price of drugs. To the extent that drug demand by addicts is price inelastic, by raising the price the addict has to work harder to obtain the drugs necessary to maintain the habit, thus, it is argued, encouraging the addict to give up the addiction and enter treatment. To the extent that drug demand is price elastic, increasing the price means that drug users will buy lesser quantities of drugs, and therefore there will be less intoxication.

However, there is evidence that the more effective law enforcement is in raising the price of drugs, the more crime has to be committed: more burglaries, more muggings, more car break-ins, more shoplifting. Stolen property is fenced, that is, it is sold for an enormous discount. The addict who has to pay $20 more per day for drugs has to steal $100 more in property. Multiply those numbers by tens of thousands of addicts.

Increasing the supply of stolen property drives down the wealth of a community. Instead of assets increasing in value, they are marked down. Imagine that every time a house in your neighborhood was sold it was sold for one-fifth or one-tenth of what was paid for it. Imagine the economic consequences for your neighborhood. A large supply of stolen goods depresses the market for legitimate retailers.

Other drawbacks from increasing the street prices of drugs are that traffickers get wealthier faster, more persons are encouraged to enter into careers of drug selling, and traffickers have access to more capital for corruption and other crime.

The enforcement efforts of the war on drugs have increased the amount of economic activity engaged in for noneconomic reasons. From 1983 through 1986 I conducted numerous hearings for the U.S. House Judiciary Committee on money laundering. The essence of money laundering is to convert the proceeds of crime into assets that cannot be traced to the crime but which the criminal can control. To carry out money laundering, one engages in numerous transactions, not because they are profitable or make economic sense, but because they serve to disguise the true parties to the transaction. This contributes to draining capital out of our neighborhoods.

Any of you who are in business know that to operate you need credit. Credit is vital to acquiring inventory, to expanding one's facilities. How do you compete with people who have access to unlimited funds, people like the drug dealers and their money launderers? Successful drug dealers control laundered assets which must be invested into legitimate enterprises to disguise their relationship to crime. To enter a legitimate business, instead of applying to a bank for a loan, the drug dealer "borrows" money from an overseas entity that he in fact controls, and which he in fact has capitalized. His "interest" payments are actually income into another pocket. Almost any kind of business is useful for laundering money—whether it makes or loses money is okay.

Let's consider the impact on legitimate investment of new law enforcement strategies to carry out the prohibition movement. You buy a house and it has a basement that you convert into an apartment. You are able to afford your mortgage because of that extra income. You rent the apartment and your tenant grows marijuana in the basement, or uses the apartment to package cocaine. You don't know about it. You have no basis to suspect. But your tenant is arrested. The government searches the apartment and seizes it, because one of the major enforcement tools of the war on drugs is "asset forfeiture." As soon as the government seizes that apartment you stop getting any rent.

Congress has given the government the power to seize property if there is probable cause to believe it is derived from drug trafficking. This is very important because "probable cause" is all that it has to show to win legal title to property it seizes. You could lose the apartment. Even though there is no evidence that could result in convicting you of a crime, there may be enough evidence to take your apartment away. The government doesn't have to prove the property was derived from drug trafficking by proof beyond a reasonable doubt. It doesn't have to prove a preponderance of the evidence. All it has to demonstrate to win permanent control of the property is the likelihood that the property was being used to conduct illegal activity. It just has to establish "probable cause"—the same level of suspicion needed to justify the arrest of someone or to satisfy a judge that he or she is authorized to issue a search warrant. There is no presumption of innocence. The burden of proof is on you who own the property to prove that the property was not derived from drug trafficking.

To make this power especially easy for law enforcement to use, the seizure of property can be made before anyone is indicted or accused of a crime. To make the use of this power especially tempting, the law enforcement agency gets to keep the property it seizes. The proceeds don't go to finance the general expenses of the government like other receipts, from fines, fees, or taxes—these funds stay in the hands of law enforcement agencies to use as they see fit.

What I have outlined is how prohibiting aggravates our crime problem, how it undermines our health care system, and how it is sapping our economy. Now some will say, drugs do that, drugs are the problem.

My response is that drugs don't exist in a vacuum. They are in our society as part of a system that we have set up. We must ask if the system is the best system. I have described what I argue are the costs of prohibition. Perhaps those costs are necessary to bear if prohibition will rid us of drugs.

Perhaps we might decide that as costly as prohibition is, we can afford it. Well, is the investment a good investment? Can prohibition succeed at some reasonable time in eliminating the cultivation of drug crops, or stopping the manufacture of drugs, or stopping the shipment of drugs or in arresting or deterring the drug sellers, or in eliminating demand? I spent nine years working with members of Congress in trying to find answers to those questions. My answer is no. The members whom I worked with want to be reelected. They will refuse to surrender. Every two years, about a month before election day, they pass a new antidrug, anticrime bill that will win the war on drugs.

Our Prohibition Strategy is Doomed to Continue to Fail

Crops of opium, coca, and marijuana can't be controlled overseas. Even in the United States, with our technology and sophisticated law enforcement, marijuana cultivation remains a major industry.

Shipments of drugs will continue to be smuggled into America. We are too big an importer of legitimate goods, over a trillion pounds of legal cargo—but we import less than half a million pounds of heroin and cocaine. Even the military can't stop drugs. Drugs become much more valuable once they're in the United States—many times their replacement cost overseas. No more than a small fraction, 10 to 20 percent, of all drug shipments can be stopped.

Domestic clandestine laboratories easily and cheaply synthesize new drugs.

Traffickers can't be eliminated. The profits are too great. New people enter the business every time someone is arrested—we can't find, let alone prosecute, more than a small fraction. If we let go every thief, robber, murderer, rapist, burglar, car thief, forger, bank robber, counterfeiter, and every other criminal who wasn't arrested for selling drugs, we would not have enough room in prison for all the drug sellers.

Drug users can't be stopped by force. Too many people like the effects from drugs. We can't punish more than a tiny fraction of the users. We can't afford to simply build more prisons. Many of the proposed punishments do more damage to the lives of the users than the drugs themselves.

So What Can Be Done?

I call my program "comprehensive intoxication management." In a fundamental way, our society must address the many different factors that contribute to the demand for drugs: the inadequacy of our schools, inadequate employment opportunities, the alienation in many types of employment, the dysfunctional nature of so many of our families, the compulsion toward success and achievement, the many factors that lead to psychic pain in our complex and stressful culture.

We must undermine the drug culture, ending the promotion of drug use (particularly alcohol and tobacco) and mute the messages that drugs are a necessary ingredient for sex, for companionship, for fun, or to demonstrate success or sophistication.

We need to become a recovery society. Instead of building monuments to individual consumption, we need to build the institutions of community enrichment. The values of our competitive culture have to change. The ethos of the 1980s, "We're Number 1, We're the greatest," are the ethos of cocaine use. It is no wonder that basketball stars, salesmen, and lawyers used cocaine so extensively. The sub-ethos, "I don't have time for the pain," is the other cultural prop for drug use.

Preventing drug abuse will be a long and slow process. Effective anti-drug education cannot simply be, "Just say no!" Drug education is more appropriately drug use education: how to make wise and informed drug use decisions. It must be comprehensive for over-the-counter drugs, prescription drugs, and "recreational" drugs (including alcohol). Rituals for controlling drug use should be reintroduced in the society. Perhaps drug use should be a licensed behavior. Why do we assume that any person over 21 should legally drink alcohol, when we know that at least 10 percent of the adult population will have problems with drinking?

Violations of public safety in the course of using drugs must be subject to sanctions, i.e. driving a vehicle under the influence of drugs or alcohol. That is true "user accountability." When a person is convicted of driving under the influence of alcohol, their alcohol consumption license is suspended.

"Vendor accountability" is also necessary. Prohibition on sales to minors must be enforced. Sales to those who have lost their drug use privileges should be prohibited.

We must offer treatment to all those who want to stop using drugs, but recognize that treatment is a slow process, and recidivism is a part of that process.

The goal of comprehensive intoxication management is temperance—temperate use of drugs and alcohol. The point is not to legalize or decriminalize drugs, the point is to reduce the harm to society and individuals from the fact that drugs are a part of the environment, and cannot be eradicated.

Ten Principles of Intoxication Management

1. Redefine our drug strategy goal: We will try to reduce to a minimum the harms from drug use in our society, and maximize the benefits.

2. There are no magic solutions to the problems of crime, violence, and drug abuse. There will continue to be addicts and crime no matter what we do.

3. Move slowly—not everything can be managed or regulated at once. Developing a regulated and policed market won't be easy or simple. Alcohol regulation (that is the regulation of just one drug) now has over 10,000 different federal, state and local laws for beer, wine, and whiskey. That is a clue that developing a regulatory scheme that is comprehensive can't be accomplished overnight.

4. Be comprehensive. We must tighten up on alcohol and tobacco, the big killers in America. Last summer, in New York a baby taken away from her "crack-addicted" mother was killed by her drunken foster mother (*New York Times*, 6-23-90). Let's end the availability of tobacco to children.

5. Adopt a public health approach, not a criminal approach, toward all drugs. Regulation has to include antidrug education. Honest prevention works. Cigarette smoking is down. Twenty-five million cigarette addicts have quit in the past 25 years. We don't jail or urine test cigarette smokers. We aren't defoliating North Carolina.

6. Make compassion the basis for dealing with drug users and drug addicts. Addicts must not be treated like Old Testament lepers. Heroin addicts who won't want to quit ought to get clean, cheap heroin to prevent crime and disease. Medical assistance has to be easily available. This is a step in researching a policed and regulated market.

7. Experiment with means of administration that are easier to control, socially and culturally, as well as legally. Smoking drugs, nicotine, cocaine, heroin, marijuana, leads to more intense rushes. Oral ingestion is less intense and less habit-forming. We don't want to legalize crack, therefore we might examine whether the availability of beverage forms of cocaine can pull crack users out of that market. Some physicians argue that opium eating, while addictive, is far less dangerous than injecting heroin. We should experiment and find out if this will improve the lives of addicts, even if it doesn't "end addiction."

8. Drug buyers should not have to patronize criminals. Therefore, marijuana could be taxed and sold to adults in packages with warning labels, minus promotion like tobacco and alcohol. Break the drugs and crime connections. Take the tens of billions of dollars in annual profits away from organized crime.

9. Drugs should not be promoted or advertised. A significant sector of the current legal drug market does not have consumer-directed advertising. The public doesn't see ads selling brands of penicillin. Other markets don't have advertising either. You don't see ads saying, "Buy IBM stock, double your money in 60 days." End the advertising of drugs to children through "Spuds McKenzie," the Camel "Smooth Character" and the like.

10. Insist upon genuine user accountability and responsibility. Drug or alcohol use cannot be an excuse for criminal or negligent conduct. In critical safety situations test for actual impairment, not for past use of intoxicants. Drug use can be dangerous. We can't save everybody from vices. But surveys show few Americans would try dangerous drugs even if they were legal.

Conclusion

The best control in a democracy is self-control, not police control. Encourage the development of self-control, not society's reliance upon police control which weakens individual responsibility.

Be confident that real pleasures are truly better than artificial pleasures, and that real accomplishments are more rewarding than imaginary accomplishments. When drug use is managed and drug sales are regulated, legally, culturally, and individually, we won't be a nation of zombies.

Ending the prohibition approach to drugs will free us from a great deal of hysteria, racial stereotyping, and scapegoating. Adopting a management approach toward the drug problems will encourage us to focus on the profound problems in all society of which drug use and abuse are symptomatic.

QUESTIONS FOR DISCUSSION

15.1 Can government legislate morality? Does the very fact that an activity is illegal affect the behavior of people?

15.2 Would the legalization of drugs deglamorize them and make their use less attractive to the young?

15.3 What is the bigger problem—the effect of drug use on society or the increase in violent crime that is associated with drug trafficking?

Chapter
16

What Explains the Inequalities of Income and Wealth in America?

INTRODUCTION

During the boom years of the 1980s (1983–1989), the disparities in wealth and income widened between America's upper middle class and the poor. The mean family income for the poorest one-fifth grew only $1000 while the richest one-fifth of American families saw their mean income increase by over $15,000. Few quarrel with these facts, but many dispute their causes. The rising economic tide of the 1980s did not raise the boats of the poor.

Liberals place a large proportion of the blame on the tax and spending policies of the Reagan administration; conservatives claim that the deterioration of the family and the growth of single-parent families with its disproportionate impact on the poor was the culprit.

Robert S. McIntyre argues in the following selection that the so-called "trickle-down" theory, whereby reduced taxes on the wealthy and the corporations would produce more savings and investment and thus more jobs and income for the poor, did not work in the 1980s. The Reagan tax cuts, he claims, enlarged the deficit and put more money in the pockets of the rich without benefitting the poor. McIntyre would rewrite the tax laws to place a greater burden of taxation on the wealthy.

Representative Bill Archer (R-Texas) defends the Reagan policies and asserts that during the 1983–1989 boom the mean income of every income quintile rose, that federal income taxes on the poor fell, and that the percentage of taxes paid by the rich increased. Archer does acknowledge that "low-income families are not sharing equally in our nation's economic growth." Archer does not place the blame for this at the feet of the national administration. He sees three primary explanations for the growing disparity between rich and poor: (1) fewer high paying jobs for those with only a high school education; (2) the growth of two-income families among the upper income groups; and (3) the increase in the number of children living with single mothers (over 40 percent of female-headed families with children live in poverty).

Both authors seem to agree that the Social Security payroll tax (in 1992 it was 7.65 percent on the first $55,500 in earnings) is the major reason for the disproportionate impact of federal taxes on the poor. Beyond that point, however, they have far different views of the responsibility of the federal government for the tragic condition of the nation's poor.

Who's the Fairest of Them All?
The Truth About the 1980s
Representative Bill Archer

The most remarkable characteristic of the last Congress was the level of misinformation that accompanied the now infamous budget debate. Democrats skillfully deployed a series of charges against the Reagan-Bush policies of the 1980s to advance their case for increased taxes and spending. The charges were repeated incessantly by the media and became a kind of muzak against which the budget minuet proceeded. When the music stopped, Americans were left with a huge new bill for an exceedingly fat troupe of federal dancers. Now that the music has started again, it seems advisable to conduct a dispassionate analysis of the critics' arguments.

The case against the Reagan-Bush policies boils down to four assertions: (1) tax cuts of the early 1980s starved the federal government of revenues; (2) reduced revenues forced Congress to slash spending, particularly on social programs, creating a "social deficit"; (3) this social deficit was exacerbated by the growth of income among the rich and the reduction of income among average and low-income families; and (4) tax policy favored the rich by shifting the tax burden to less wealthy families.

These bumper-sticker slogans belie the facts. In reality, during the 1980s, Congress had an additional $1.9 trillion to spend on favored programs, including $1.1 trillion from higher tax revenues; social spending on children and families increased 18 percent; the mean inflation-adjusted income of families reached an all-time high of $41,506, about 11 percent above its level at the peak of the last business cycle in 1979; the mean income of every income quintile rose every year between 1983 and 1989, though the bottom quintile in 1989 still had a lower mean income than in 1979; and the percentage of federal taxes paid rose for the top 5 percent of families while falling for the remaining 95 percent.

CONGRESS'S $2.4-TRILLION SPREE

The first charge, that tax cuts have led to lower federal revenues, is the starting point in most media debates about the economy. Like much conventional wisdom, it's simply not true. Revenues stood at $1.07 trillion in 1990, 35 percent above the 1980 level when adjusted for inflation. Federal revenues in 1980, the last year of the Carter administration, were $796 billion in 1990 dollars. Over the next 10 years, federal revenues averaged $906 billion annually in 1990 dollars, about 14 percent higher than in 1980. Over the decade, a total of $1.1 trillion flowed into the treasury in excess of that which the treasury would have received if revenues had remained at the 1980 level.

Of course, revenues are not the only source of money available to Congress. Congress occasionally borrows money to maintain—or create new—levels of federal spending. The federal deficit was $114 billion in 1980. Over the next 10 years, the deficit averaged $196 billion, about $82 billion above the 1980 level. Over the decade, Congress had at its disposal a total of $822 billion in borrowed money above the 1980 level of borrowing adjusted for inflation.

With its $1.1 trillion in additional revenue and $822 billion of borrowed money, Congress had more than an additional $1.9 trillion to spend. But even this figure is an underestimate of the additional money at the disposal of Congress during the decade. The famous Reagan spending cuts, to be discussed in greater detail below, resulted in substantial savings in some government programs. The federal government spent less in 9 of the 18 federal budget functions over the 10-year period than it would have spent had the 1980 spending level, adjusted for inflation, been maintained. The major reductions came in energy, employment and training, community and regional development, and general government. Taken together, about $500 billion was cut from these various functions.

Add this to the $1.9 trillion in new revenue and borrowing, and Congress had a grand total of $2.4 trillion additional or reallocated money to spend over the decade. Not bad for a pauper like Uncle Sam.

"SAVAGE BUDGET CUTS"

As a result of budget starvation, so the media and Democratic folklore goes, Congress was forced to cut spending, especially on social programs. Members of Congress, special interests, and members of the media hummed a refrain of deprivation, claiming that millions of Americans lost vital government benefits because safety net programs were savagely slashed to the bone. A careful examination of government budget figures, however, reveals that over the eight-year period beginning in 1981, during which the population increased 8 percent, the population under age five increased 11 percent, and the number of people in poverty increased by less than 1 percent, federal spending on children and families increased 18 percent.

Table 16.1 summarizes federal spending on major federal programs designed primarily to help families with children. In constant dollars, the federal government spent $19 billion more in 1989 than in 1981 on 38 different programs that provided income support, nutrition, social services, education and training, health services, and housing to America's children and families.

Table 16.1 does not include the nation's two largest social programs, Social Security (except the small fraction of benefits paid to dependent children) and Medicare. These programs were excluded in order to focus attention on programs that provide primarily for nonelderly families, the very programs critics assert were most devastated by cuts. If Social Security and Medicare had been included, the increase in social spending over the period would have been $89 billion rather than $19 billion and 25 percent rather than 18 percent.

The Reagan-Bush years were hardly a period of declining federal spending on social needs; indeed, social spending during the period sometimes seemed exceedingly generous. Consider developments in the funding of child-care programs. Throughout the period, but especially after 1985, the nation was subjected to insistent claims that families were experiencing a day-care crisis. Census Bureau reports showed that the federal government was already paying about one-third of the nation's total day-care bill, not including $4 billion or so provided directly to low-income families with children through the Earned Income Tax Credit (EITC). Even so, a lively three-year battle was fought over additional funding for day care and the EITC.

Table 16.1   CONSTANT DOLLAR SPENDING ON MAJOR SOCIAL PROGRAMS IN 1981 AND 1989

Spending program	Year		Change	
	1981	1989	In $	In %
Income support				
Aid to Families with Dependent Children	$ 9,112	$ 9,000	$ −112	−1%
Earned Income Tax Credit*	2,562	6,632	4,070	159
Child Support Enforcement	588	941	353	60
Supplemental Security Income	8,576	11,300	2,724	32
Social Security Dependents	15,410	11,000	−4,410	−29
Military Survivors	441	804	363	82
Workers Compensation–Federal	840	988	148	18
Black Lung	2,144	1,400	−744	−35
Subtotal	**$39,673**	**$42,065**	**$ 2,392**	**6%**
Nutrition				
Food Stamps	10,988	10,300	−688	−6
School Lunch	3,216	3,100	−116	−4
School Breakfast	430	510	80	19
Child-Care Food	390	669	279	72
Commodity Assistance	847	530	−317	−37
WIC	1,206	1,900	694	58
Subtotal	**$17,077**	**$17,009**	**$ −68**	**0%**
Social service				
Social Services Block	4,020	2,700	−1,320	−33
Dependent Care Credit*	1,538	2,442	904	59
Head Start	1,072	1,200	128	12
Foster Care	407	1,023	616	151
Community Services Block	705	381	−324	−46
Subtotal	**$ 7,742**	**$ 7,746**	**$ 4**	**0%**
Education and training				
Education of Disadvantaged	3,484	4,000	516	15
Education Block Grant	686	463	−223	−33
Handicapped Education	1,172	1,475	303	26
Vocational Education	820	826	6	1
Impact Aid	914	733	−181	−20
Defense Schools	512	821	309	60
Training Disadvantaged	2,814	1,800	−1,014	−36
Jobs Corps	752	742	−10	−1
Summer Youth Training	1,124	709	−415	−37
Subtotal	**$12,278**	**$11,569**	**$ −709**	**−6%**

(continued)

Table 16.1   (continued)

Health				
Medicaid	5,494	7,700	2,206	40
Maternal & Child Block	519	554	35	7
Community Health Centers	434	415	−19	−4
Alcohol, Drug Abuse Block	695	806	111	16
Indian Health	925	1,081	156	17
Federal Employees	3,350	7,800	4,450	133
Military Health	7,638	12,700	5,062	66
Subtotal	**$ 19,055**	**$ 31,056**	**$12,001**	**63%**
Housing				
Public Housing	3,216	3,200	−16	0
Leased	4,154	9,800	5,646	136
Rental	891	626	−265	−30
Subtotal	**8,261**	**13,626**	**5,365**	**65**
Grand Total	**$104,086**	**$123,071**	**$18,985**	**18%**

*These are updated figures taken from *Background Material and Data on Programs within the Jurisdiction of the Committee on Ways and Means.* Washington, D.C.: U.S. Government Printing Office, 1991, pp. 901, 907.

Note: All figures are millions of constant 1989 dollars; some of the figures include expenditures for adults other than parents.

Source: House, S.L. *Federal Programs for Children and Their Families* (90–131 EPW). Washington, D.C.: Congressional Research Service, 1990, Table 3, pp. 25–29.

Republicans argued that whatever funds were available should be used to expand Head Start and to give money directly to working families with children through an expanded EITC. Democrats agreed that Head Start should be expanded and that some money should be spent on the EITC. But many congressional Democrats, and their allies in the day-care community, countered with their traditional big-government message that the day-care crisis could be effectively addressed only by a huge federal program that would impose federal standards on state authority to regulate, would professionalize care, and would provide day-care subsidies to families earning up to $40,000. Against these two positions, both notable for the amount of new federal spending involved, only a few isolated voices could be heard making the quaint argument that whatever Congress decided to do, only moderate new funds should be spent.

Although the original bill sponsored by the Bush administration proposed spending about $10 billion over five years, every round of the debate resulted in more expensive proposals. By the time Congress actually passed a bill, most of the major players got at least part of what they wanted—at a price tag of $23 billion over five years.

The federal government expects to spend about $85 billion over the next five years on "old" day-care and children's tax credit programs that existed before last year's bill. This figure includes, among other programs, $19.8 billion for Head Start, $6.6 billion for the Child Care Food Program, $34.5 billion for the Earned Income Tax Credit, and $16.6 billion for the Dependent Care Tax Credit. Adding to this amount the $23 billion in new spending approved in last year's bill brings total spending on day care, Head Start, and the EITC to the spectacular sum of $108 billion.

INCOME STAGNATION FOR THE POOR

The third charge levied against Republican policies is that family income declined or remained stagnant during the 1980s. Unlike congressional pauperism and reduced social spending, the issue of income stagnation and decline for some families is real and serious. But we must peel through several layers of rhetoric to get at the real problem.

The basic claim that average family income has declined is hopelessly incorrect. After 1983 the economic recovery increased the income of families in every quintile, including the lowest, and families in every quintile except the lowest achieved and then surpassed their highest income ever. In 1989, the mean inflation-adjusted income of families increased for the seventh straight year and reached its all-time high of $41,506, about 11 percent above its level at the peak of the last business cycle in 1979 and 17 percent above its low during the recession year of 1982. (During this same period, median family income increased nearly 13 percent, from $30,394 in 1982 to $34,213 in 1989.)

A more sophisticated version of the declining family income charge is that the income of families at the bottom of the income distribution decreased. There is some truth in this assertion. In 1989, the mean income of families in the lowest 20 percent (quintile) increased for the sixth straight year to $9431 (see **Table 16.2**). Unfortunately, this amount was still about 4 percent below the mean income of $9801 registered by families in the bottom quintile in 1979. And in relative terms, at 4.6 percent, their share of the total income pie in 1989 was lower than at any time since at least the 1960s.

It is troubling that low-income families are not sharing equally in our nation's economic growth. But before we rush to blame government policy for this disparity, we should examine the underlying causes of income stagnation at the bottom of the income distribution.

DECLINING MALE WAGES

One problem is wages. Again, despite claims to the contrary, average wages increased throughout the economic recovery if we include supervisory as well as production workers and all forms of employee compensation including fringe benefits. However, if we examine wage growth at various points in the

Table 16.2   MEAN FAMILY INCOME BY QUINTILE IN CONSTANT 1989 DOLLARS, 1970–1989

| Year | Income quintile | | | | |
	Lowest fifth	Second fifth	Third fifth	Fourth fifth	Highest fifth
1970	9,070	20,341	29,412	39,674	68,224
1971	9,103	20,047	29,331	39,723	68,419
1972	9,518	20,968	30,799	42,059	72,945
1973	9,783	21,351	31,370	42,872	73,557
1974	9,636	21,035	30,783	42,172	72,121
1975	9,291	20,235	30,153	41,288	70,541
1976	9,509	20,740	31,017	42,379	72,440
1977	9,361	20,817	31,394	43,325	74,276
1978	9,650	21,475	32,319	44,530	76,566
1979	9,801	21,623	32,657	44,970	77,922
1980	9,286	20,852	31,588	43,828	75,049
1981	8,906	20,144	30,916	43,411	74,419
1982	8,427	19,834	30,381	43,093	75,903
1983	8,409	19,869	30,634	43,668	76,823
1984	8,692	20,406	31,554	45,123	79,518
1985	8,808	20,677	31,985	45,845	82,510
1986	9,095	21,396	33,204	47,447	86,423
1987	9,248	21,734	33,749	48,301	88,271
1988	9,284	21,712	33,787	48,524	89,033
1989	9,431	22,018	34,206	49,213	92,663

Note: Mean incomes are in 1989 CPI-U-X1 adjusted dollars.

Source: U.S. Bureau of the Census, *Money Income and Poverty Status in the United States,* 1989, Series P-60, No. 168. Washington, D.C.: U.S. Government Printing Office, 1990, p. 30.

income distribution during the 1980s we find some very unsettling numbers. For males, real hourly earnings decreased for all but earners in the top quintile. The decline in hourly earnings was less than 0.3 percent for males in the next-to-highest income quintile, slightly under 1 percent for those in the middle quintile, and slightly greater than 1 percent for those in the bottom two quintiles.

Most economists agree that education plays an important role in this wage decline. Over 85 percent of Americans, including 81 percent of blacks and 62 percent of Hispanics, now receive a high school degree before the age of 29. Unfortunately, our economy no longer has very many high-paying jobs for young people who have only a high school education or less. Richard Freeman of Harvard and his colleagues have shown that between 1973 and 1987 the real wages of high school dropouts fell by about 20 percent. Wages of those with 12 years of education fell by over 13 percent. The reality of today's global marketplace is that high wages go to the highly educated. Brawn and stamina are not as well rewarded as they were in a less technological society.

We now offer one of the most expensive, if not the most effective, public education systems in the world. We provide generous college grants and loans to students from low-income families. Last year the Congress significantly expanded the already extensive tax breaks we provide for low-wage workers, especially those with families. Thus, the federal government continues to maintain and even expand programs that help young Americans assume a productive place in the nation's economy; Congress also subsidizes the wages of those who are able to command only low wages. But the major responsibility for low wages does not lie with government programs. At some point we simply must help young adults face the cold facts: If they want good wages in our technological society, they must obtain education or training beyond high school. Those who emphasize the role of government programs obscure the extensive and difficult changes in personal behavior upon which our future depends.

THREE MILLION SINGLE MOTHERS IN POVERTY

Another important contributor to income stagnation is family breakdown. In 1989, married-couple families had median incomes of $38,547. By contrast, female-headed families had median incomes of $16,442. Similarly, the poverty rate for married-couple families was under 6 percent as compared with over 32 percent for female-headed families.

Between 1980 and 1988 the number of female-headed families with children increased by 830,000. Worse, this increase was accounted for almost entirely by out-of-wedlock births. Earnings of never-married mothers are even lower than those of divorced mothers. These disastrous demographic trends added substantially to the number of Americans receiving low wages or living in poverty. The most generous social policies will be ineffective in greatly reducing poverty and dependency, so long as the number of children living with single mothers, and especially with never-married mothers, continues to increase.

In addition to declining wages and the increasing number of out-of-wedlock births, a third factor contributing to problems with family income is lack of participation in the work force. Unfortunately, there are several indications that the level of nonwork among low-income families increased even during a period of rapid job creation. Between 1959 and 1989, for example, the percentage of poor families reporting some earnings declined from 67.5 to 50. Over the same period, the percentage of poor families headed by a full-time worker declined from 31.5 to 16.2.

Table 16.3 illustrates the problem in the starkest terms. Families in the highest income quintile had an average of 1.28 year-round, full-time workers in 1970. By 1986, these families had increased work output substantially to an average of 1.42 workers. By contrast, as shown in the last panel, families in

Table 16.3   NUMBER OF FULL-TIME, YEAR-ROUND WORKERS IN VARIOUS FAMILY TYPES BY INCOME QUINTILE

Family type	Year		
	1970	1980	1986
Highest quintile			
All Families with Children	1.28	1.38	1.42
Married Couples	1.31	1.41	1.45
Single Mothers	0.75	0.93	0.92
Middle three quintiles			
All Families with Children	0.95	0.99	1.06
Married Couples	0.99	1.09	1.18
Single Mothers	0.31	0.39	0.39
Bottom quintile			
All Families with Children	0.42	0.28	0.27
Married Couples	0.63	0.57	0.61
Single Mothers	0.05	0.02	0.03

Source: Congressional Budget Office. *Trends in Family Income: 1970–1986.* Washington, D.C.: U.S. Government Printing Office, 1988, Table A-15.

the bottom quintile had only an average of 0.42 workers in 1970. Over the next 16 years, as the number of workers in wealthier families increased, the number of workers in families in the bottom quintile decreased to 0.27—a decline of over 35 percent.

The reason for this decline is apparent. Married-couple families in the bottom quintile had an average of about 0.6 workers, but single-mother families had only 0.03 workers. Neither of these figures varied much over the 1970–1986 period. As the proportion of single-mother families relative to married-couple families in the bottom quintile increased, the average number of workers in all families was pulled down.

In 1989, there were about 7.4 million female-headed families with children; approximately 3.2 million of them lived in poverty. Here is the heart of America's greatest social problem: over 3 million single mothers in poverty, virtually none of them working full-time.

Partisan congressional debate on changing family income during the 1980s was too simplistic. Yes, average wages of production workers declined. Yes, family income at the bottom of the income distribution failed to reach the levels reached in the 1970s. Democrats were only too glad to ascribe these developments to alleged help-the-rich, forget-the-poor instincts of Republicans. Republicans, overly sensitive to this charge, acted as if denying the problem would make it disappear. But careful analysis, by both liberal and conservative scholars, has shown that education, family composition, and work effort play the lead roles in the drama of family income.

Only on the editorial pages can government play the role of *deus ex machina*. In the real world, the solution is for the nation to return to strong family values, for our children and young people to once again take effort and responsibility seriously, and for adults to turn away from welfare and choose instead the uncertainty that inevitably comes with self-reliance. Social policy can play no more than a supporting role in these achievements.

LOWER INCOME TAXES FOR ALL

Yet another charge against the policies of the 1980s is that changes in the tax code favored the rich. This accusation is the centerpiece of the onslaught against Republicans and the issue of "tax fairness" became a central theme of the budget wars.

According to estimates made by the Congressional Budget Office, in 1980 the 20 percent of families with the highest earnings paid 27.3 percent of their income in taxes. This percentage then declined to 25.8 in 1990. By contrast, the percentage of income paid in federal taxes by the lowest quintile of earners increased over the same period from 8.4 to 9.7.

Mountains of myth and $165 billion in new taxes were built on the foundation provided by these data. The plausibility of the fairness case was further advanced by the fact that marginal tax rates in the top brackets had declined in 1981 and again in 1986. When Ronald Reagan became president in 1981, the top tax rate was 70 percent; by the end of his second term it was 33 percent.

Both the changes in percentage of income paid by low-income and wealthy taxpayers and the decline in tax rates provide plausible evidence that fairness—defined by Democrats as making middle-income and wealthy citizens pay an ever-increasing percentage of their income in taxes—decreased during the 1980s. But before we leap to any conclusions, a more detailed analysis is in order.

Total federal taxes are a summary measure of several quite different types of taxes. The biggest revenue producer is the individual income tax, which is explicitly designed to collect a higher percentage of income from the rich than the poor. As we have seen, families in the top quintile paid a lower percentage of their income in total federal taxes in 1990 than in 1980. Similarly, they paid lower effective *income* taxes (as opposed to total taxes) over this period; the decline was from 17.1 to 15.6 percent.

Families in the bottom four quintiles also paid less in income taxes. A major purpose of the tax code changes of 1981 and 1986 was to reduce everyone's income tax rates—and that is precisely what happened. Between 1980 and 1990, the decline in effective income tax rates for the highest quintile was about 9 percent, the decline for the middle three quintiles was around 20 percent, and the decline for the bottom quintile was 275 percent (in part because the 1986 reforms removed around six million families from the tax rolls altogether).

REGRESSIVE PAYROLL TAXES

Next to the income tax, the federal tax that has the biggest impact on taxpayers is the Social Security payroll tax. In fact, counting both the employer and employee share of the tax, roughly 75 percent of American families pay more in Social Security taxes than they do income taxes. Unlike the income tax, the payroll tax is a flat percentage for everybody. Moreover, it applies only to the first $51,300 (in 1990) in earnings. Any amount above $51,300 goes untaxed (although the tax increases of 1990 included raising the wage base for the Medicare portion of the payroll tax to $125,000).

Unfortunately, the payroll tax has increased several times since its inception in 1935. Just between 1977 and 1990, both the rate for employers and the rate for employees increased nine times from 5.85 percent to 7.65 percent.

The CBO tax model shows that payroll tax increases during the 1980s were regressive if measured as a percentage of family income. For the lowest-income quintile, the effective payroll tax rate increased by 41 percent from 5.4 to 7.6 percent; for the middle quintile by 23 percent from 8.7 to 10.7 percent; and for the upper quintile by only 15 percent from 5.9 to 6.8 percent.

This regressivity of the payroll tax is the major cause of the disproportionate impact of federal taxes on low-income families. By direct contrast, the income tax is progressive and getting more so. Thus, the most direct way to increase progressivity in the federal tax code would seem to be to reduce the payroll tax for low-income earners. But before anyone starts writing legislation, consider the following three points about payroll taxes.

First, in addition to increased rates, the taxable wage base was raised from $22,900 in 1980 to $51,300 in 1990, thereby subjecting more of the income of wealthier families to taxation.

Second, concerned with the impact of payroll taxes on families with children, in 1975 Congress enacted an earned income tax credit (EITC) that provided income tax forgiveness or, in the case of families that did not earn enough to owe income taxes, actual cash rebates. Substantially expanded several times since 1975, the credit now provides tax relief or cash rebates of as much as $1,000 to nearly 10.5 million families earning less than $20,000.

When the expansions enacted last year are fully implemented in 1994, the maximum value of the EITC will leap to $3,000.

Even now, the EITC more than offsets the entire amount of federal income tax paid by families in the lowest quintile. In 1980, families in the bottom quintile "paid" federal income taxes equal to a negative 0.4 percent of their income. In other words, the amount these families received back from the EITC was greater than the income tax paid in by an aggregate of around $600 million (in 1990 dollars). By 1990, the amount forgiven or returned to these families had more than tripled.

Third and most important, emphasizing payroll tax regressivity without paying attention to Social Security benefits produces approximately the same result as estimating the size of an iceberg by measuring the part sticking out of the water. A recent study by the Social Security Administration indicates that in 1987, the highest quintile of earners paid 42 percent of Social Security taxes, but received only 12 percent of the benefits. By contrast, the lowest quintile of earners paid 2 percent of the taxes, but received 19 percent of the benefits.

The famed regressivity of the Social Security tax, then, is mitigated by several factors that do not often find their way into speeches and editorials about the regressive impact of Social Security taxes on American families.

RICH MAN'S BURDEN

Thus far, our discussions of tax fairness have been confined to effective tax rates—the percentage of income paid in taxes by families at various points in the income distribution. Another useful measure of tax fairness is what might be called the tax burden, that is, the percentage of federal taxes paid by each income group. As a percentage of the federal income taxes actually paid between 1981 and 1987, the burden on the upper 5 percent of earners increased while the burden on the remaining 95 percent of families decreased. **Table 16.**4 contains actual tax return data collected by the Internal Revenue Service for 1981 through 1988. Here we see that the tax burden of both the upper 1 percent and 5 percent increased between 1981 and 1988, the former by nearly 56 percent and the latter by about 31 percent. Meanwhile, the tax burden of the bottom 50 percent declined by 25 percent.

Perhaps the most arresting number in Table 16.4 is the burden ratio. The burden ratio is obtained by dividing the average tax bill for families in the upper 1 percent by the average tax bill for families in the bottom 50 percent. In 1981, the burden ratio was $118; families in the upper 1 percent of the income range paid an average of $118 for each dollar paid by families in the bottom half of income. By 1988, the burden ratio had more than doubled to $240.

Table 16.4   PERCENTAGE OF FEDERAL INCOME TAXES PAID BY VARIOUS INCOME
GROUPS, 1981–1988

Year	Income group				Burden ratio*
	Top 1%	Top 5%	51st–95th percentile	Bottom 50%	
1981	18%	35%	57%	8%	$118
1982	19	36	56	7	129
1983	20	37	56	7	142
1984	21	38	55	7	143
1985	22	39	54	7	152
1986	25	42	52	7	191
1987	25	43	51	6	202
1988	28%	46%	49%	6%	$240

*Computed by dividing the average tax paid by families in the upper 1 percent by the average tax paid by families in the bottom 50 percent.

Note: Based on IRS tax return data; income data is for families.

Source: Frenze, C. The Federal Income Tax Burden, 1981–1987: A Senate Staff Report, Washington D.C.: Joint Economic Committee, Republican Staff, 1990.

INCENTIVES THAT WORKED

A final set of numbers from federal tax returns also deserves consideration. A fundamental tenet of incentive economics is that low tax rates encourage investment and growth while discouraging tax dodges and shelters. As a result, low tax rates can lead to increased tax revenue, as well as more fairness. The first post-war president to practice incentive economics was John Kennedy, who led the move to cut the top tax bracket from 91 to 70 percent in 1961. An economic boom followed, perhaps by coincidence. The next president to enroll in the incentive club was Ronald Reagan, who convinced Congress to reduce the top bracket from 70 to 50 percent in 1981 and 1982. An economic boom followed, again perhaps by coincidence. Reagan liked the results so much he lobbied for further reductions in tax rates amidst an overall reform of the tax code to abolish many deductions and credits and to encourage investment and saving. The 1986 simplified rate structure of 15, 28, and 33 percent became effective in the midst of an economic recovery. The recovery subsequently became the greatest in post-war history, with a 30 percent increase in GNP and around 18 million new jobs created between 1981 and 1990.

Critics maintained that cutting taxes would reduce federal revenues. The incentive economists countered that cutting the rates would increase revenues both because taxpayers would shelter less of their income and because new investments would stimulate growth and thereby increase the tax base. The incentive economists were right.

In constant dollars the federal individual income tax produced revenues of $360 billion in 1980 and $416 billion in 1988. That's an increase of over 15 percent in real dollars. Meanwhile, income taxes paid by the upper 1 percent increased from $66 billion to $106 billion, an increase of over 60 percent. The increase for the top 10 percent was from $177 billion to $237 billion, an increase of 34 percent. The remaining 90 percent of taxpayers actually paid $5 billion less in taxes in 1988 than in 1980, a decline of 2.5 percent. Thus, tax policy of the 1980s might be fairly summarized by three developments, all felicitous: lower rates, increasing revenues, increasing progressivity.

ALL-TIME SPENDING HIGHS

Ronald Reagan and George Bush tried to alter the course of the nation by reducing the size of government and the scope of its authority to interfere in almost every aspect of American social and economic life. Theirs was a view of limited, efficient, effective government that would leave in place the major programs of the New Deal and the Great Society. The safety net was not simply left intact; it was expanded substantially throughout the decade.

The three most significant domestic achievements of the era were reforming the tax code by reducing rates, broadening the tax base, and removing millions of poor and low-income families from the tax rolls; slashing inflation from about 10 percent in the Carter years to an average of around 4 percent during the Reagan-Bush years; and inspiring an economic expansion that created 18 million new jobs, raised average family income to an all-time high, and carried the GNP to nearly $5.5 trillion by 1990.

But the government containment strategy had limited success. On the tax side, the reforms of 1981 produced worthwhile reductions. Federal taxes declined from over 20 percent of GNP in 1981 to just under 20 percent in 1982 and to 18.1 percent in both 1983 and 1984. But after 1984, taxes once again began to rise. By the time of last year's budget debate, they were at historic highs: 1990 was the fourth consecutive year in which taxes were greater than 19 percent of GNP, a sustained level of taxation that has never before afflicted the nation.

The reason, of course, was monstrous levels of federal spending and borrowing. If we take federal spending as a percentage of GNP in five-year chunks beginning in 1955, the relentless rise is astounding: 17.9, 18.8, 19.3, 19.6, 21.3. Even the average during the first five years of the 1980s, including three years of the "savage" Reagan cuts, was 23.2—by far the highest in history. The combination of Reagan spending cuts working on the numerator and a rapidly expanding economy working on the denominator, abetted by the Gramm-Rudman-Hollings law and universal concern about the deficit, managed to reduce federal outlays slightly as a percentage of GNP in the years after 1985. During 1987, 1988, and 1989, spending did not exceed 23 percent of GNP. This level of spending was still higher than that of any peacetime period before the 1980s. But at least the federal giant had been contained.

Alas, the containment was only temporary. In 1990, the year of the great budget war, spending again jumped almost a full 1 percent of GNP, from 22.3 to 23.2, and was projected to grow even more in subsequent years. Under assault from the four charges examined above, Republicans were unable to defend either the tax reforms or spending containments they had achieved during the 1980s. As a result of the 1990 budget agreement, outlays will be at 25 and 24 percent of GNP in 1991 and 1992—their highest ever except during World War II. That's the bad news. The good news, such as it is, is that if Congress adheres to the budget agreement, spending will decline to about 21 percent of GNP by 1994. In view of the fact that this level of spending, though lower than the level for 1991 and 1992, was virtually unheard of before the 1980s, one's enthusiasm may be somewhat muted. Moreover, taxes will not decline at all. At 19.9 percent of GNP in 1994, they will be the third-highest in peacetime history.

Budget and tax reforms that had done so much for the nation during the 1980s are now being overcome by bumper-sticker arguments: Uncle Sam is a pauper; the safety net is tattered; family income is depressed; tax policy favors the rich. While the truth value of these arguments ranges from moderately incorrect to spectacularly false, proponents of the Reagan-Bush policies are now on the defensive. The facts are on our side. But unless we marshall them at every opportunity, we are guaranteed additional setbacks on the major tax and spending issues that define our political parties and chart the nation's future.

Borrow 'n' Squander

Robert S. McIntyre

Have you ever felt you're paying too much for what you get from the government? One of the legacies of the Reagan-Bush era is that middle-income families are paying more of their income in federal taxes than they used to, while getting far less back in programs and services. So why is the government running such huge deficits? Lower spending and higher taxes are supposed to be the standard prescription for reducing the deficit, not enlarging it. The answer is quite simple. Tax cuts for the very richest people and interest on the debt that was built up to pay for those cuts can explain the entire increase in the federal deficit over the past fifteen years.

Based on data from the Congressional Budget Office, I calculate that the richest million Americans—the top 1 percent of all families—will pay 30 percent less in federal taxes in 1992 than they would owe had the tax code remained as progressive as it was in 1977. (I use 1977 as the base year because it is just before the two "supply-side" tax acts: the 1981 Reagan tax act and its precursor, the 1978 capital gains tax cut.) That 30 percent tax cut amounts to an average tax reduction of $83,460 per super-rich family. In total, it comes to almost $84 billion in 1992.

But that's not all. The tax reduction for the very rich was not a one-shot, one-year event. It has been a growing cost to the treasury over the past 15 years, and it was paid for with borrowed money. The federal government did not have to increase its borrowing rate in the 1980s to pay for additional spending on programs and services. Social Security has amassed a large surplus, and the overall cost of all non-Social Security programs except interest and deposit insurance actually declined as a share of the gross national product from 1980 to 1990.

But the government did have to borrow—heavily—to pay for corporate and upper-income tax cuts. In fact, if everything else had been the same except for those tax cuts, then government borrowing over the past 15 years would have been more than a trillion dollars lower than it was. What does adding more than a trillion dollars to the national debt mean to the annual budget deficit? A huge increase in yearly interest payments. In fact, the interest due on the debt built up to pay for previous years' tax cuts for the very wealthy will be nearly $81 billion in 1992.

Thus the total 1992 cost of the supply-side tax reductions for the richest million families—adding up the $84 billion tax cut that they will enjoy in 1992 and the $81 billion in interest the government must pay on the debt incurred due to tax cuts for the rich in previous years—comes to a staggering $164 billion! Now, from fiscal 1977–1978 to fiscal 1992–1993, the federal deficit will have almost doubled as a share of the GNP—from 2.8 percent to 5.1 percent. That's an increase of $143 billion in fiscal 1992–1993. So the deficit is up by $143 billion, while tax cuts for the wealthy cost $164 billion.

This is hardly a coincidence. The growing cost of tax cuts for the rich closely parallels the growth in the deficit over the past decade. From fiscal 1982–1983 to fiscal 1990–1991, the average budget deficit was 1.7 percent of the GNP larger than in fiscal 1977–1978. In that same period, the cost of tax cuts for the richest 1 percent since 1977 (including interest) averaged 1.9 percent of the GNP. Of course, the correspondence is not perfect in every year. In the early 1980s, with the defense build-up, deficit growth outpaced the rich's tax cuts. In the late 1980s, after defense had passed its peak as a share of the GNP, the opposite took place. In the fiscal 1991–1993 period, however, the relationship is almost exact: The deficit is up by 2.6 percent of the GNP and tax cuts for the wealthy cost 2.6 percent of the GNP.

How can tax cuts for such a small proportion of our population cause such a large drop in tax revenues, and loom so large in the deficit picture? It's simple arithmetic. The really rich get a huge share of our nation's total income. In 1992 the richest 1 percent of the population will make $678 billion before taxes. That's more than the total income of the bottom 40 percent of all families. The $2.4 trillion of income concentrated on the top fifth of the nation's population is greater than the total income of the remaining four-fifths of American families.

While the rich got tax cuts, what about the rest of us? The CBO data show that for three out of four families (all but those in the poorest fifth and best-off 5 percent) federal taxes are now higher than in 1977. (Taxes on the poor were up for most of the 1980s but were cut back to pre-Reagan levels in last year's deficit reduction act.) For families in the middle fifth of the income spectrum (making about $32,000 a year), for instance, the average tax hike is $280.

The deal that the federal government offers average families looks even worse when you factor in spending changes. In fiscal 1990 interest on the national debt was up by 1.7 percent of the GNP compared with fiscal 1980—an increase of $94 billion in fiscal 1990 dollars. The cost of deposit insurance—zero in fiscal 1980—was almost $60 billion due to the savings and loan fiasco. And though down from its lofty mid-1980s apex, defense still cost $28 billion more in fiscal 1990 than in fiscal 1980 (in GNP-adjusted dollars).

Over the same period, however, spending on the entire rest of the government excluding Social Security fell from 9.9 percent of the GNP to 7.4 percent—a drop in 1990 dollars of $130 billion! Spending on the justice system and general government was 42 percent lower. Education and training outlays were down by 40 percent. Programs for the environment and natural resources were cut by 39 percent. Spending on roads and transportation dropped by 32 percent. Welfare and unemployment outlays went down by 21 percent. In total, the $130 billion decline in those traditional federal programs and services means that the typical family now gets an average of $1260 less from the government each year in such benefits.

George Will has quipped that the public liked Reaganomics because it gave them $1 worth of government for only 75 cents in taxes (the rest being borrowed). But for most families, the truth is exactly the opposite. Compared with a decade ago, middle-income families are getting a fourth *less* in traditional federal government services for every dollar they pay in taxes.

The "supply-side" redistribution of taxes and spending occurred even as incomes were shifting as well. The CBO estimates that from 1977 to 1992, average constant-dollar pretax income will decline by 13 percent for the poorest fifth of all families; fall by 10 percent for the next fifth; and drop by 7 percent for the middle fifth. The average income of families in the next 20 percent will rise by only 1 percent. But the richest 1 percent of the population will see its average inflation-adjusted income rise from $314,500 in 1977 to $675,900 in 1992—an increase of 115 percent.

The combination of the tax and income shifts in favor of the wealthy caused the share of total after-tax income going to the richest 2 percent of Americans to jump from 7.3 percent to 13.4 percent of the total—an increase of 84 percent. Meanwhile, the share of after-tax income fell for every other group except the best-off 5 percent.

Had the tax code remained as progressive as in 1977, there still would have been a shift in after-tax income toward the wealthy. But it would have been considerably less than actually occurred. On its own, the 30 percent tax cut that the top 1 percent will enjoy in 1992 explains almost two-fifths of this group's increased share of after-tax income. Without that tax cut, the rich's share of total income would be 11.1 percent of the total, rather than 13.4 percent. In addition, the tax changes contributed substantially to the huge gains that rich people obtained in their *pretax* incomes, due to their increased investment earnings on the portion of their tax cuts that they didn't immediately spend.

The purported rationale for the redistributionist supply-side policy, of course, was the old "trickle-down" theory that lower taxes on wealthy people and corporations would produce a boom in savings and investment. To its credit, Congress eventually recognized that the trickle-down approach was an abject failure, and reversed course. The monumental 1986 Tax Reform Act took back a quarter of the tax cuts that the richest 5 percent had received in earlier tax-giveaway bills and rolled back some of the previous tax increases that had hit most nonwealthy families, particularly the poor. And it made critical structural changes in the tax code to curb tax shelter abuses.

Last year Congress resisted the efforts of the Bush administration to raise taxes sharply on middle- and low-income families and to cut taxes even further on the rich. Instead, the deficit reduction act took back another small portion of the wealthy's tax cut and reduced taxes on the poorest families to their pre-Reaganomics level. But the sorry legacy of the Borrow 'n' Squander 1980s still looms over us. Only by restoring real tax fairness can we hope to solve our deficit problem—and start getting the government services and investments that our tax dollars are supposed to provide.

QUESTIONS FOR DISCUSSION

16.1 How much moral responsibility should the government take for the condition of the poor? During the 1960s President Lyndon Johnson declared a war on poverty with the hope of eradicating it in this country. Is this a proper and realistic goal for government?

16.2 Should the Social Security tax be altered from a flat 7.65 percent tax on the first $55,500 in earnings (1992 rates) to a progressive tax on all earnings?

16.3 Did the Reagan tax and budget policies contribute to the disparity in wealth and income or are these disparities the result of forces and behaviors beyond the control of government?

Chapter
17

Have Congressional Budget Reforms Helped or Hindered Our Deficit Problems?

INTRODUCTION

Since the mid-1970s Congress and the president have wrestled with various mechanisms for building some fiscal restraint into the budgetary process. The Congressional Budget and Impoundment Control Act of 1974 established timetables for the budget review process and created the Congressional Budget Office (CBO); the Balanced Budget and Emergency Deficit Control Act of 1985 (known as Gramm-Rudman-Hollings after its senatorial sponsors) mandated progressive cuts in the deficits to achieve a balanced budget in 1993; the Budget Enforcement Act of 1990 amended Gramm-Rudman and placed spending caps on specific categories—defense, international, and discretionary domestic spending.

Despite these well-intentioned efforts, the federal deficit grew unabated. In fiscal 1993, the year Gramm-Rudman set for a balanced budget, the CBO projected a budget deficit of over $350 billion. In fact, the CBO has projected large deficits continuing into the next century. The process was not supposed to work that way. Why has the deficit defied these reforms? In the mid-1980s, some blamed the increase on defense spending, but such spending declined in the late 1980s and early 1990s with the end of the Cold War.

By 1995, under the plan of President Bush, the defense budget should be only 3.4 percent of the gross national product (GNP)—the lowest percentage since before World War II.

Democrats blamed the Reagan tax cuts; Republicans blamed the failure of the Democratic Congress to cut domestic programs. Many blamed the failure of both parties to control entitlement spending. The 1990 Act did impose tough pay-as-you-go restrictions on the expansion of entitlement programs, but failed to control the rising costs of the existing programs, particularly Medicare, Medicaid, food stamps, and agricultural subsidies. Such entitlements, at about 45 percent of the federal budget in 1992, were projected to rise to 61 percent of the budget in 1995.

Stephen Moore argues that the 1990 budget agreement, which anticipated deficit reduction of $500 billion, was "a spectacular flop." He blames this upon forecasting methods that do not account for the debilitating impact of new taxes on the economy.

The Congressional Quarterly article by George Hager, "Budget Rules Under Fire," explains the complexities of the 1990 budget agreement and the temptations of the Congress to postpone the tough budget choices to later years. In "The Deficit: Trouble Ahead," the charts project the deficit rising well past the year 2000, and the text gives a brief explanation of the reasons.

All Pain, No Gain

Stephen Moore

Of all the gloomy economic news from Washington in recent months, perhaps the most frightening was the prediction by Office of Management and Budget Director Richard Darman that Congress and the president may hold another bipartisan budget summit in 1993. This would seem about as advisable for George Bush as it would have been for someone safely in a lifeboat to reboard the *Titanic*. The 1990 budget summit has already helped produce a sagging economy, soaring federal spending, and record deficits. America quite literally cannot afford any more of the budget summits.

Of course, if success in Washington is measured purely in terms of winning the rhetorical battle, then the budget deal has been a stunning triumph for the White House. The national media continue to speak of the summit package in reverential tones. The headline on an article by Alan Murray of the *Wall Street Journal* this July was typical: "Last Year's Budget Pact Gains New Admirers for Curbing Spending."

Seemingly no one has an unkind word to say about the deal. Rudolph Penner, former director of the Congressional Budget Office, says, "If you look at the fundamentals of the budget, the situation is improving." Even conservative Representative Newt Gingrich, a vocal opponent of the agreement when it was originally unveiled, now echoes the conventional wisdom: "The agreement has worked far, far better than I thought it would."

One can only wonder what possible criteria Mr. Gingrich and his colleagues use to measure success. If the primary objective of the $500-billion "deficit reduction" package was to, well, reduce the deficit, then the agreement could only be labeled a spectacular flop. Almost exactly one year ago, shortly before the start of the budget summit, the Congressional Budget Office predicted that the deficit would be $161 billion in 1991 and $124 billion in 1992. The budget summit was convened to *lower* these numbers.

Unfortunately, the budget numbers released show that it did the reverse. The 1991 deficit will be $282 billion—shattering by some $60 billion the previous record for red ink. And that was the report's good news. The White House now admits that next year's deficit spending will surge to $348 billion—almost triple the prebudget-summit estimate and $70 billion above the forecast when the president signed the deficit "reduction" package into law.

Darman and his co-conspirators have attempted to explain away this ocean of red ink by saying the higher deficits are due simply to "technical re-estimates." Only in Washington could a $70-billion budget revision— roughly the size of the combined net incomes of the 50 largest Fortune 500 companies—be blamed on an accounting glitch.

Even if Darman is telling the truth, however, there can be no denying the unhappy bottom line: If these new forecasts hold true, from 1991 through 1994 Congress will add close to $1 trillion to the national debt. This will be the nation's worst four-year fiscal performance ever. And remember those budget savings of $500 billion we were told over and over again the summit would generate? Sorry—sometime this summer they mysteriously vanished.

WHERE ARE THEY NOW?

Remarkably, these stratospheric deficits have hardly evoked a peep of protest in Washington. The mere suggestion that the budget summit has run amok is treated as politically incorrect speech. There is a conspiracy of silence among the national media, the pro-tax liberal Left, and the moderate, balanced-budget wing of the Republican Party—that is, all the people who, since the early 1980s, have hysterically predicted economic collapse unless deficits were reduced immediately. Where are these deficit fear-mongers now? They, too, have mysteriously vanished.

"Apparently there are two kinds of deficits," Reagan administration economist Paul Craig Roberts concludes sarcastically. "Reagan deficits deindustrialize America, force up interest rates, doom future generations, and suck up the world's savings. But Bush deficits, resulting from the old routine of taxing, regulating, and spending, cause hardly a ripple in the domestic or world economy." This indeed has become the prevailing view, despite the observable fact that the evil Reagan deficits corresponded with eight years of economic prosperity while the benign Bush deficits—and the pro-spending policies that created them—ground that prosperity to a halt.

The critical issue for Congress and the president now is not *whether*, but *why*, the budget summit led to this debacle. A primary reason is that Congress and the White House stubbornly refused to acknowledge the debilitating impact that their new taxes would have on the economy. In fact, the congressional forecasting models actually predicted that the budget deal would have a *favorable* economic impact, because higher taxes would reduce government borrowing and thus lower interest rates.

These same models were long ago exposed as defective. Two years ago, to demonstrate the intellectual bankruptcy of the congressional forecasting methods, Senator Bob Packwood asked the Joint Tax Committee of Congress to estimate how much revenue could be raised by imposing a 100 percent tax on all earnings over $200,000. As anyone with even an elementary understanding of economics knows, the answer is zero. But after the JTC ran the numbers through its computers, Packwood was told the tax would raise more than $100 billion per year. Evidently, the number crunchers on Capitol Hill have never been told that confiscatory taxation reduces the incentive to earn reportable income.

Table 17.1   THE FEDERAL DEFICIT BEFORE AND AFTER THE 1990 BUDGET AGREEMENT

	Pre-summit forecast July 1990	Current forecast July 1991
1991	$161	$282
1992	124	348
1993	132	246

Sources: Congressional Budget Office, "The Economic and Budget Outlook: An Update," July 1990; Office of Management and Budget, "Mid-Session Review of the Budget," July 1991.

TAXES WITHOUT REVENUES

This year's tax increase provides a case study of the Laffer Curve in action. For the previous six years, with almost no new taxes, federal revenues climbed by a healthy 8 percent per year. This year, with an increase in income-tax rates, a hike in the gasoline tax, the introduction of a 10 percent surcharge on luxury items, and a variety of other new levies, total federal revenues are crawling ahead by an anemic half a percentage point.

A particular source of embarrassment for the White House and congressional leaders has been the 10 percent tax on boats, aircraft, jewelry, and other luxury items. Masterminded as a fail-safe method of collecting from the "super rich," the levy has instead crippled the domestic boat and small-aircraft industries. What the masterminds seemed to have forgotten was that boats and airplanes are built by people almost none of whom are named Trump or Rockefeller. This year alone, some 9400 nonrich Americans will have lost their jobs—all because of a tax that has actually *cost* the treasury nearly $20 million. As one laid-off boat worker complained, "This Congress views jobs as luxuries."

What Congress still views as an absolute necessity, however, is spending money. Federal outlays are up 8 percent over last year, or double the rate of inflation, making a mockery of Darman's persistent claims that the summit agreement contains "the toughest budget enforcement system ever."

In its defense, the Bush administration has been courageously trying to hold the last vestiges of the budget agreement together, but the congressional Democrats long ago lost interest in belt-tightening. This summer they have rolled out their entire arsenal of New Deal, Keynesian, anti-recession spending ideas. Highlights include: a $5.8-billion unemployment-insurance extension bill, to show some compassion for the thousands of boat-industry employees and other workers thrown out of their jobs by the tax hike; Dan Rostenkowski's universal-health-insurance bill, to be paid for through a massive payroll-tax hike; and a $153-billion highway bill, containing more than four hundred porkbarrel road and transit projects—nearly one for every congressional district.

Herein lies the rub for Republicans. While the White House is determined, come hell or high water, to abide by the terms of the budget agreement, the Democrats clearly do not feel similarly honor bound. President Bush has thus committed the Republican Party to a path of unilateral economic-policy disarmament. The Democrats are free to spend, but the Republicans are forbidden to cut taxes.

Indeed, under the GOP's new politics of austerity, the White House has been immovable in its opposition to cutting any taxes. Social Security payroll-tax cuts? Bush lobbied to defeat them. The DeLay-Wallop Job Creation Act, linking cuts in payroll taxes and capital-gains taxes with expanded IRAs? Bush is against it. A proposal by Senator John McCain to repeal a pernicious provision of the budget deal requiring a three-fifths vote in the Senate to approve any tax cut? Bush wants to retain the super-majority requirement. Incredibly, Bush has even waffled on a Republican proposal to exterminate the luxury tax—the tax that doesn't raise any revenue!

Remember Bush's idea of cutting the capital-gains tax—the pillar of the Republicans' 1988 economic program? That became the first casualty of the 1990 budget summit; it has not been seen nor heard from since January, when Bush said he could not "find a way to pay for it."

Ironically, this is the line that liberal Democrats used exactly ten years ago in a futile attempt to block the Reagan supply-side tax cuts. Those income-tax-rate reductions eventually pulled America out of the deepest recession since the Great Depression and sparked a record 80 months of continuous prosperity. In contrast, for more than 20 months now Bush has presided over an economy that has recorded zero real GNP growth—one of the longest periods of stagnation.

The message should be obvious: By chaining himself to a budget agreement that has not spurred economic expansion, has not reined in spending, and has not reduced the deficit (and cannot do so), Bush is persuasively substantiating the Democrats' claim that this administration has no domestic agenda. In short, the 1990 budget deal is not a triumph, it is an albatross. Unless the White House soon recognizes this, the American public will be faced with two unattractive choices in the 1992 elections: a nonexistent Republican economic-growth agenda and a nonsensical Democratic one. The worry for the GOP is that you can't beat something with nothing.

Budget Rules Under Fire

George Hager

Tough new budget rules agreed to just a little over a year ago, after the 1990 budget summit, are under heavy attack and will almost certainly be revised, stretched, or even thrown out altogether this year.

Here is a guide to those rules:

Discretionary spending caps. Individual caps on defense, domestic, and international appropriations were originally set to last throughout fiscal 1993 before collapsing into a single cap on all discretionary spending for fiscal

1994–1995. But enormous pressure for a "peace dividend" has generated enthusiasm for knocking down the walls a year early. Total discretionary spending would be the same, but an unlimited amount of defense spending could be shifted to domestic appropriations in fiscal 1993. Under current rules, defense savings can be used only for deficit reduction.

If the walls simply come down a year early, the Democratic-controlled Congress would likely take the lead in determining the size of the defense budget through the usual budget and appropriations process. There are bills in the House (HR 3732) and the Senate (S 644) to knock down the walls for fiscal 1993, and Democratic strategists in both houses say such legislation is a high priority.

But congressional Republicans say that any agreement to cut defense further this year and shift the savings to domestic spending should come at a price: extending the individual caps at least through fiscal 1994–1995, and possibly through fiscal 1998. Continuing the caps would give the White House a tool for limiting cuts in the defense budget because there is little political incentive to cut defense spending below the cap when the savings can be used only for deficit reduction.

Democrats are expected to flatly oppose any extension of the walls, and Republicans are expected to insist on an extension or some negotiated floor for defense in exchange for an increase in domestic spending.

Appropriators want the issue resolved early so they can proceed with the lengthy process of turning out the 13 regular fiscal 1993 spending bills. If there is no quickly negotiated settlement, House appropriators could conceivably proceed with spending bills based on the expectation of an eventual

Table 17.2   DISCRETIONARY CAPS
(In billions of dollars, by fiscal year; totals may not add due to rounding)

	1991	1992	1993	1994	1995
Domestic					
Budget authority	$182.9	$202.7	$206.1		
Outlays	200.5	215.1	225.4		
International					
Budget authority	21.2	34.5	22.8		
Outlays	20.3	19.8	20.6		
Defense					
Budget authority	332.9	301.7	289.0		
Outlays	330.8	309.2	296.8		
TOTAL					
Budget authority	537.1	538.9	517.9	515.3	522.0
Outlays	551.6	544.2	542.8	538.5	541.6

Source: Fiscal 1993 budget.

Box 17-1 **The Deficit: Trouble Ahead**

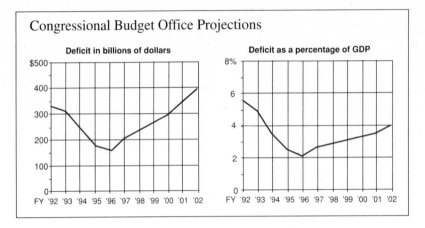

Congressional Budget Office Projections

Deficit in billions of dollars

Deficit as a percentage of GDP

OMB Projections

(Dollar amounts in billions[a])

Fiscal Year	1991	1992	1993	1994	1995	1996	1997
Outlays	1,323.0	1,475.1	1,516.7	1,474.8	1,535.5	1,607.5	1,683.6
Revenues	1,054.3	1,075.7	1,164.8	1,263.4	1.343.5	1,427.5	1,501.8
Deficit	268.7	399.4	351.9	211.4	192.1	180.0	181.8

[a]*Totals include Social Security, which is off budget, and exclude comprehensive health reform.*
Source: Fiscal 1993 Budget

The above graphs demonstrate why Congress and the White House will have to return to the bargaining table to try again to reduce the deficit—very likely next year, following the presidential election.

Instead of the deficit gradually declining to zero and then turning into a surplus, as lawmakers had hoped, Congressional Budget Office (CBO) figures show it shrinking to a smaller but still troublesome $178 billion, or 2.4 percent of the gross domestic product (GDP), in fiscal 1996. That would mark the lowest level since 1979, when the deficit was a comparatively anemic $40.2 billion, or 1.6 percent of the gross national product (GNP).

(The chart below the graphs, which is based on Office of Management and Budget figures, also shows the deficit declining through 1996.)

But instead of continuing downward, the deficit would then begin another steady rise, to $407 billion and 4 percent of the gross domestic product by 2002, according to CBO. (CBO has switched from the GNP to the GDP index for measuring deficits.)

The 1990 budget-summit agreement was not supposed to work that way. Architects of the deal believed that once temporary problems such as the recession and the savings and loan bailout faded away, the deficit would also fade. But the optimists failed to reckon on what now is seen as a major flaw in the agreement—its failure to control mandatory spending, chiefly for entitlement programs such as Medicare, Medicaid, food stamps, and agricultural subsidies. The budget rules imposed tough, pay-as-you-go restrictions on new entitlement programs and the expansion of existing programs. But they did nothing to control the rapidly rising costs of current programs, which by law must serve all qualified beneficiaries. Mandatory spending accounts for almost half the budget, and CBO identifies explosive growth in those programs as the primary reason for the expected deficit rebound.

CBO says its projections are based on uncertain economic assumptions, but that they "nevertheless call into question the comfortable assumption that the deficit will eventually go away of its own accord."

Source: Congressional Quarterly (Washington, D.C.: Congressional Quarterly Press, 1992), p. 222.

defense-domestic transfer. But President Bush would ultimately have the upper hand: If domestic appropriations bills combined to exceed the domestic ceiling, all domestic appropriations would be subjected to an across-the-board cut, or sequester, at the end of the session.

Pay-as-you-go restrictions. So-called PAYGO rules cover tax cuts and mandatory spending (chiefly for entitlement programs such as Medicare, Medicaid, and food stamps). Any changes must be deficit neutral. A tax cut, a new entitlement program, or a change that increases spending in an entitlement program must be offset by a tax increase or cutbacks in entitlement spending.

Despite the fact that PAYGO strangled virtually all new entitlement spending initiatives in 1991 except an extension of unemployment benefits, Democrats and Republicans alike favor keeping the rule as a brake on runaway spending. Some Democrats say, however, that they would like to be able to pay for a tax cut or new entitlement spending over several years. PAYGO rules require that changes be offset in the same year.

Enthusiasts say that such a change would permit critical spending now and defer repayment until the economy was stronger. But budget purists say it is a formula for smoke-and-mirrors budgeting, with real expenses now and illusory paybacks sometime in the future.

PAYGO rules also bar using savings made in discretionary accounts such as defense to pay for a tax cut. Budget experts warn against using tenuous, year-to-year cuts in appropriations bills to fund tax cuts or entitlement spending increases, which tend to stay locked in place for many years after they are enacted.

Maximum deficit targets. The 1990 budget deal included maximum deficit targets, but the limits are toothless for at least one more year. The intention was to let lawmakers off the hook for deficit increases that result from forces beyond their control—the recession or the savings and loan bailout, for example—while holding their feet to the fire for spending they can limit. The only way Congress can trigger a sequester this year is by exceeding the discretionary spending caps or violating the PAYGO rules. The president can change that rule for fiscal 1994 and bring back year-end Gramm-Rudman across-the-board spending cuts. But for the moment, Congress need not pay any attention to the size of the deficit, which is expected to easily set a new record this year.

Suspending the budget rules. As early as April, the Senate could be forced to vote again on whether to suspend the budget rules. Such a vote is mandatory after two back-to-back quarters of low or negative economic growth, which could occur in the last quarter of 1991 and the first quarter of 1992. The Senate overwhelmingly rejected three such motions to shelve the budget rules last year, but as the recession has lingered, support for the budget restrictions has eroded.

QUESTIONS FOR DISCUSSION

17.1 One student of the budget process has concluded that, "no tinkering with process can substitute for a general political consensus on substantive matters." Do you agree?

17.2 Why have the budget reforms been so ineffective in reining in the problem of deficit spending?

17.3 Would a constitutional amendment requiring a balanced budget be a wise solution to this problem? Or would it simply require the Congress to find another ingenious way around its commands?

Chapter 18

What Are the Major Causes of Homelessness in America?

INTRODUCTION

Despite recessions and economic downturns America is still a land of plenty, with one of the largest per capita incomes in the world. Yet, as one walks the streets of any of our great cities, one is confronted with numerous homeless people who have made the streets, subways, alleyways, and sidewalks their homes. Thirty years ago when the country was not as rich, the homeless were far less visible or numerous.

How did this present situation come to be? Policy analysts, commentators, and advocates have given different answers to this question: the increase in drug addiction and alcoholism that cause many to squander their resources and destroy their lives; the mentally ill who are given drug therapy rather than institutional care and cannot provide for themselves; the disappearance of the extended family that once cared for its own unfortunates; the displacement of low-income single-room-occupancy buildings with more profitable townhouses and condominiums; rent control programs, which reduce the financial incentive for building more low-cost housing.

In the following article John Belcher and Jeff Singer see the problem of homelessness as a manifestation of the inadequacies of capitalism. Free market economics in their view simply discards the unproductive. There is, they argue, "no market mechanism to assure services for the homeless." The deinstitutionalization of the mentally ill gave fiscal conservatives an excuse to reduce the costs of government. The homeless, these authors contend, symbolize the inadequacies of the welfare state which serves "business interests by controlling the poor and providing them with such a minimal level of support that they may be forced to work for low wages and in hazardous conditions."

E. Fuller Torrey argues that the homeless are not a monolithic group and consist of three general categories—the very poor, those with serious mental illness, and the alcoholics and drug abusers. Each, according to Torrey, requires a different approach and solution. For the poor, he would increase the stocks of low-income housing such as single-room-occupancy hotel units and an entire panoply of job retraining programs. For the mentally ill, he would provide incentives for the states to fund psychiatric care following release from mental hospitals. For the drug and alcohol abusers, he would require regular attendance at Alcoholics Anonymous or Narcotics Anonymous along with vocational retraining.

While Belcher and Singer see homelessness as endemic to capitalism, Torrey feels it is a product of misguided and mismanaged government programs. Homelessness is an inexcusable phenomenon in an advanced technological society, but where do we go to find the solution to it?

Homelessness: A Cost of Capitalism

John R. Belcher and Jeff Singer

It is no mystery why or how people become homeless in America. Reasons include economic policies designed to control the economy, corporate mergers, movements by American businesses overseas, housing policies that subsidize the wealthy, and deinstitutionalization. Efforts to help the homeless have focused on building more shelters, expanding health and mental health care, providing job retraining, and reeducation about how to look for work. Missing from these efforts is the recognition that homelessness is a direct result of the welfare state's role in the maintenance of profits for business interests in America.

THE INTENT OF THE WELFARE STATE

Some conservatives have argued that the modern welfare state threatens corporate America through excessive taxation and burdensome regulations (cf. Gilder, 1981; Murray, 1984). However, New Left historians have observed that the discontent and reform movements that brought about the Progressive Era and the New Deal were used by corporate elites to create a welfare state that served the interests of business (Kolko, 1963; Weinstein, 1968). The impact of the welfare state has been "an attempt to bring order and predictability to the social costs of production" (Adams, 1985, p. 388).

In general, the state may be said to fulfill two sets of roles, those associated with accumulation and those associated with legitimation. Habermas (1975), delineates four classes of tasks that allow the modern rational state to "become[s] the complementary arrangement to self-regulative market commerce" (p. 21), that is, to promote accumulation. These include the protection of commerce by police and by the administration of civil justice, guarding market mechanisms from destructive side effects (e.g., insider trading), providing investment in infrastructure (e.g., public education and roads), and adapting civil law to promote the process of accumulation (e.g., tax and banking laws). Piven and Cloward (1971) outline the legitimation functions that are specifically carried out by relief arrangements in the welfare state. It is this latter set of functions with which discussions relating to homelessness are usually concerned. However, the role of those functions associated with accumulation is ignored at the risk of substantially limiting understanding of causes and of solutions.

Politicians' efforts to convince the American electorate that there are limited dollars for social welfare and that hard choices must be made as to who is deserving of support illustrate this phenomenon. Three types of individuals generally are eligible for benefits from the welfare state: those capable of producing goods and services (but who are temporarily unemployed), women with children (who raise future workers), and those disabled by physical or mental conditions. Providing benefits to the first two groups is clearly a means of enabling production and accumulation. The latter group, while not involved in processes of accumulation, are deserving only because not serving them would raise a furor from progressive social forces; thus, providing services to this vulnerable population may be seen as a legitimation function.

The intent of the welfare state to maintain the structures of capitalism is highlighted in the Reagan administration's efforts to curb the inflation of the early 1980s and control the economy. In 1981, unemployment was 7 percent, the consumer price index had risen 24 percent over the previous two years, and interest rates were high. In response to a stagnant economy and high inflation, the administration instituted massive tax cuts, mandated less growth in federal spending, instituted regulatory relief, and slowed down the money supply. By 1982 the unemployment rate stood at a postwar high of 10.7 percent and the average person's income had been reduced by $1000 (Palmer and Sawhill, 1984).

Business benefited from the recession by laying off thousands of workers and shifting the cost of maintaining these workers to the welfare state. Threatened with further layoffs, workers were forced to agree to significant reductions in wages. Welfare benefits kept many of those laid off alive, yet desperate enough to return to work when businesses realized adequate cost savings through these reduced wages. Cost savings to business resulted in higher costs to the welfare state in the form of direct welfare support and indirect support through police and fire departments, hospitals, and jails.

The economy recovered in 1983 and a temporary gain was made against inflation, but the victory was not painless. Many had already begun the dead-end road to homelessness. The jobs created by the 1983 recovery were largely low paying and in the service sector. Standards of living for many decreased, making them more vulnerable to financial problems, emotional stress, family conflict, marital problems, and homelessness. These stresses were not experienced equally by the well-to-do who historically have managed "to keep their high-paying jobs and lucrative professional practices, and continue to realize some returns on investments" (Bell, 1987, p. 57).

The late 1970s and the 80s have witnessed business mergers and corporate takeovers in which thousands of workers have lost their jobs. Business leaders argue that corporations have become healthier by expanding their buying capabilities and purging unhealthy capital investments (Burck, 1981). However, capital that could be used for business expansion and the creation of new jobs is often used unproductively in the merger process (Associated Press, 1978). Ultimately, mergers result in fewer jobs and more unemployment, and business interests are able to exercise increasing control over wage rates and, through economies of scale, reduce the size of their work forces.

The overseas flight of American business has saved millions and shifted the fiscal burden of maintaining an increasing number of workers and markets to the welfare state. Locating outside of the United States saves businesses money because they encounter fewer government controls, less stringent pollution standards, lower wage rates, few fringe benefits, and a more desperate (and therefore more compliant) labor force (Seamonds, 1985). In 1981, overseas tax shelters allowed large corporations with profits between $1.1 billion and $9.6 billion to receive tax refunds or owe no taxes, thus providing no resources to the welfare state (Bell, 1987, p. 81). Meanwhile, the welfare state maintained a pool of workers and consumers supported by welfare payments and services from charitable organizations, productivity declined, and profits increased.

Those who lost their jobs because of attempts to curb inflation, displacement by corporate mergers, and plant closure due to the flight of business overseas are confronted by a welfare system that concentrates its efforts on women and children and those who are physically or mentally disabled. Support for able-bodied single adults who do not meet draconian standards relating to work history is practically nonexistent. These individuals are likely to become homeless in an economy that does not want their services and does not provide them with adequate welfare benefits.

Public policies and private practices relating to housing have also contributed to the dramatic increase in homelessness. Over the past 15 years, housing costs have increased more rapidly than have other consumer goods. From 1972 to 1983, median gross rent rose from 22 to 29 percent of median income, and increases were greater for those with smaller incomes. Mortgage delinquencies are at an all time high, while 6.3 million families pay more than 50 percent of income for rent (Hartman, 1987, p. 13).

Two-and-a-half million Americans are displaced annually from their homes, and public policies must accept a large measure of the blame for this. Urban economic development, skewed toward expensive housing and upscale retailers and financed with large proportions of public funds, has caused much of this displacement. Equally at fault are tax expenditures that subsidize homeownership at a cost of $44 billion annually (70 percent of which benefits persons with annual incomes exceeding $30,000). This sum represents more than three times the annual federal expenditure for housing for the poor (Hartman, 1987, p. 15).

The current imbalance in housing is reflective of a more general economic crisis. The employed as well as the unemployed are feeling a "sense of insecurity" relating to the

> collapse all around them of the traditional economic base of their countries. . . . Counting only those effects that are "countable"—plant closings, relocations, and estimated physical contractions—a sizeable fraction of all the private sector jobs that existed at the beginning of the . . . 1970s had been destroyed by the end of the decade through private disinvestment in the productive capacity of the American economy (Bluestone and Harrison, 1982, pp. 145–146).

This "sense of insecurity" is tolerated by the welfare state and further buttresses business interests in America by "cooling off" those who must survive on inadequate welfare payments (Piven and Cloward, 1971).

Unlike many European nations that have made a commitment to the right to employment and provide opportunities to work, unemployment is accepted in America (Alperovitz and Faux, 1984). The availability of jobs is left to chance factors, business cycles, corporate mobility, and corporate decisions. Workers must adapt to the workplace instead of the workplace adapting to the needs of workers, and the democracy that is proclaimed as the foremost American attribute disappears once workers set foot in the workplace.

Homelessness becomes a repository for those who are judged to be expendable. Its present existence on a massive scale is unprecedented in a period characterized by economic growth, and the reticent response of the welfare state may seem to be equally unprecedented. However, when viewed within the context of the balancing of the state's legitimation and accumulation functions, this response may be understood. Services for the homeless such as temporary shelters and soup kitchens provide barely enough resources to sustain many of them, but this may prevent them from acting out the frustrations of their desperate lives.

The able-bodied who have become homeless are the least wanted by the welfare state. They are more likely to have health problems and to lack resources such as clothes, transportation, and personal hygiene items necessary to make them productive assets for American business, so a small investment is made on their behalf by the welfare state. Much of the funding for those services that are provided comes indirectly in the form of tax relief for organizations willing to support the homeless, rather than direct expenditures that might distribute wealth.

The welfare state must also control the cost of serving those individuals such as the physically and mentally impaired who are the most needy and the most likely to become homeless, because they have the least to offer with respect to the processes of accumulation. An example of how the welfare state limits access to benefits is the conceptualization and implementation of deinstitutionalization, which has been cited as a major source of homelessness (Bassuk, 1986; Appleby and Desai, 1985).

Reformers of mental health care saw deinstitutionalization as a "bold new approach" that would provide more appropriate treatment in the community for the mentally ill. However, fiscal conservatives realized an opportunity to reduce overall funding of mental health services by state governments, and to shift the cost of care to the federal government through Supplemental Social Security Income (SSI) (Rose, 1979; Scull, 1979). The federal government responded by tightening requirements for SSI, purging the roles, and maintaining benefits at low enough levels to make homelessness a likely outcome. An Ohio study found many mentally ill persons in desperate conditions where choices for survival included deciding between paying the rent and eating (Belcher, 1987).

Homelessness as a result of deinstitutionalization should not have been unexpected; indeed, it was a direct result of preclusive hospital admission policies, inadequate SSI payments, inadequate community facilities, and inadequate funding mechanisms. The policies associated with deinstitutionalization are exemplary of the state's role in a capitalist society to enhance accumulation by limiting access to social resources by nonproductive citizens.

This review of welfare state activities has highlighted how these activities serve business interests in America by controlling the poor and providing them with such a minimal level of support that they may be forced to work for low wages and in hazardous conditions. Policies such as deinstitutionalization and programs such as Medical Assistance offer aid, but also act as a means to limit cost to an acceptable level of expenditure by the welfare state. For those who "fall through the safety net," and are thus of little value to business interests in America, the process of homelessness is a method of reducing government costs while providing an object lesson to other working persons.

This view rejects the notion that the American welfare state is based on democratic and humanitarian influences; instead, well-meaning social reformers have unwittingly become allies of business interests. The prevailing class structure determines the functions of both the public and the private sectors.

TOWARD A MORE PROGRESSIVE PUBLIC POLICY

There is no market mechanism to assure services for the homeless. Business will not find it profitable and the welfare state, fulfilling the interests of business through the promotion of accumulation and the maintenance of legitimation, will invest little capital in aiding the homeless. Current efforts to help the homeless only disguise the structural changes in society necessary to address the problem.

Welfare policy in the United States may be characterized as a risk-by-risk approach to human problems instead of a cradle-to-grave program. Most government activities are planned and implemented without consideration of the interests of the vulnerable and the indigent. Thus, the first step toward addressing the needs of the homeless is to ensure that government policies are viewed holistically. For example, those policies oriented toward improving the economy must be designed so that they do not create more homelessness.

Reducing the cost of inflation by increasing unemployment is an example of a government policy in need of reexamination. We offer no magic way to reduce inflation; however, many economists suggest that reductions like the Reagan effort in 1981 did not result in significant long-term savings to the economy. The burden posed by inflation needs to be rethought and alternatives found for lowering inflation that do not include increases in unemployment.

Legislation inhibiting corporate mergers and business flight to overseas locations is also necessary. Preconditions to mergers and relocation should require businesses to assess the impact on workers of the proposed change and to delineate the efforts they are willing to make to address negative impacts on workers. This legislation would have to be accompanied by taking mechanisms that penalize companies who do not comply with the impact studies and do not implement ways of retraining and placing workers.

Central planning in economic matters is necessary to address both micro and macro changes in the economy. Decision-making within the Council of Economic Advisers must include social welfare experts who are skilled in assessing the impact on workers of proposed government policies. Currently, decisions are made that involve significant human costs, but social welfare experts are not consulted.

The American welfare state historically has ignored the human consequences of business cycles. Many American businesses produce large inventories and pay workers overtime in order to avoid hiring larger work forces. Once business inventories are built up to a high level, workers are laid off so businesses can avoid paying wages while they sell their inventories. This standard business practice makes sense for business only if the welfare state is willing to support unwanted workers.

An alternative approach is for the welfare state to refuse to support these business decisions by raising unemployment taxes on business to reflect the true cost of maintaining unemployed workers. While at present it may be unrealistic to expect government to force business to become responsible for its workers, government can make the cost of engaging in certain actions prohibitively expensive through tax legislation. Taxation of business to pay for the costs of their decisions that have a negative impact on workers is among the least expensive means of combating homelessness.

Change in demand by consumers because of changing life styles and generational change means businesses will have to adjust their services and products. Currently, there is no way of determining how businesses will change, what kinds of workers will be displaced, or what new skills will be necessitated by the change. Both the public and private sectors must take larger roles in providing job retraining and financial support to displaced workers, and public agencies must be assigned to coordinate these activities. Those businesses that do not provide current information to public agencies responsible for the coordination of such activities would be penalized through taxation.

Influencing the decision-making process of business interests in America through taxation is congruent with capitalistic thinking that bases decision-making on the "bottom line." If the cost of a business decision is prohibitively expensive, business interests are more likely to find a less costly alternative. Estimating the "true" cost of business decisions for workers must begin by determining the cost, or economic value, of a human life. Interestingly, the U.S. Department of Transportation recently placed the value of a human life at $1 million and the Occupational Safety and Health Administration placed the figure at $2 to $5 million (Waldman, 1988).

In addition, the welfare state must implement programs that lessen the vulnerability of workers to negative business decisions. This suggests that the welfare state must change the way it addresses social problems. Instead of waiting until there is a consensus that a problem is significant enough to warrant intervention, social welfare policies must be designed to prevent problems.

The best example of this is health care. Thirty-seven million Americans are not covered by health insurance and must wait until they become sick enough to warrant costly emergency treatment. This increases the risk of the illness becoming life threatening and creates an increased financial burden on already underfinanced public health problems. Preventive care provided by paying for routine medical examinations and earlier diagnosis would save the welfare state millions of dollars. Obviously, this form of care could only be provided in a nationalized health care system.

Increasing the cost to American businesses of conducting their affairs without regard to the human costs of their decisions suggests that changes are needed in society's view of U.S. business interests. Similarly, lessening the impact of business decisions by developing new programs such as nationalized health care poses difficult challenges and means transforming the function of the welfare state. We believe, however, that homelessness is the high cost of allowing business interests to make decisions without regard to their human cost.

The American welfare state is held hostage by corporate giants who threaten to move out of the country, close plants, or lay off workers, if their tax burden is increased. Localities compete for these enterprises by promising services and financial incentives, while the ranks of the homeless increase steadily. Our social resources are increasingly invested in the conspicuous consumption of the wealthy, while basic needs of large numbers of citizens are neglected. The welfare state can ignore the consequences of capitalism that causes homelessness by building more shelters and asking business interests in America for donations. However, until society holds corporate America accountable for its decisions, homelessness will increase and we will continue to bemoan the fate of millions of our relatives and neighbors whose only home is the street.

REFERENCES

Adams, P., "Social Policy and the Working Class," *Social Service Review*, 9 (1985), pp. 387–402.

Alperovitz, G. and Faux, J., *Rebuilding America* (New York: Pantheon, 1984).

Appleby, L. and Desai, P., "Documenting the Relationship between Homelessness and Psychiatric Hospitalization," *Hospital and Community Psychiatry*, 36 (1985), pp. 732–7.

Associated Press, "Henry's Brother Speaks out against Company Takeovers: Kissinger vs. Conglomerates," *Cleveland Plain Dealer* (June 9, 1978), p. 32.

Bassuk, E. L., "Homeless Families: Single Mothers and their Children in Boston Shelters," in E. L. Bassuk (ed.), *The Mental Health Needs of Homeless Persons* (San Francisco: Jossey-Bass, 1986).

Belcher, J. R., "Adult Foster Care: An Alternative to Homelessness for some Chronically Mentally Ill Persons," *Adult Foster Care Journal*, 1 (1987), pp. 212–25.

Bell, W., *Contemporary Social Welfare* (New York: Macmillan, 1987).

Bluestone, B. and Harrison, B., *The Deindustrialization of America* (New York: Basic Books, 1982).

Burck, A., "A Different Opinion: A Merger Specialist Who Hates Mergers," *Fortune*, 108 (1981), pp. 221–8.

Gilder, G., *Wealth and Poverty* (New York: Basic Books, 1981).

Habermas, J., *Legitimation Crisis* (Boston: Beacon Press, 1975).

Hartman, C., "The Housing Part of the Homelessness Problem," in *Homelessness: Critical Issues for Policy and Practice* (Boston: The Boston Foundation, 1987).

Kolko, G., *The Triumph of Conservatism: A Reinterpretation of American History, 1900–1916* (New York: Free Press, 1963).

Murray, C., *Losing Ground: American Social Policy, 1950–1980* (New York: Basic Books, 1984).

Palmer, J. L. and Sawhill, I. V., *The Reagan Record* (Cambridge: Ballinger, 1984).

Piven, F. F. and Cloward, R. A., *Regulating the Poor* (New York: Pantheon, 1971).

Rose, S., "Deciphering Deinstitutionalization: Complexities in Policy and Program Analysis," *Milbank Memorial Fund*, 57 (1979), pp. 429–60.

Scull, A., "Rights of the Deviant," *Journal of Social Issues*, 37 (1981), pp. 6–33.

Seamonds, J. A., "When States Go all out to Lure Industry," *U.S. News & World Report*, 98 (May, 1985), pp. 40–42.

Waldman, S., "Putting a Price Tag on Life," *Newsweek* (Jan. 11, 1988), p. 40.

Weinstein, J. *The Corporate Ideal in the Liberal State: 1900–1918* (Boston: Beacon Press, 1968).

Who Goes Homeless?

E. Fuller Torrey, M.D.

Should the homeless be included in the statement, "Ye have the poor always with you"? Given the array of individuals who have become permanent fixtures on the streets of every American city in the last decade, the answer would appear to be yes. In fact, however, homelessness has evolved from being a homogeneous, sphinx-like problem to being a heterogeneous cluster of interrelated problems for which many of the solutions are known. The mystery no longer is what to do, but rather why we do not do it.

One change in homelessness has been the perceived magnitude of the problem. Until 1987 some advocates were claiming that more than two million Americans were homeless. A 1987 study by the Urban Institute initially estimated the number to be between 567,000 and 600,000; the primary author later revised this downward to between 355,000 and 445,000. Peter H. Rossi, in his 1989 book, *Down and Out in America*, concluded that "the most believable national estimate is that at least 300,000 people are homeless each night in this country, and possibly as many as 400,000 to 500,000." In 1990, Census takers claimed to have found 228,621 homeless on the night of March 20, including 49,793 persons "visible at preidentified street locations." If it is assumed that only one-third of those actually living on the streets were counted by the Census, the total number of homeless persons would be 328,207, a number consistent with the estimates by both the Urban Institute and Rossi.

CHANGING CLIMATES

Another change is a decrease in the public's tolerance for the homeless. In New York City, labeled by one newspaper as "Calcutta on the Hudson," police evicted the homeless from Penn Station and razed their temporary shelters in Tompkins Square Park. In Washington, D.C., a right-to-shelter law was rescinded in a 1990 referendum, and local police began enforcing a city ordinance against begging. Atlanta's Mayor Maynard Jackson in 1991 asked the City Council to impose stiff penalties, including up to 60 days in jail, for aggressive behavior or sleeping in vacant buildings.

Perhaps most surprising has been the decreased sympathy for the homeless in towns and cities traditionally thought of as bastions of liberalism. In Santa Monica, which serves free meals daily on the City Hall lawn, a 1990 poll showed voters favoring tougher law enforcement against the homeless. In Berkeley, police regularly make sweeps of People's Park, and across the Bay, San Franciscans overwhelmingly picked homelessness as the city's biggest problem—bigger than drugs, crime, or AIDs—in a newspaper poll. Indeed, according to *San Francisco Chronicle* columnist Cyra McFadden, "You could get rich in this town right now by selling T-shirts reading, 'Eat the homeless.'" Decreasing public tolerance does not by itself produce any more solutions to the homelessness problem than did the earlier indulgences of public guilt, but it does tend to force harder thinking about solutions. Shelters and soup kitchens provide short-term respite from serious thinking about long-term solutions.

Probably the most significant shift in debates about the homeless has been a growing consensus that they are not a monolithic group, but rather composed of three distinct groups. Eliciting the most sympathy from the public are the down-on-my-luck individuals and families, especially children. Economic recession, shrinking availability of low-income housing, and marginal job skills have affected this group. Eliciting somewhat less sympathy are homeless individuals with serious mental illnesses, especially schizophrenia, because many people are frightened of them and do not realize that they have a brain disease that places them in the same category as people with Alzheimer's disease. It has been estimated that there are now twice as many schizophrenics living in public shelters and on the streets as there are in all state and county psychiatric hospitals. Eliciting by far the least public sympathy are the alcoholics and drug abusers. Many of them use public shelters and soup kitchens in order to save their money to feed their addiction, and they panhandle the most aggressively.

It is widely agreed that approximately half of all the homeless have an alcohol and/or drug problem; some of these are also mentally ill and/or have marginal job skills. The mentally ill account for approximately one-third; this percentage is lower in cities with relatively good public psychiatric services (e.g., Salt Lake City) and higher in cities where such services are abysmal (e.g., Los Angeles, Houston, Miami). The pure down-on-my-luck group is relatively small (about 15 percent) although very visible in stories about the homeless; advocates learned long ago that this group most effectively elicits support for their cause.

SEPARATING THE STRANDS

Henry J. Kaiser once wrote that "problems are only opportunities in work clothes." This is certainly true for homelessness, which is really three separate problems corresponding to these three groups.

The easiest of the three problems is what to do with the mentally ill. Their homelessness is a consequence of deinstitutionalization and the subsequent breakdown of public psychiatric services. A 1983 study of discharges from Metropolitan State Hospital in Boston, for example, found that 27 percent of all discharged patients became at least intermittently homeless within six months of discharge. A similar study in 1986 of discharges from Columbus State Hospital in Ohio reported that 36 percent were homeless within six months. Furthermore, the number of beds in state mental hospitals was reduced from 552,000 in 1955 to 108,000 in 1986. As was pointed out in *The 1990 Annual Report of the Interagency Council on the Homeless*, given the 41 percent increase in the population of the United States since 1955, if there had been no deinstitutionalization there would be 800,000 state psychiatric beds today, nearly eight times the actual number.

The major reason for the failure of public psychiatric services has been a fiscal one. It is not, however, a question of *how much* is being spent, as is commonly supposed; the approximately $20 billion in public funds currently being spent each year is probably sufficient to buy first-class services if it were utilized properly. Rather, the problem is *how these services are funded.* Until the early 1960s, approximately 96 percent of public psychiatric services were funded by the states, with the other 4 percent split between federal and local sources. As deinstitutionalization got under way, the released patients were made eligible for federal Supplemental Security Income (SSI), Social Security Disability Income (SSDI), Medicaid, Medicare, food stamps, and other federal subsidies. By 1985 it was estimated that the states' share of the cost for the mentally ill had fallen to 53 percent of the total, while the federal share had risen to 38 percent (it is undoubtedly several percentage points higher by now).

The shift of the fiscal burden from the states to the federal government was not, by itself, a disaster. The problems arose out of how the various fiscal supports were related to each other. For example, the patients in Metropolitan State Hospital and Columbus State Hospital mentioned above were primarily the fiscal responsibilities of the states of Massachusetts and Ohio as long as they were in the hospitals. Once discharged, they became primarily the responsibility of the federal government. If such patients relapse and need rehospitalization, as most of them do, they typically are sent to the psychiatric ward of a general hospital, where Medicaid pays most of the bill. Elderly psychiatric patients were similarly transferred from state hospitals to nursing homes not because the care was necessarily better (often it was worse) but rather because such a transfer made them eligible for Medicare and Medicaid. Even with the states coming up with Medicaid matching funds, it was extremely cost-effective, from the point of view of state government, to shift the fiscal burden to the federal government.

The fiscal organization of public psychiatric services in the United States is more thought-disordered than most of their patients. The incentives all lead to discharging psychiatric patients from state facilities as quickly as possible; there is no incentive to worry about where they go, whether they get aftercare, or whether they become homeless. Indeed, if you tried to set up a system for funding public psychiatric services in a way which would guarantee its failure, you would set up just such a system as we have created.

The solution is to meld federal and state funding streams into a single stream with responsibility placed at the state level, unless states wish to delegate to the county level (as do California, Minnesota, and Wisconsin). All incentives to shift the fiscal burden to the federal government must be removed. States would rapidly learn that it is cost-effective to provide good psychiatric aftercare, because the costs of repeated rehospitalizations are very high. Continuity of care between inpatient and outpatient programs would become the rule rather than the exception. Existing model programs for the homeless mentally ill such as Seattle's El Rey Residential Treatment Facility or the widely praised Weingart Center in Los Angeles, which combine treatment, housing, and rehabilitation, would spread quickly. State laws making it difficult to hospitalize obviously impaired individuals would be amended as it became apparent that good psychiatric care does not cost more in the long run than not-so-benign neglect. And the homeless mentally ill, including the emblematic bag ladies, would become a thing of the past.

NOW FOR THE HARDER ONES

The problem of the homeless mentally ill is easy to solve compared with the problems of the other groups. Alcoholics have always made up a significant percentage of the homeless population, from the days of the early American almshouses to the hobos who rode the rails in the years before World War II. When one is addicted to alcohol or drugs the highest priority is to save as much money as possible to feed that addiction. Present homeless policies, which in some cities have guaranteed free beds and food for everyone who asks, have probably exacerbated rather than relieved the problem of homeless substance abusers.

Although there is no policy which can force a person to help himself, it stands to reason that public programs should not make alcohol and drug problems worse. All substance abusers who have any income should be required to pay a certain proportion of it for shelter and food and should also be required to attend regular meetings of Alcoholics Anonymous or Narcotics Anonymous. Rehabilitation programs including vocational training should be readily available, but abstinence should be a requirement for participation. For those who refuse to meet minimal requirements for such publicly funded programs, there is a network of private and church-run shelters (such as the Salvation Army's) which have provided exemplary care for alcoholics and drug abusers for many years.

Solutions to the down-on-my-luck homeless are both easy and difficult at the same time. Many of them are victims of reduced stocks of low-income housing. It does not take a Ph. D. to realize that when single-room-occupancy (SRO) hotel units were reduced from 127,000 to 14,000, as happened in New York City between 1970 and 1983, or from 1,680 to 15, as happened in Nashville between 1970 and 1990, some people would be left with nowhere to live.

But housing is the easy half to solving the down-on-my-luck problem. Many of these people have a poor education and marginal job skills. As the workplace demands increasing technological skills for even entry-level positions, this group is likely to continue to grow. Solutions require the whole panoply of often discussed but rarely available services from remedial education to vocational training, job coaching, transitional employment, supported employment, and counseling. This is certainly the most difficult and most expensive segment of the homeless population to rehabilitate, but not rehabilitating them is also expensive.

As long as programs for the mentally ill, substance abusers, and consumers of low-income housing are part of the ongoing political tug-of-war between federal and state governments, solutions to the problems of the homeless will be elusive. The homeless are, in one sense, daily reminders of the lack of resolution of this issue.

In the area of public psychiatric and substance-abuse services, the federal government has a miserable record of achievement. Exhibit A is the federally funded Community Mental Health Centers program, which wasted over $3 billion setting up 769 centers, most of which never did what they were intended to do. It seems likely that service programs conceived by federal officials, who are too far removed from the real world, will almost inevitably fail.

What, then, should be the federal government's role? The setting of minimal standards and enforcement of such standards through fiscal incentives and disincentives is necessary, for example, expecting states to reduce the mentally ill homeless to a specified level and reducing federal subsidies if they fail. The enforcement function should probably be vested in the Office of Inspector General in departments such as Health and Human Services (HHS) or Housing and Urban Development (HUD). Model programs such as those under the McKinney Act, the HHS-HUD collaborative program to improve housing and services for the homeless mentally ill, or Senator Pete Domenici's recently introduced "Projects to Aid the Transition from Homelessness" bill, should be encouraged. The problem is that from most states' point of view, such programs are not regarded merely as models, but rather as an ongoing federal commitment to replace the efforts of the states themselves.

The homeless, then, will be with us until we are able to resolve the issue of federal versus state responsibility for social programs. Hallucinating quietly next to vacant buildings, lying under bushes in the park, or aggressively accosting strangers on the street, the homeless represent not only a failure of social programs, but more broadly a failure of government at all levels.

QUESTIONS FOR DISCUSSION

18.1 To what extent does society have responsibility for those whose condition is a result of alcohol or drug abuse? Is society's responsibility greater for those who are mentally ill? Should such moral judgments shape public policy?

18.2 Should homelessness—whatever its cause—be permitted in a modern, technological society such as the United States?

18.3 Why, despite the great increase of wealth in America, is homelessness a greater problem today than it was in the 1950s?

Chapter
19

Is Nuclear Power a Serious Threat to Our Environment?

INTRODUCTION

The fears about nuclear power dramatized by the accident at Three Mile Island in 1979 and the more serious event at Chernobyl in the Ukraine in 1986 have led to a decline in the nuclear industry. No new reactors have been ordered in the United States since 1978. This is largely due to public fears about a potential environmental disaster even greater than that at Chernobyl and concerns that we have yet to resolve the problem of nuclear waste. Despite these apprehensions, what is the alternative to nuclear power?

While the prospects for more nuclear power plants decline, oil imports increase, and now make up approximately 50 percent of our consumption. In large part our desire to liberate Kuwait from Iraqi control in the Gulf War was motivated by a fear of Saddam Hussein's controlling a major portion of the world's oil reserves. Must American national security policy be driven by fears over who controls oil in the Persian Gulf?

Beyond the questions of national security and overreliance upon foreign oil are the environmental concerns associated with our dependence upon fossil fuels. The burning of coal and oil have long been associated with such problems as acid rain, urban smog, and global warming. Is nuclear power the answer to both our foreign and environmental policy dilemmas?

The two selections in this chapter give contrasting answers to this question. Bill Harris gives a vigorous defense of nuclear power. He argues that if we build more nuclear plants we could reduce our dependence upon foreign oil and meet the growing demand for electricity without doing any damage to the environment. Alan Miller and Irving Mintzer fear that building more nuclear plants would do more damage to the environment than good. In order to meet the recommendations of an international conference that met in Toronto in 1988 to suggest a 20 percent reduction in global carbon emissions by 2005, a crash program for building nuclear power plants might be considered. But the authors fear that the construction of so many plants would consume a disproportionate amount of energy, drain capital resources, and would actually increase carbon emissions.

This is a policy dilemma of great complexity whose answer cannot possibly be reduced to a bumper sticker.

Nuclear Energy
Toward U.S. Energy Independence

Bill Harris

The Persian Gulf contains most of the oil reserves to fuel the industrialized world. Whoever controls that oil . . . controls western economies . . . and destinies. The United States cannot let a regional bully wield that kind of power.

It's easy to hate Saddam Hussein. It's very easy to blame him for our involvement in Mideast madness. But we need to be honest. He had some help—unintentional though it was—right here in the United States. No one in the Middle East got us hooked on oil. No one over there put our heads in OPEC's noose by importing half of all the oil we use. Most important, no one over there kept us from developing energy that's Made in the U.S.A. We did that to ourselves.

It's not as if we didn't have warning. Twice before, unrest in the Persian Gulf has caused oil shocks in the West. In 1973, as you may well remember, with the Arab oil embargo. And in 1979, after the Iranian Revolution. Yes, we were warned . . . and warned again . . . that foreign oil addiction was bad for America's health. But we ignored the risk. And now our young men and women are in Saudi Arabia, a hair trigger away from war.

What more will it take for us to kick the foreign oil monkey off our back . . . to develop more domestic sources of energy . . . so we'll never again risk shedding American blood to defend a vulnerable lifetime of oil.

As you know, I'm here today to talk about nuclear energy. There are many important reasons it must be a major part of our energy mix. But none more important than this: It's in our national interest. The more electricity we make using nuclear energy, the less we must make with imported oil. Since the 1973 Arab oil embargo, nuclear energy has saved this country over 4 billion barrels of oil . . . enough to fuel every motor vehicle in America—cars, buses, trucks, you name it—for well over a year. And nuclear energy has kept $125 billion U.S. from flowing into the pockets of foreign oil producers. That amounts to almost half of America's entire 1991 budget for national defense.

Those are just the savings in the United States. Throughout the world, 426 nuclear electric plants in 26 nations displace six million barrels of OPEC oil each day. So you can see that nuclear energy furthers not just U.S. energy independence, but that of our allies, as well.

But there's still a ways to go toward real energy independence. Earlier I pointed out that nearly 50 percent of U.S. oil is now imported. If you think that's a problem . . . just hold on . . . because it's going to get worse. Some experts believe that by the year 2000, we could be importing more than 12 million barrels a day . . . nearly two-thirds of our total oil needs. That kind of dependence is bad enough . . . but the price tag is even worse: over $100 billion a year paid to foreign suppliers.

Given that frightening forecast, wouldn't you think every sector of our economy should try to cut back its use of oil? Well, the electric utility industry has cut back—dramatically. Between 1973 and 1987, utilities did a superb job of reducing their use of oil. Oil went from producing 17 percent of U.S. electricity in 1973 . . . to only about 5 percent in 1987. How did they manage to do it? Most of the credit goes to the new coal and nuclear energy plants that came into service during that time, to take the place of oil. In fact coal and nuclear energy have provided 95 percent of *all* new electricity supply since 1973.

But during the 1980s, building large plants—like coal and nuclear energy—became financially risky for utilities. So they began to turn back to oil. Since 1987, utility oil use has increased 34 percent. New England now gets 35 to 40 percent of its electricity from oil-fired plants. On Long Island, it's close to 100 percent.

Does this make any sense? At a time when we're importing nearly half our oil, when we're paying $1.5 billion a week to foreign suppliers . . . when imported oil represents over 40 percent of the U.S. trade deficit . . . does it make sense to compound that problem by importing oil for electricity generation? I don't think so.

Using more nuclear energy and other domestic sources strengthens America strategically . . . there's no doubt about that. But nuclear energy also helps strengthen us economically. The U.S. economy is hungry for new electric supply. Demand for electricity is growing faster than supply. Just look around you, at all the ways we use electricity that our parents never dreamed of . . . microwave ovens . . . personal computers . . . new industrial technologies . . . like infrared and laser and robots . . . that make our industrial sector more productive than ever before.

No one knows exactly how much new electric capacity we'll need in the next 10 years. But make no mistake, there's a problem. History shows that if our economy grows by 2–3 percent a year, demand for electricity will grow at about the same pace—2–3 percent a year. That works out to between 100,000 and 200,000 megawatts of new capacity in only 10 years. That's *at least* as much electric capacity as there is today in all of California, Arizona, Colorado, New Mexico, Nevada, Idaho, Maine, New Jersey, and Connecticut.

Will those additional megawatts be there when we need them? It doesn't look very good. Right now, we have only 84,400 megawatts of new capacity planned, and 57 percent of that is not yet under construction. If that's not a supply side problem, I don't know what is.

The first signs of trouble have already appeared. In the last few years, we've seen brownouts, and public appeals to conserve, all the way from New England to Florida. Electric utilities across the country report electric demand not expected 'til the mid-1990s or even later. There's no getting around the fact that we need to build new power plants. The last nuclear energy plant was ordered in 1978. We're starting to pay the price for that . . . in less reliable service . . . and growing dependence on foreign oil. It seems to require a crisis to alert America to its energy problems. I hope it won't take an electricity crisis to help us all wake up to our urgent need to build new plants.

It is equally important to pursue conservation and efficiency to help solve our energy problems. Nobody supports energy efficiency more than the nation's electric utilities . . . in fact, they are leading the way. Utilities have in place about 1300 programs—and spend $1 billion each year—to help their customers either use less electricity or shift our usage to off-peak hours. These programs have saved the equivalent of 21 large plants. And certainly even greater savings can be achieved in the future.

But we must be realistic. Conservation and energy efficiency alone won't solve the problem of supply. The simple fact is, the United States will need to produce more electricity than we're capable of producing now. Today, nuclear energy supplies nearly 20 percent of U.S. electricity. We will need every available generating source—including nuclear energy—to meet our nation's growing demand.

It is encouraging to note that Americans feel strongly that we must protect our environment as we meet our energy needs. And even with the crisis in the Gulf, I believe Americans will continue to care a great deal what energy production does to our environment. Nuclear energy is one of the cleanest sources of electricity. It emits no sulfur oxides . . . no nitrogen oxides . . . no carbon dioxides . . . or other greenhouse gases.

Take away the nation's 112 nuclear energy plants, and utility sulfur oxide emissions would be five million tons a year higher. That's one-half the reduction mandated in the new Clean Air Act.

Take away our nuclear energy plants, and utility nitrogen oxide emissions would be two million tons a year higher. That's equal to the reduction required in the Senate version of the new law.

In France, where over 70 percent of electricity comes from nuclear energy—far more than in the United States—there have been even more dramatic environmental benefits. Back in 1979, when France was still heavily dependent on oil and coal-fired power, their plants emitted large amounts of nitrogen oxides and sulfur dioxide. By 1987 . . . in less than 10 years . . . the use of nuclear energy had tripled . . . and those emissions had dropped dramatically. Total pollution from the French electric power system decreased by 80–90 percent. You don't hear many French environmentalists opposing nuclear energy.

The nuclear industry has no higher priority than the safe operation of its plants. The industry was severely jolted by the accident at Three Mile Island in 1979 . . . even though no one was injured. The result of Three Mile Island was a concerted industry drive for excellence. Every aspect of plant operations was examined . . . and reexamined. Nothing was taken for granted. The independent Institute of Nuclear Power Operations was created in 1979. It examines the operation of all plants and sets and enforces high standards of training and good practices. The U.S. Nuclear Regulatory Commission, which keeps close watch on the industry, reports dramatic improvements in all areas of performance. The industry is committed to maintaining and improving those high marks.

The only deaths that ever resulted from nuclear electric power happened at Chernobyl, in the Ukraine. The Chernobyl plant was a very unique Soviet design. It lacked essential safeguards that Western plants have . . . which is why it could never have been licensed to operate in the United States. There could not be a Chernobyl *accident* in the United States . . . because there could never be a Chernobyl-type *plant* in the United States. By the way, you should know that one of the benefits of perestroika is that the Soviet Union is now fully cooperating in a worldwide network to assure safe operation of nuclear electric plants.

What about the waste from nuclear energy plants? Often, people don't realize that we're talking about a very small amount. A typical plant produces about 30 tons of used fuel each year. Contrast this with the more than 300 million tons of chemical waste created each year in our country. And no other industry has managed its waste as scrupulously as we have. Every bit of used fuel ever produced by a nuclear electric plant is safely stored—mostly on plant sites in concrete storage pools lined with steel. And it will remain there, in its solid form, carefully monitored and fully accounted for, until a permanent storage facility is in place.

Clearly, nuclear energy holds out a host of benefits. It can help America avoid even greater dependence of foreign oil. Nuclear energy can help meet growing demand for electricity to fuel economic growth. And it can do these things safely, without environmental damage. It's really not surprising that a broad cross-section of Americans support using nuclear energy. Over 80 percent of Americans think nuclear energy should play an important role in the new National Energy Strategy being developed by the Department of Energy. That's according to a recent, independent public opinion poll. Even more interesting, among Americans who identify themselves as active environmentalists . . . 69 percent say nuclear energy will be important in the years ahead.

That's what the American people think. And their political leaders agree. Out of 48 key congressional votes on nuclear energy legislation during the 1980s, 41 favored nuclear energy. On the state level, the National Governors Association and the National Council of State Legislatures have enacted a number of resolutions in support of nuclear energy. So you see, anyone who tells you nuclear energy has no support . . . doesn't know what he's talking about. Nuclear energy is good for this nation . . . and Americans are smart enough to know it.

I know the American Legion already has adopted a resolution supporting nuclear energy. And I understand you'll soon consider renewing this solution. I sincerely hope you will. Let's learn from what is happening in the Persian Gulf. Let's not wait for another crisis . . . to put America on a sound energy footing. Energy security goes hand in hand with national security. Let's become as strong . . . secure . . . and energy independent as we possibly can. We owe that to our fellow citizens and to our young people. And with the help of nuclear energy, we can do it.

Global Warming: No Nuclear Quick Fix

Alan Miller and Irving Mintzer

Growing concern about the buildup of greenhouse gases and possible climate change has fueled new debate about the global energy future, especially on ways to expand use of nonfossil fuels. One controversial alternative is to rapidly expand use of nuclear fission, since nuclear power plants do not release carbon dioxide into the atmosphere. Nuclear power advocates have begun to cite global warming as a reason to continue developing this technology.[1]

Many of these advocates acknowledge that nuclear electric technology poses major problems: the high capital and energy costs of plant construction, the safety of plant operations, the long-term disposal of radioactive waste, and the risks of nuclear proliferation. But they argue that the risks associated with rapid climate change are equal or greater, and that efforts to resolve nuclear power problems should be expanded in order to take advantage of this currently available alternative to fossil sources of electricity.

We do not address the issues of safety, waste disposal, or proliferation. Instead, we maintain that there are other, equally compelling reasons why nuclear electric generating capacity should not be expanded rapidly worldwide. And we believe that although fission power is likely to be part of the energy economy for decades to come, a sudden expansion of nuclear power would not reduce the risks of global warming for many years.

RAPID ROAD TO BANKRUPTCY

The energy needs of rapidly growing populations in developing countries have been a source of much concern about the buildup of greenhouse gases. Developing nations were responsible for just 7 percent of global carbon dioxide emissions in 1950, but in 1987 they accounted for about 28 percent.[2] China is the largest coal-consuming nation and the world's third largest source of carbon dioxide emissions, after the United States and the Soviet Union. China, India, and Brazil together emit more carbon dioxide annually than does Western Europe.

Most analysts project that developing countries will produce increasing levels of carbon emissions, and a larger share of global emissions, because per capita energy consumption is growing along with population. Electrification is proceeding steadily. According to one study, installed generating capacity in 13 major developing countries grew an average of 7.5 percent between 1979 and 1987, and planned additions for 1987–2000 imply an average growth rate of 6.3 percent per year. Much of the new capacity will depend on coal.[3] By 2020, developing nations could be responsible for over 40 percent of energy use and more than half of global carbon emissions.

A recent study prepared for the U.S. Congress by the Environmental Protection Agency emphasized the implications of energy growth in developing countries. It found that if greenhouse gas emissions are limited only in industrialized countries, rapid atmospheric warming could still be expected because of increasing emissions from developing countries.[4]

In order to make a significant dent in greenhouse gas emissions, hundreds of nuclear power plants would have to be operating in the Third World by the year 2010. It is extremely unlikely that such a buildup could be sustained over the next two decades, for a number of reasons:

The existing base of operating experience is small. As of 1988, just 23 reactors were operating in developing countries, many only intermittently. Nuclear power is currently expected to approach 10 percent of installed capacity in only two developing countries—South Korea and Taiwan—by the year 2000. Both are among the more affluent nations in the Third World.

Capital costs are high. Nuclear power is the most capital-intensive form of energy supply, with the possible exception of a few large hydroelectric projects. Interest payments on existing international debt are crippling the development plans of many countries, and capital continues to be a scarce resource in most of the rest of the Third World. International borrowing for electric power already exceeds 40 percent of total annual public investment in Argentina, Brazil, Colombia, South Korea, and Mexico. A recent report by the U.S. Agency for International Development estimates that in order to meet currently projected needs in two decades, countries receiving U.S. assistance would need to more than double current borrowing rates.[5]

Nuclear power would increase the debt burden in these countries even further. And because the World Bank, an important source of funds for power development, does not finance nuclear projects, borrowers must seek loans at higher costs in the private capital markets.

Nuclear plants are traditionally large scale. Conventional fission electric plants are most efficient in gigawatt-scale installation. Because the cost of extending the distribution grid into rural areas is often prohibitive, nuclear energy seems useful only in large urban centers which already have distribution systems. The development of more efficient, smaller reactors has been a goal of the Indian nuclear program, however. This would have important implications for nuclear prospects.[6]

Nuclear power requires a strong supporting infrastructure. Planning, regulating, and operating nuclear plants and disposing nuclear waste demand high technical expertise, including many doctorate and master's-level engineers and physicists. Training these specialists adds lead time and cost to a commercial nuclear program. Lack of domestic expertise has no doubt contributed to the poor performance of many existing reactors in developing countries.

Solving these problems requires more than engineering improvements in the design of nuclear power systems: It calls for extensive cooperation from the industrialized countries to provide the necessary technology, financing, and training. Public opposition to nuclear power in these countries would no doubt have to be assuaged before such assistance could be offered. Even in Japan, which has one of the most extensive nuclear power programs in the world, more than 60 percent of the public oppose building more reactors.[7] Only a new generation of nuclear technology seems likely to satisfy public concerns—and the process of designing, developing, testing, and reviewing new systems could take decades.

Only the most optimistic studies suggest that traditional nuclear systems can ever compete in cost with fossil fuel plants in developing countries, particularly those with indigenous resources. One study indicated that coal prices would have to rise to $70 a ton—they are now about $30 a ton—and nuclear costs would have to drop from their present level of over $2000 per installed kilowatt to $1200 per kilowatt in order for nuclear power to be competitive.[8]

Global agreements to impose carbon-based fuel taxes or other policies to control emissions could shift the balance of costs somewhat. But nuclear power is not the only low-emission technology. And while nuclear costs show no sign of declining, the costs of turbine and solar technologies are rapidly improving.

In the modern sector of developing countries, increasing energy efficiency will be equally important as developing new supplies. Widespread evidence suggests that improving efficiency is cheaper, faster, and safer than any alternatives. A 1986 study indicated, for example, that investing $4 billion in efficiency improvements in Brazil could offset the need for 22 new power plants by the year 2000 and, in the process, save almost $20 billion.[9]

CRASH PROGRAM A NET LOSS

Regardless of where the plants are built, it is not clear that a crash nuclear power program would reduce the risks of global warming. In order to produce energy, the fission-electric fuel cycle requires large amounts of energy for construction and fuel enrichment—much of it before a commercial power plant begins operating and most derived from fossil fuels. Therefore one must ask, at what rate of expansion would a program begin to draw more energy from the conventional sector than it produces? Conceivably, at some rate of growth in the global network of nuclear plants, the energy required for the complete ensemble of activities—mining and concentrating uranium resources, constructing facilities, enriching fuel, and disposing of radioactive wastes—would result in an increase in carbon emissions rather than a decrease. And if this is so, a sustained program of nuclear plant construction could temporarily increase the risk of rapid global warming.

One widely endorsed goal for reducing global carbon emissions is the "Toronto target"—a 20 percent reduction from the 1988 level by 2005—based on recommendations of a June 1988 international meeting hosted by the Canadian government. Discussions on how that goal might be achieved are now under way in the Intergovernmental Panel on Climate Change, a group formed in November 1988 by 40 nations meeting under the aegis of the World Meteorological Organization and the United Nations Environmental Program.

If current trends continue and primary energy demand increases by about 2.2 percent annually, total world energy supply will need to reach approximately 450 exajoules (EJ) in 2005; the global supply was about 290 EJ in 1986.[10] If the fuel mix remains similar, approximately 140 EJ of this energy would be provided by solid fuels, about 190 EJ from liquids, and about 94 EJ from gas—a scenario that would produce about 8.3 gigatons (billion metric tons) of carbon per year. The Toronto target would require reducing carbon emissions to 4.2 gigatons per year, which could be accomplished by substituting nuclear electricity for three-fourths of the solid fuels and about half of the liquid projected by current trends—an increase in the global nuclear electric supply from about 19.5 EJ in 1989 to about 205 EJ in 2005, or an average growth rate of almost 16 percent per year.

To understand the implications of such a program, we analyzed the effect of growth rate on the net energy yield from a system of nuclear power plants. We made the most optimistic assumptions possible:

- the average plant would take only five years to construct and test;
- the construction of the generating station, the fabrication and delivery of the initial fuel load, and the preparation of the decommissioning facilities would require energy equal to only 5 percent of the lifetime output from the generating station;
- the annual energy required for routine operations of the power plant and for other plants needed to provide regularly scheduled fuel reloads would be equivalent to only 5 percent of the annual output from the generating station;
- the plant would operate continuously for 40 years.

Under these conditions, the global system of nuclear fission plants could only expand about 7 percent a year and still produce a net energy gain. Meeting the Toronto target by nuclear power alone, which requires a 16 percent annual growth rate, would mean finding a way to reduce the energy put into construction, fuel load, and decommissioning to less than 3.75 percent of a plant's lifetime production. (Reducing the fraction of annual output required for routine operation by a similar amount does not materially affect the rate at which the system could be expanded.)

In today's world, optimistic assumptions are seldom realized. Recent plants in Western Europe and Japan have required years to build; in the United States they have taken 12–15 years to complete. Traditional pressurized-water reactors fed with uranium fuel enriched in U.S. facilities have required substantially more than 5 percent of their output for operations and maintenance, even without taking into account the energy requirements for long-term waste disposal.

This analysis suggests that it will be nearly impossible to meet the Toronto target with nuclear power alone, without making the construction and operation of the nuclear plants themselves an energy drain on the world economy. Yet none of the problems we have cited are unresolvable, particularly over the long time frames appropriate to thinking about global warming. In our view, fission electric systems can eventually help to reduce the risk of global warming. But rapidly expanding the global system of present-day nuclear power plants would contribute to the problem rather than the solution, and it would severely complicate the economic difficulties that currently plague many developing countries.

NOTES

1. See "Nuking the Greenhouse," *New Scientist* (Nov. 5, 1988), p. 20.
2. *World Resources Report 1988–89* (Washington, D.C.: World Resources Institute and United Nations Environment Program, 1988), p. 336.
3. S. Meyers et al., *Plans for the Power Sector in Thirteen Major Developing Countries* (Berkeley, Calif.: Lawrence Berkeley Laboratory, Oct. 1989).
4. U.S. Environmental Protection Agency, *Policy Options for Stabilizing Global Climate* (draft, Feb. 1989), p. VI-15.
5. *Power Shortages in Developing Countries* (Washington, D.C.: U.S. Agency for International Development, 1988).
6. Iengar, "India," in P.M.S. Jones, ed., *Nuclear Power: Policy and Prospects* (Chichester, N.Y.: Wiley, 1987).
7. *Japan Quarterly* (Jan.–March 1989), p. 110.
8. *China: The Energy Sector* (Washington, D.C.: World Bank, 1985), p. 131.
9. Howard S. Geller et al., "Electricity Conservation in Brazil: Potential and Progress," *Energy*, vol. 13, no. 6 (1983), pp. 469–83.
10. *World Resources Report, 1988–89.*

QUESTIONS FOR DISCUSSION

19.1 Was the Gulf War a warning to the United States that dependence upon foreign oil could lead to an open-ended military involvement in the Middle East?

19.2 Is the case for nuclear power driven more by environmental or energy concerns?

19.3 What political choices would decision-makers confront in deciding whether or not to increase our reliance upon nuclear power?

Chapter
20

Should America Be the Global Policeman?

INTRODUCTION

With the end of the Cold War and the collapse of the Soviet Union, some foreign policy critics argued that it was time for America to withdraw from its numerous commitments around the world and put America first. Others claimed that as the only remaining superpower the United States had an obligation to lead the world toward a new era of peace and democracy. President George Bush talked of the importance of American leadership in creating a New World Order. In his 1992 State of the Union address Bush declared, "Among the nations of the world, only the United State of America has both the moral standing and the means to back it up. We are the only nation of this Earth that could assemble the forces of peace."

But the American instinct to mind its own business and leave the world to its own devices has its roots in George Washington's warning to America in his Farewell Address to "steer clear of permanent alliances with any portion of the foreign world." Those instincts asserted themselves prior to World War II when a powerful citizens' group, America First, argued against our involvement in the wars then raging in Europe and Asia. The Japanese attack on Pearl Harbor brought the United States into the war and ended the debate. World War II and the Cold War that followed led to an era of continual American involvement in world affairs and to the triumph of internationalism over isolationism.

In the 1990s, Americans were struggling with a massive government debt and wondering if the costs of world leadership were too high. In the following essay Ted Galen Carpenter argues that the United States should only be concerned with threats to its political independence, domestic freedom, and physical survival. The search for global stability, Carpenter warns, can only lead to American involvement in a host of regional quarrels, which will continue the costs of the Cold War. Charles Krauthammer, on the other hand, argues that the United States, as the only superpower, should defend its interests and values around the world. For example, Krauthammer claims that the United States must act to prevent weapons of mass destruction from falling into the hands of irresponsible governments.

The debate that raged in this country prior to Pearl Harbor has now reappeared and Americans are again asking fundamental questions about our role in the world. Will a world that reflects our commitment to individual liberty and democratic pluralism be a safer place or will our efforts to achieve such a world lead to perpetual war for perpetual peace?

Uncle Sam as the World's Policeman
Time for a Change?

Ted Galen Carpenter

The Bush administration apparently intends to preserve the principal features of America's activist Cold War strategy in a post–Cold War world and to maintain unnecessarily high levels of military spending. Its proposed $306 billion 1991 defense authorization bill is 16 percent higher in real terms than was the 1981 budget adopted immediately after the Soviet invasion of Afghanistan and the collapse of détente. Even the original projections for the 1995 budget were nearly 8 percent higher. The Bush administration gradually has been retreating from that position, with the president announcing plans for a 25 percent reduction in military personnel. That action is a belated step in the right direction, but we can and should make far deeper cuts, both in personnel and weapon systems.

More disturbing than the grudging nature of the administration's budget cuts has been the pervasive attitude that the fundamentals of America's Cold War strategy of global interventionism should remain intact despite vastly altered international conditions. Typical of the reasoning is the comment in Secretary of Defense Richard B. Cheney's 1990 report to the president and Congress that the United States must strive to "attain the same basic strategic objectives with a somewhat smaller defense budget." The president himself has sought to preserve venerable Cold War institutions such as NATO by formulating vague alternative missions. NATO and the U.S. military presence in Europe, he affirms, will be needed for decades, not to deter a Warsaw Pact invasion (which even he concedes is now utterly improbable), but to prevent "instability and unpredictability."

That approach is a blueprint for the indefinite prolongation of expensive and risky U.S. military commitments around the globe. The international system always has been quite unstable and unpredictable, and there is little evidence that the future will be significantly different. However, instability *per se* does not threaten America's security. Indeed, in a post–Cold War world, there may be many local or regional disputes that are (or at least should be) irrelevant to the security interests of the United States.

Iraq's invasion of Kuwait is a case in point. Baghdad's aggression unquestionably is odious, but that expansionist drive, however unpleasant it may be for Kuwait and other nations in the region, does not threaten vital American interests. Even the most "realistic" reason for the U.S. intervention—the supposed need to protect the Persian Gulf oil supply—fails to withstand scrutiny. The takeover of Kuwait gives Iraq control of only 7 percent of world oil production; a subsequent conquest of Saudi Arabia would have increased the total to 15.7 percent. That degree of control might be enough to nudge up oil prices, but it hardly would give Saddam Hussein a stranglehold on the economies of the West. Because any major rise in oil prices would have to be predicated on Iraq's willingness to withdraw a substantial portion of existing supplies from the market—a most unlikely step since oil is its only significant source of revenue—even a worst-case scenario of Iraqi preeminence in the Persian Gulf region would have meant an increase in oil prices to approximately $30 a barrel. By leading the fight to impose an embargo on Iraqi and Kuwaiti oil exports, and by creating the prospect of a war in the Middle East (with the disruption of the oil flow war would cause), Washington has succeeded in driving prices far higher.

Even assuming the United States can thwart the "threat" to Persian Gulf oil supplies by taking military action against Iraq—and by no means will success be assured—such a victory must be measured against the probable cost of achieving it. Just maintaining forces to protect the Persian Gulf oil flow in peacetime is extremely expensive—nearly $40 billion per year. These ongoing deployments in the Gulf region are costing an additional $1.2 billion to $1.5 billion per month, and sustained combat operations would be vastly more expensive. Some defense experts estimate that combat expenses could approach $1 billion *per day.* If those military costs are factored into the price of oil, it is far less expensive to risk a price increase resulting from unpredictability of Persian Gulf supplies, and that is only taking into consideration the financial factors—not the inevitable loss of life that will ensue if the United States goes to war against Iraq. In short, the stakes in the Persian Gulf are not worth the costs or risks that American military action would entail.

U.S. leaders must learn to distinguish between vital and peripheral—much less nonexistent—security interests. During the Cold War, American policy-makers tended to regard even the most trivial geopolitical assets as essential. However, to be considered a threat to a vital interest, a development should have a direct, immediate, and substantial, connection with America's physical survival, its political independence, or the preservation of its domestic freedoms. Threats to truly vital interests are relatively rare, and they may be even rarer in a post–Cold War setting where no potential adversary is capable of making a bid for global domination.

In that context, the preservation of America's Cold War system of alliances is ill-advised. Not only are such commitments expensive, they are profoundly dangerous. As Cato Institute senior fellow Earl C. Ravenal has noted, alliances are "lethal transmission belts for war," converting what should be minor, localized conflicts into wider confrontations between great powers.

There are various flash points around the world where Cold War–era commitments to clients could entangle the United States. In addition to the volatile Persian Gulf, the tense situations involving Pakistan and India, Syria and Israel, and the two Koreas are the most visible examples. The Balkans and other portions of Eastern Europe also could become caldrons of ethnic strife.

There has been much discussion of a "peace dividend" emerging from the end of the Cold War, but without an entirely new defense strategy, there will be no such dividend for Americans to enjoy. Instead, Washington will perpetuate a vast array of increasingly irrelevant commitments and the military forces to defend them. The statements of Secretary of State James A. Baker III and other administration officials that the United States will need a long-term military presence in the Persian Gulf even if Iraq's expansionist bid is stymied exemplify both the logic and the consequences of global interventionism.

The pursuit of stability is a chimera. Even when a problem is "solved" and stability in a particular region is restored, it is rarely more than a temporary achievement. New revisionist powers invariably arise, revolutions can replace pliant regimes with hostile ones, and the maneuvering for advantage on the part of rival states continues unabated. That is especially true of the volatile Middle East, but it also applies to most regions. If the United States insists on linking its security interests to the achievement of global stability, and thereby injects itself into a host of regional quarrels, it will need military forces that are larger, more diverse, and more expensive than those maintained to wage the Cold War.

The connection between force levels and commitments is crucial. Military units do not exist for their own sake, but to fulfill specific missions, and creating and maintaining those forces is inherently costly. For example, 11 of the Army's 18 divisions exist to help defend Western Europe from a Warsaw Pact invasion. Similarly, the Navy's alleged need for 14 aircraft carrier battle groups is predicated on the continuation of U.S. commitments to allies and clients in Europe, the Far East, and the Persian Gulf. Even the size of the U.S. strategic arsenal is largely the result of embracing the doctrine of extended deterrence—shielding other nations with our nuclear umbrella.

The pertinent question is whether such commitments serve America's security interests, especially now that the Cold War is over. With the decline of the Soviet threat and no other would-be hegemonic power on the horizon, a global network of U.S.-dominated alliances appears to make little sense— particularly given its enormous expense. NATO alone costs American taxpayers more than $130 billion each year. Washington's commitments to Japan, South Korea, and other nations in the Far East run $40 billion and our Persian Gulf commitments add another $40 billion.

It was one thing to undertake such expensive and risky obligations to prevent Soviet global domination, as improbable as that danger may seem in retrospect. It is quite another to perpetuate those obligations merely to prevent vaguely defined instability or discourage the outbreak of local quarrels that have little or no relevance to America's security interests.

IT'S TIME TO TRANSFER POWER

Washington fails to recognize that other democratic powers are now important actors in the global arena—the Bush administration proceeds on the assumption that only the United States can deter aggression. That may have had some validity in the years following World War II when Europe lay in ruins, Germany and Japan were occupied and disarmed, and the geostrategic environment was starkly bipolar, but today the situation is changed radically. It no longer is necessary or desirable for the United States to play the role of Atlas, carrying the security burdens of the planet on its shoulders. The time has come—indeed, it is long overdue—to transfer the entire responsibility for their own defense to prosperous and capable world powers.

It is quite clear, however, that those nations will not volunteer to protect their own security interests as long as the United States is willing to do so on their behalf. That point has been underscored by the meager allied support for the U.S. military intervention in the Persian Gulf. The so-called multinational force arrayed against Iraq is an overwhelmingly American enterprise, with little more than token military contributions from Japan, the members of the European Community, and even the Middle Eastern nations that would seem to be the most directly threatened by Iraqi expansionism. Those countries exhibit little inclination to accept meaningful financial burden-sharing and even less inclination to undertake meaningful risk-sharing.

Instead of attempting to preserve expensive and dangerous alliances and other military commitments, the United States should adopt a new policy of strategic independence from the post–Cold War era. This would be based on three factors: a recognition that the Soviet threat has declined, a narrower and more rigorous definition of America's vital security interests, and the appreciation that other nations now have the economic strength to provide for their own defense needs without a U.S. subsidy.

By phasing out its global network of alliances and adopting a course of strategic independence, the United States radically could downsize its military establishment. The most important changes would include reducing the number of aircraft carrier battle groups from 14 to 6 and tactical air wings from 40 to 17; cutting the number of Army divisions from 18 to 2 and combining the remaining units with the Marine Corps in a new mobile strike force; scaling down the strategic arsenal from more than 12,000 warheads to 3,000–3,500; eliminating such unnecessary systems as the MX and Midgetman missiles, the B-2 Stealth bomber, and the C-17 transport plane; and placing greater emphasis on defending American territory and lives than on power projection in distant regions, which requires the development of an effective defense against ballistic missiles.

Under a regime of strategic independence, the United States eventually could defend its legitimate security interests with a military force of only 905,000, compared with the 2,044,000 proposed in the administration's 1991 budget—and the force of 1,635,000 contemplated in the revised 1995 projections. Adopting that strategy would enable the United States to reduce its military spending to $120 billion within five years. That is a sizable peace dividend by any definition. It not only would eliminate the alleged need for a tax increase to narrow the budget deficit, it could (and should) lead to substantial tax reductions. The American people have borne great risks and burdens throughout the Cold War; they now deserve to reap the benefits from the end of that long, twilight struggle.

The Lonely Superpower

Charles Krauthammer

A Marxist-led rebel coalition overthrows a Soviet satellite regime in Ethiopia. Whom do both sides call upon to mediate, to arrange terms of the rebel take-over, and to support the new government? The United States. Boris Yeltsin becomes the first freely elected leader of Russia in 1000 years. What is his first destination? Washington. Chinese students, Kurdish rebels, Bangladeshi disaster victims seek aid and succor. To whom do they turn? America.

We live in a unipolar world. The old bipolar world of the Cold War has not given birth to the multipolar world that many had predicted and some insist exists today. It has given birth to a highly unusual world structure with a single power, the United States, at the apex of the international system. Multipolarity will come in time. But it is decades away. Germany and Japan were to be the pillars of the new multipolar world. Their paralysis in the face of the Gulf crisis was dramatic demonstration that economic power does not inevitably translate into geopolitical power. As for the other potential pillar, "Europe," its disarray in response to the Gulf crisis made clear that as an international player it does not yet exist.

We have today no lack of second-rank powers. Germany and Japan are obvious economic powers. Britain and France are able to deploy diplomatic and, in some cases, military assets around the world. The Soviet Union possesses several elements of power—military, diplomatic, and political—but all are in rapid decline. There is no prospect in the immediate future of any power to rival the United States. This situation is almost unknown in the history of the modern nation-state: 1815 and 1945 come to mind, but even then the preeminent power was faced with at least one rival of roughly equal strength.

The world's unipolarity became blindingly clear this year when, with a prodigious act of will, the United States turned history in the Arabian peninsula. But the new structure of the international order has nothing to do with the Persian Gulf. It is a direct result of the collapse of the Soviet empire. One might place the birth of the unipolar world at Stavropol last July where, at the Kohl-Gorbachev summit, the Soviet Union ceded to NATO the jewel of its European empire, East Germany.

The end of the Cold War changed the structure of the world. The Gulf war merely revealed it. And in doing so it exploded two myths about the current international system. Some have misinterpreted the war as reinforcing the first myth, the myth of multilateralism. That victory is said to be an example of a new era of collective security, of the indispensability of coalition politics, of the resurgence of the U.N. This is pious nonsense. The Gulf War was an example of pseudo-multilateralism. The United States recruited a ship here, rented a brigade there, bought (with skillfully deployed sticks and carrots) the necessary U.N. resolutions to give its actions a multilateral sheen. The Gulf was no more a collective action than was Korea, still the classic case of pseudo-materialism.

The only people who willingly acknowledge today's pseudo-materialism are those rather indisposed to the United States. Former French Defense Minister Jean-Pierre Chevenement (forced to resign because of his pro-Iraqi sentiments) charged that the United States has never considered the Security Council anything other than "a blessing and a guarantee for its own actions." But of course. Would not any great power? Would not France if given the chance?

But Americans insist on the multilateral pretense. A large segment of American opinion doubts the legitimacy of unilateral American action, but accepts action taken under the rubric of the "world community." Why it should matter to Americans that their actions receive the Security Council blessing of Deng Xiaoping and the butchers of Tiananmen Square is a mystery to me. But to many Americans it matters. It is thus largely for domestic reasons that American political leaders make sure to dress up unilateral action in multilateral clothing. The danger, of course, is that they may ultimately come to believe their own pretense.

The second myth most recently exploded is the myth of American decline. Before the Gulf crisis American declinists were lamenting America's fall from its perch atop the world in—their favorite benchmark year—1950. Well, in 1950 the United States engaged in a war with North Korea. It lasted three years, cost 54,000 American lives, and ended in a draw. Forty-one years later the United States engaged in a war with Iraq, a country of comparable size. It lasted six weeks, cost 143 American lives, and ended in a rout. If the Roman empire had declined at that rate, you would be reading this in Latin.

But, say the declinists, you cannot compare the two wars. In Korea, did not the United States have to contend with China as well as North Korea? That is precisely the point. In the 1950s our adversaries had strategic depth. They had the whole Communist world behind them. That is why we were not able to prevail in Vietnam and Korea. In 1991, with the Cold War won, our great adversaries are in retreat. The enemies we do encounter today, like Saddam, have to face us on their own. Because of that, they don't stand a chance. The difference between Korea and Iraq lies in the fact that in the interim the Cold War was won and the world became unipolar.

Now, the response of Americans to this extraordinary state of international affairs is decidedly unenthusiastic. Americans do not enjoy their hegemony. They can rouse themselves for a one-day parade to celebrate the most lopsided military victory since Agincourt, but even that merriment, which elicited considerable editorial grumbling about hubris and expense, seemed a bit forced. Of all the great imperial powers, America is probably the least imperially minded. Britain and France, at their height, would have stayed in the Gulf after such an extraordinary military victory to rearrange the map and establish themselves as hegemons. The United States, in contrast, could not wait to get out and go home.

That is the American way. Hence our evacuation of Europe after World War I and our mass demobilization after World War II. Americans are endlessly resourceful in trying to escape the responsibilities that history has placed on their shoulders. The most notable example, of course, is the isolationism of the 1920s and 1930s. But even during the years of Cold War engagement, a significant element, sometimes a majority, of the American intelligentsia counseled abdication. Indeed, for years, until the revolutions of 1989, "cold warrior" was a term of abuse.

When the Cold War was won the first response was euphoria, coupled with the demand for a "peace dividend," that is, unilateral disarmament. Having won the latest war to end all wars, there were calls in Congress for huge and immediate cuts, up to 50 percent, in defense expenditures. The mood was best caught at a press conference at the White House early last year when a celebrated correspondent, disturbed by the president's "out of sync" $300 billion defense budget, asked Bush skeptically, "Who is the enemy?"

Six months later we got our answer. It took Saddam to remind us that the world is a nasty place, even without the Soviet threat. Americans do not appreciate the reminder. Hence the determined search for evasions to escape our superpower responsibilities.

There are two principal modes of evasion. The first, on the rise before the Gulf War, and now in embarrassed but only temporary retreat, is old-style isolationism. With the end of the Cold War, native American isolationism, always a powerful political undercurrent, is beginning to reassert itself openly. This neoisolationism, like its interwar forebear, has two factions. The more well known, left isolationism, is a child of Vietnam. The newer phenomenon (for this generation) is right isolationism, which has its roots in the 1920s and 1930s but which took a holiday during the Cold War when it gave itself over to a passionate anti-communism. The holiday is over. The return of right isolationism as a respected intellectual stance might be dated to Russell Kirk's notorious Heritage Foundation speech (October 1988) attacking neoconservatives, which included a thrust at their "fanciful democratic globalism." Pat Buchanan has followed up in the popular press, leading the charge for a foreign policy of "America first" and declaring, "When this cold war is over, America should come home."

"America first" is a deliberate echo of a right-wing isolationist slogan of the 1930s. "Come home America" is a deliberate echo of McGovern's anti-Vietnam slogan of 1972. This overt borrowing is a clear sign that left and right strains of isolationism will produce alliances that will confound ideological distinctions. It is true that left isolationism refuses to engage the world because it fears that America will corrupt the world, whereas right isolationism refuses to engage the world because it fears that the world will corrupt America. But as the Soviet threat recedes into history, ideological lines among isolationists will blur. Conservatism, however, will be isolationism's great new growth area. After all, on the left, those who were propelled toward isolationism by Vietnam (much of the Democratic Party) are already there. New converts to isolationism will come from the right, now that the anti-Communist emergency is over.

Isolationism is the first and the most obvious means of escape from the burdens of the new world order. The other, more subtle, means is multilateralism. Rather than say, Come home America, the multilateralist says, Stay engaged but let someone else do the real work. That someone else is the Organization of American States, collective security, the Security Council, or some other multilateral invention. Let them police the world. We want out.

Multilateralism is fine. It provides cover for what are essentially unilateral American actions. But it carries two dangers. The first is that we will mistake the illusion—world opinion, U.N. resolutions, professions of solidarity—for the real thing, which is American power. And that we will assume that if we dispense with the real thing, the illusion will get us where we mean to go. It will not.

The second danger is that multilateralism will become a fetish. If it becomes an end in itself, the need to nurture it can become a hindrance to the exercise of real power. Before the war, for example, many in Congress argued against undertaking any military actions on the grounds (among others) that it might jeopardize the grand coalition that the president had assembled. But the whole point of the coalition was to get Iraq out of Kuwait. If the coalition stood in the way of that end, it had to yield. To do otherwise would be to confuse ends and means.

The ultimate problem with multilateralism is that if you take it seriously you gratuitously forfeit American freedom of action. You invite China and the Soviet Union, countries indifferent when not hostile to our interests, to have a decisive say and even a veto over our interests and those of our friends. Why should the preeminent power on the globe invite such a needless constraint on its action?

Multilateralism is the isolationism of the internationalist. Those who would like to appear internationalist but have tired of real engagement know that if they tie themselves up in enough coalitions and international structures they will quite effectively be taken out of the game. And that, of course, is the point.

But both the multilateral dodge and the isolationist abdication are no answer to the dilemmas of a unipolar world. There is no escape. If we want stability and tranquility in the world, we will have to work for it, impose it, sometimes on our own. It will not come as a gift from the Security Council. It will not come of itself. It will come only from an America working to shape a new world order.

The phrase "new world order" is George Bush's. He likes it so much that, since last August, he has been using it constantly. He would like New World Order to be as much his legacy as New Deal is FDR's. What exactly is it? The departed Minister Chevenement charges that the only thing new about the new world order is that it is an American order. Right again. If the new world order means anything (as yet, not a certain proposition) it is as an assertion of American interests and values in the world.

What interest and what values? Here we can see contradictory strains developing within the administration itself. One vision of the NWO, a conservative vision, was offered by the president on April 13 in a speech at Maxwell Air Force Base. For the first time Bush set out the principal elements of his NWO: "Peaceful settlements of disputes, solidarity against aggression, reduced and controlled arsenals, and just treatment of all peoples."

Now, peace, collective security, arms control, and justice are fine goals. But the list provocatively omits the values that have been traditionally invoked by the modern presidency to justify intervention abroad: self-determination (Wilson); freedom (FDR, Truman, and Kennedy); human rights (Carter); democracy and the democratic revolution (Reagan). Bush did invoke justice, but last and least. His principal passion is something quite different: "The quest for the new world order is, in part," he said at Maxwell, "a challenge to keep the dangers of disorder at bay." For Bush, the new world order is principally about order.

Order is indeed a high value. But maintaining order is a rather pinched vision of America's mission in the world. Under this NWO, the United States does the work of the Congress of Vienna. The international system becomes a club of existing nation-states, acting together if necessary, to maintain the status quo. Under this NWO, the United States expresses a preference for Yugoslavia over its republics; is most tepid in support of Baltic independence (to say nothing of that of Georgia, Armenia, or Moldavia); deals with Deng Xiaoping of Tiananmen Square in the name of stability; saves Saddam after the Gulf War rather than risk the dissolution of the Iraqi state.

This is a highly constrained vision of the world. Order is the watchword, stability the goal, sovereignty the most sacred principle. The president favors this conservative vision. But even he does not completely embrace it. Some of his actions suggest a far more expansive, morally self-confident, indeed, radical NWO II.

Three days after the Maxwell speech, the president, despite himself, gave a glimpse of this unarticulated NWO II. Having finally been persuaded that the Kurds needed saving, the president intervened, almost unilaterally, to save them. Together with the British and the French, he sent thousands of troops to occupy a faraway piece of sovereign territory.

The legal basis for what he did is, to be generous, thin. As the *New York Times* put it none too subtly: "Helicopter teams moved into Iraq against a backdrop of confusion over the diplomatic and legal foundations of the American plan." Not that we could not round up the usual international lawyers to mine Security Council resolutions for retrospective legal justification for our action. That, after all, is what international lawyers are for. But let us be honest. We acted unilaterally in Kurdistan because it was the right thing to do. A couple of allies did join us. But we did not occupy northern Kurdistan in the name of international legality. We did so in the name of right, self-evident right.

Hence the fundamental law of NWO II: When, as in Kurdistan, the existing international rules conflict with basic American values, to hell with the rules. And the corollary: The new world order should be an assertion of American interests and values in the world, if necessary asserted unilaterally. Where possible, we should act in concert with others. Where not, we should proceed regardless.

Of the two versions of the new world order, the president is clearly more comfortable with NWO I. But NWO I will not do. First, because it cannot command domestic support. The idea of being involved in the world in defense of a desiccated notion of international stability or a subtle maintenance of the balance of power is extremely uncongenial to Americans. Americans will venture abroad to do right things, but only to do right things. Otherwise they would rather stay home. In the Gulf, for example, the Kuwait policy commanded support when presented not as an issue of oil and jobs but as a war of liberation. In contrast, the postwar policy of allowing Saddam to stay in power as a way of maintaining a delicate balance of power in the region engendered dismay and disgust.

Second, NWO I is too weak an idea to deal with the crisis of the post–Cold War world. Specifically, it is not flexible and bold enough to confront the two looming revolutionary developments in the international system that will haunt it—and us—for the next decades.

First among these is a technological revolution; the advent of the age of weapons of mass destruction and the means to deliver them. According to the Pentagon, by the year 2000, now only nine years away, there will be two dozen developing nations with ballistic missiles, 30 with chemical weapons, 10 with biological weapons, and almost as many with nuclear weapons. Iraq is the prototype of this kind of threat; tomorrow perhaps it will come from North Korea, Libya, Pakistan, Iran, South Africa.

It is banal to say that modern technology has shrunk the world. But the obvious corollary is rarely drawn: In a shrunken world the divide between regional superpowers and great powers is radically narrowed. Missiles shrink distance. Nuclear (or chemical or biological) devices multiply power. Both can be bought at market. Consequently, the geopolitical map is irrevocably altered. Fifty years ago, Germany had to be centrally located, highly industrial, and heavily populated to pose a threat to world security and to the other great powers. It was inconceivable that, say, a relatively small Middle Eastern state with an almost entirely imported industrial base could do anything more than disturb its neighbors. The central truth of the coming era is that this is no longer the case: Relatively small, peripheral, and backward states will be able to emerge rapidly as threats not only to regional but to world security.

The second great challenge of the coming era is geopolitical: the breakup of the great multinational states (the Soviet Union, Yugoslavia, perhaps India) and possible emergence among the rubble of raw, aggressive, perhaps virulent nationalism. The Sikhs and Kashmiris, the Croats and Georgians, the Russians too, enlist our sympathy today when they are down. When they are up, they and others now struggling to be free may act in ways that elicit horror.

These two challenges will have to be met by the new world order or the term has no meaning. There are no magic answers to how to deal with them. But any answers will likely involve breaking international rules and making new ones, a boldness that requires the radicalism of NWO II rather than the deep, almost paralytic conservatism of NWO I.

For example, in dealing with the threat of weapons of mass destruction it will become essential to confront and deter and, if necessary, disarm states that brandish and use these weapons. Doing so may violate current norms of international legality. It will certainly infringe on cherished ideas of sovereignty. Today, in the case of Iraq, we get international support for breaking these rules. (In fact, the "international community" sitting in the Security Council makes up the rules as it goes along.) Tomorrow we may not be so lucky. In which case, the United States will have to act alone, backed by as many of its allies as will join the endeavor. There may not be many.

As for the second threat, the rise of aggressive nationalisms, here too the United States will have to try to create new norms and rules. To satisfy small national groups seeking independence without totally fracturing the world, we will need to invent some concept of subsovereignty—a kind of autonomy that grants peoples an intermediate status between subservience and full statehood. Subsovereignty might offer some way out of the Soviet, Yugoslav, Indian, even the Palestinian conundrum. Our unplanned intervention in Kurdistan may actually show the way: A new world order that does not just enforce rules, but breaks old rules and makes new ones.

As in 1946–1949, it is the United States that will create a new world order. The only question is, what kind? Bush seems to prefer the merely orderly order of NWO I. The coming crises, heralded by the minicrisis in Kurdistan, will require the boldness of NWO II, a more American order.

I say this with little enthusiasm. I find these challenges stirring but at the same time deeply dismaying. I would much have preferred that after the long twilight struggle America enjoy the respite from toil and danger to which it is richly entitled. Alas, there is no end to toil, and it is not just naive but dangerous to pretend otherwise. Even after the defeat of the Soviet threat, we face a highly dangerous new world from which there is no escape. Our best hope for safety in such times, as in difficult times past, is in American strength and will: the strength to recognize the unipolar world and the will to lead it.

QUESTIONS FOR DISCUSSION

20.1 Should the United States maintain a military force large enough to discourage another superpower (Germany, Japan) from emerging?

20.2 Is the protection of American vital interests best preserved by the spread of democratic systems around the world?

20.3 Even if another hostile superpower should not emerge, what are threats to American security that may require a policy of intervention?

Credits

CHAPTER 1

"Judicial Review and Democracy" by Robert H. Bork, from *Society*, Nov./Dec. 1986, pp. 5–8. Copyright © 1986 by Transaction Publishers. Reprinted by permission.

"The Democratic Character of Judicial Review" by Eugene V. Rostow, from *Harvard Law Review*, LVI (December 1952), pp. 193–224. Copyright © 1952 by the Harvard Law Review Association. Reprinted by permission of the Harvard Law Review Association and the author.

CHAPTER 2

"Operation Domestic Order" by Raymond L. Flynn, from *Commonweal*, April 19, 1991, pp. 251–256. Copyright © 1991 Commonweal Foundation.

"The *Real* Story Behind State Governments' Financial Crisis" by Stephen Moore, from *USA Today*, March 1992, pp. 10–13. Reprinted from *USA Today Magazine*, March copyright 1992 by the Society for the Advancement of Education.

CHAPTER 4

"In Defense of Affirmative Action" by Herman Schwartz, from *Dissent*, Fall 1984, pp. 406–414. Reprinted by permission.

"Race, Scholarship, and Affirmative Action: Campus Racism" by Walter E. Williams, from *National Review*, May 5, 1989, pp. 36–38. © 1989 by National Review, Inc., 150 E. 35th Street, New York, NY 10016. Reprinted by permission.

CHAPTER 5

"Neoconservatism: Myth and Reality" by Dan Himmelfarb. Reprinted from *Commentary*, May 1988, by permission. All rights reserved.

CHAPTER 6

"Why Young People Don't Vote" by Curtis Gans, from *The Education Digest*, February 1989, pp. 40–43. Reprinted with permission by Prakken Publications, Inc.

"Turning On Youth to Politics" by Harry C. Boyte, from *The Nation*, May 13, 1991, pp. 626–628. This article is reprinted from *The Nation* magazine/The Nation Company, Inc., © 1991.

CHAPTER 7

"The Art of Capitol Hill: Shilling in the Senate" by David Corn, from *The Nation*, July 17, 1989, pp. 84–87. This article is reprinted from *The Nation* magazine/The Nation Company, Inc., © 1989.

CHAPTER 8

"Congress on the Auction Block" by David L. Boren, from *USA Today*, May 1990, pp. 10–12. Reprinted from *USA Today Magazine*, May copyright 1990 by The Society for the Advancement of Education.

"Campaign Reform: An Exercise in Cynicism" by William L. Armstrong, from *USA Today*, November 1990, pp. 13–14. Reprinted from *USA Today Magazine*, November copyright 1990 by The Society for the Advancement of Education.

CHAPTER 9

"Privates of Parade" an editorial from *The New Republic*, November 13, 1989, pp. 7–9. Reprinted by permission.

"How Pure Must Our Candidates Be?" by Garry Wills, from *American Heritage*, May–June 1992. Reprinted by permission of *American Heritage* Magazine, a division of Forbes Inc., © 1992.

CHAPTER 11

"Quid Pro Whoa" by Michael Waldman, from *The New Republic*, March 19, 1990, pp. 22–25. Reprinted by permission.

CHAPTER 12

"The Poison of Professional Politics" by Mark Petracca, from *USA Today*, January 1992, pp. 10–13. Reprinted from *USA Today Magazine*, January copyright 1992 by the Society for the Advancement of Education.

CHAPTER 13

"How to End the Health Care Crises" by Marty Russo, from *USA Today*, March 1992, pp. 20–21. Reprinted from *USA Today Magazine*, March copyright 1992 by the Society for the Advancement of Education.

"Can We Put the Brakes on Health Care Costs?" by Louis W. Sullivan, table from *USA Today*, March 1992, p. 26. Reprinted from *USA Today Magazine*, March copyright 1992 by the Society for the Advancement of Education.

CHAPTER 14

"Courting Rituals" by Max Lerner, from *The New Republic*, February 1, 1988, pp. 16–18. Reprinted by permission.

"A Record That Speaks for Itself" by Francis Flaherty, from *Commonweal*, September 11, 1987, pp. 477–480. Copyright © 1987 Commonweal Foundation.

CHAPTER 15

"Legalizing the Intolerable Is a Bad Idea" by Richard A. Hawley, from *Phi Delta Kappan*, September 1991, pp. 62–65. Reprinted by permission.

"What Should We Do About Drugs? Manage the Problem Through Legalization" by Eric E. Sterling, from *Vital Speeches*, Vol. 52, 20, August 1, 1991, pp. 626–632. Speech sent by Eric Sterling, the Criminal Justice Policy Foundation, 200 L Street NW, Suite 702, Washington, D.C. 20036.

CHAPTER 16

"Who's the Fairest of Them All? The Truth About the '80s" by Bill Archer, from *Policy Review*, Summer 1991, pp. 67–73. Reprinted with permission from the Summer 1991 issue of *Policy Review*, the flagship publication of The Heritage Foundation, 214 Massachusetts Avenue, NE, Washington, D.C. 20002.

"Borrow 'N' Squander" by Robert S. McIntyre, from *The New Republic*, September 30, 1991, pp. 11–13. Reprinted by permission.

CHAPTER 17

"All Pain, No Gain: The Darman Deficit" by Stephen Moore, from *National Review*, September 9, 1991, pp. 33–35. © 1991 by National Review, Inc., 150 E. 35th Street, New York, NY 10016. Reprinted by permission.

"The Deficit: Trouble Ahead" by George Hager, from *Congressional Quarterly*, February 1, 1992, pp. 222–226. Reprinted by permission.

CHAPTER 18

"Homelessness: A Cost of Capitalism" by John R. Belcher and Jeff Singer, from *Social Policy*, Spring 1988, pp. 44–48. Published by Social Policy Corporation, New York, NY 10036. Copyright 1988 by Social Policy Corporation.

"Who Goes Homeless?" by E. Fuller Torrey, from *National Review*, August 26, 1991. Copyright © 1991 by National Review, Inc., 150 East 35th Street, New York, NY 10016. Reprinted by permission.

CHAPTER 19

"Nuclear Energy: Toward U.S. Energy Independence" by Bill Harris, from *Vital Speeches*, October 15, 1990, pp. 24–26.

"Global Warming: No Nuclear Quick Fix" by Alan Miller and Irving Mintzer, from *The Bulletin of the Atomic Scientists*, June 1990. Copyright © 1990 by the Educational Foundation for Nuclear Science, 6042 South Kimbark, Chicago, IL 60637. A one-year subscription is $30.

CHAPTER 20

"Uncle Sam as the World's Policeman: Time for a Change?" by Ted Galen Carpenter, from *USA Today*, January 1991, pp. 21–22. Reprinted from *USA Today Magazine*, January copyright 1991 by the Society for the Advancement of Education.

"The Lonely Superpower" by Charles Krauthammer, from *The New Republic*, July 29, 1991, pp. 23–27. Reprinted by permission.